TEACHER WRAPAROUND EDITION

P9-DDH-456

Experiencing
Choral Music

TENOR/BASS

Developed by

HAL•LEONARD® CORPORATION

Mc Graw Hill **Glencoe**

New York, New York   Columbus, Ohio   Chicago, Illinois   Peoria, Illinois   Woodland Hills, California

The portions of the National Standards for Music Education included here are reprinted from *National Standards for Arts Education* with permission from MENC—The National Association for Music Education. All rights reserved. Copyright © 1994 by MENC. The complete National Standards and additional materials relating to the Standards are available from MENC, 1806 Robert Fulton Drive, Reston, VA 20191 (telephone 800-336-3768).

A portion of the sales of this material goes to support music education programs through programs of MENC—The National Association for Music Education.

 **Glencoe**

The *McGraw-Hill* Companies

Copyright © 2005 by Glencoe/McGraw-Hill, a division of The McGraw-Hill Companies. All rights reserved. Except as permitted under the United States Copyright Act, no part of this publication may be reproduced or distributed in any form or by any means, or stored in a database or retrieval system, without prior written permission from the publisher.

Printed in the United States of America.

Send all inquiries to:
Glencoe/McGraw-Hill
21600 Oxnard Street, Suite 500
Woodland Hills, CA 91367

ISBN 0-07-861125-3 (Student Edition)
ISBN 0-07-861126-1 (Teacher Wraparound Edition)

2 3 4 5 6 7 8 9   045   09 08 07 06 05

Table of Contents

| SECTION | | National Standards | | | | | | | | |
Selection	Concepts and Skills	1	2	3	4	5	6	7	8	9
LESSONS										
Let All Men Sing	Major second intervals; describe music-related careers; describe music representing the Contemporary period.	a, b, c			a	a	b	b		a
Spotlight On Posture & Breath Management	Proper singing posture.	b								
Annie Laurie	Interval of an octave; musical phrasing; music representing the Scottish culture.	a, b, c				a	c	a, b	c	a
Spotlight On Physiology Of The Voice	Relate science and music; describe how the knowledge of vocal physiology is important to musical vocal performance.	b							a, b	
Cape Cod Girls	Diphthongs; read music with rhythmic accuracy; perform American sea chantey.	a, b, c		b	a	a	b, c	a, b	c	b, c
Gabi, Gabi	Describe and perform call and response; perform music of South African culture.	a, b, c		b		a	c	a, b	a	a
Tolite Hostias	Perform music of the Romantic period; define and interpret *maestoso*; dynamics.	a, b, c				a	a, b	a	c	a
Ose Shalom	Minor tonality; sing phrases expressively; perform music of the Hebrew culture.	a, b, c			c	a, b	b	a, b	a, b	a
Pastores á Belén	Compound meter; Spanish diction; perform music of the Puerto Rican culture.	a, c			a	a, b		a, b		a
Still, Still, Still	Describe suspension; identify the melody and harmony parts.	a, c					b	b	a	
Spotlight On Arranging	Create and arrange music within specified guidelines.				b					
All Ye Who Music Love	Rhythmic clarity; compare contrapuntal and homophonic style; perform music of the Renaissance.	a, c					a, b, c	a, b		a
Die Katze lässt das Mausen nicht	Perform music of the Baroque period; German text; identify homophony and counterpoint.	a, b, c			a	a	b		c	a
O Isis und Osiris, welche Wonne!	Falsetto register; style of an opera chorus; describe music of the Classical period.	a, c, f					a, b, c, d, e, f	a, c	a	a, d
Spotlight On Vowels	Proper use of vowels.	b								
The Pasture	Expressive phrasing and word stress; the relationship between music and poetry.	a, c			a	b		a	a, c	
MUSIC & HISTORY										
Renaissance, Baroque, Classical, Romantic and Contemporary periods	Describe, listen to and analyze music from the five main historical periods.						a, b, c, e, f		a, b, c, d, e	a, c, d, e
Spotlight On Concert Etiquette	Exhibit informed concert etiquette in a variety of settings.							a, b		

SECTION		National Standards								
Selection	Concepts and Skills	1	2	3	4	5	6	7	8	9
CHORAL LIBRARY										
Away From The Roll Of The Sea	Legato phrases and staggered breathing; dotted notes and ties.	a, b, c, f				a, b	a, e	a, c	a, b, c, d, e	a, b, d, e
Spotlight On Improvisation	Create rhythmic and melodic phrases; improvise musical melodies.	a, b, c		a, b, c						
Buffalo Gals	Swing style; define *minstrel* and discuss its role in American music history; music of American heritage.	a, c			a	a, b		a, c	b	a
Come To The Music	Mixed meters; perfect fifth; uses of music in society and culture.	a, c				b	a	b	b	
Do You Hear The People Sing?	Triplets; relate music to history and culture; American musical theater.	a, c			a		b	b	b	
Honey-Little 'Lize Medley	Accurate intonation; key of B♭ major; music representing the American heritage.	a, b, c				a		a, b		b
Spotlight On Careers In Music	Music-related career opportunities; relationship of other subjects and those of music.								b	c
Kalinka	Define *accelerando* and *crescendo*; music representing the Russian culture.	a, c				b	a, b	a		
Spotlight On Diction	Proper diction.	b							b	
Linden Lea	Identify melodic contour; sing independently in small ensembles; music representing the British culture.	a, c				a	b	a		
Spotlight On Musical Theater	Relate music to history; identify the relationships between the other fine arts and music; describe music-related career.							b	a	b
Loch Lomond	Sing with accurate intonation and balance; expressive phrasing; music representing the Scottish culture.	a, c				b	a	a		a
The Star-Spangled Banner	Accidentals; dotted rhythms; relate the music to history, to society and to culture.	a, b				b	b	a		a
Tears In Heaven	Uses of music in society; perform music expressively; smooth transition between registers.	a				b		b	b	c
Spotlight On Physiology Singing	Sing individually; relationship between other subjects and music.	b							b	
Two Excerpts from *Liebeslieder Walzer*	Describe music from the Romantic period; demonstrate proper use of head voice; 3/4 meter.	a, c			a	b		a	a	
Spotlight On Gospel Music	Classify aurally presented music representing diverse styles.	a, b, c						a, b		
Witness	Call-and-response music representing the African American spiritual.	a, c				a, b	a, b	a		a
Spotlight On Vocal Health	To introduce and experience healthy vocal production.	b								

National Standards High School Grades 9–12

The National Standards for Music Education were developed by the Music Educators National Conference. Reprinted by permission.

MUSIC

The study of music contributes in important ways to the quality of every student's life. Every musical work is a product of its time and place, although some works transcend their original settings and continue to appeal to humans through their timeless and universal attraction. Through singing, playing instruments and composing, students can express themselves creatively, while a knowledge of notation and performance traditions enables them to learn new music independently throughout their lives. Skills in analysis, evaluation and synthesis are important because they enable students to recognize and pursue excellence in the musical experiences and to understand and enrich their environment. Because music is an integral part of human history, the ability to listen with understanding is essential if students are to gain a broad cultural and historical perspective. The adult life of every student is enriched by the skills, knowledge and habits acquired in the study of music.

Every course in music, including performance courses, should provide instruction in creating, performing, listening to and analyzing music, in addition to focusing on its specific subject matter.

1. **Content Standard:** Singing, alone and with others, a varied repertoire of music
   Achievement Standard, Proficient:
   Students
   a. sing with *expression and *technical accuracy a large and varied repertoire of vocal literature with a *level of difficulty of 4, on a scale of 1 to 6, including some songs performed from memory.
   b. sing music written in four parts, with and without accompaniment.
   c. demonstrate well-developed ensemble skills.

   Achievement Standard, Advanced:
   Students
   d. sing with expression and technical accuracy a large and varied repertoire of vocal literature with a level of difficulty of 5, on a scale of 1 to 6.
   e. sing music written in more than four parts.
   f. sing in small ensembles with one student on a part.

2. **Content Standard:** Performing on instruments, alone and with others, a varied repertoire of music
   Achievement Standard, Proficient:
   Students
   a. perform with expression and technical accuracy a large and varied repertoire of instrumental literature with a level of difficulty of 4, on a scale of 1 to 6.
   b. perform an appropriate part in an ensemble, demonstrating well-developed ensemble skills.
   c. perform in small ensembles with one student on a part.

   Achievement Standard, Advanced:
   Students
   d. perform with expression and technical accuracy a large and varied repertoire of instrumental literature with a level of difficulty of 5, on a scale of 1 to 6.

3. **Content Standard:** Improvising melodies, variations and accompaniments
   Achievement Standard, Proficient:
   Students
   a. improvise stylistically appropriate harmonizing parts.
   b. improvise rhythmic and melodic variations on given pentatonic melodies and melodies in major and minor keys.
   c. improvise original melodies over given chord progressions, each in a consistent *style, *meter and *tonality.
   Achievement Standard, Advanced:
   Students
   d. improvise stylistically appropriate harmonizing parts in a variety of styles.
   e. improvise original melodies in a variety of styles, over given chord progressions, each in a consistent style, meter and tonality.

4. **Content Standard:** Composing and arranging music within specified guidelines
   Achievement Standard, Proficient:
   Students
   a. compose music in several distinct styles, demonstrating creativity in using the *elements of music for expressive effect.
   b. arrange pieces for voices or instruments other than those for which the pieces were written in ways that preserve or enhance the expressive effect of the music.
   c. compose and arrange music for voices and various acoustic and electronic instruments, demonstrating knowledge of the ranges and traditional usages of the sound sources.
   Achievement Standard, Advanced:
   Students
   d. compose music, demonstrating imagination and technical skill in applying the principles of composition.

5. **Content Standard:** Reading and notating music
   Achievement Standard, Proficient:
   Students
   a. demonstrate the ability to read an instrumental or vocal score of up to four *staves by describing how the elements of music are used.
   Students who participate in a choral or instrumental ensemble or class
   b. sight-read, accurately and expressively, music with a level of difficulty of 3, on a scale of 1 to 6.

Achievement Standard, Advanced:
Students

    c. demonstrate the ability to read a full instrumental or vocal score by describing how the elements of music are used and explaining all transpositions and clefs.

    d. interpret nonstandard notation symbols used by some 20th-century [sic] composers.

Students who participate in a choral or instrumental ensemble or class

    e. sight-read, accurately and expressively, music with a level of difficulty of 4, on a scale of 1 to 6.

6. **Content Standard:** Listening to, analyzing and describing music
Achievement Standard, Proficient:
Students

    a. analyze aural examples of a varied repertoire of music, representing diverse *genres and cultures, by describing the uses of elements of music and expressive devices.

    b. demonstrate extensive knowledge of the technical vocabulary of music.

    c. identify and explain compositional devices and techniques used to provide unity and variety and tension and release in a musical work and give examples of other works that make similar uses of these devices and techniques.

Achievement Standard, Advanced:
Students

    d. demonstrate the ability to perceive and remember music events by describing in detail significant events[1] occurring in a given aural example.

    e. compare ways in which musical materials are used in a given example relative to ways in which they are used in other works of the same genre or style.

    f. analyze and describe uses of the elements of music in a given work that make it unique, interesting and expressive.

7. **Content Standard:** Evaluating music and music performances
Achievement Standard, Proficient:
Students

    a. evolve specific criteria for making informed, critical evaluations of the quality and effectiveness of performances, compositions, arrangements and improvisations and apply the criteria in their personal participation in music.

    b. evaluate a performance, composition, arrangement or improvisation by comparing it to similar or exemplary models.

Achievement Standard, Advanced:
Students

    c. evaluate a given musical work in terms of its aesthetic qualities and explain the musical means it uses to evoke feelings and emotions.

8. **Content Standard:** Understanding relationships between music, the other arts, and disciplines outside the arts
Achievement Standard, Proficient:
Students

    a. explain how elements, artistic processes (such as imagination or craftsmanship), and organizational principles (such as unity and variety or repetition and contrast) are used in similar and distinctive ways in the various arts and cite examples.

    b. compare characteristics of two or more arts within a particular historical period or style and cite examples from various cultures.

    c. explain ways in which the principles and subject matter of various disciplines outside the arts are interrelated with those of music.[2]

Achievement Standard, Advanced:
Students

    d. compare the uses of characteristic elements, artistic processes and organizational principles among the arts in different historical periods and different cultures.

    e. explain how the roles of creators, performers, and others involved in the production and presentation of the arts are similar to and different from one another in the various arts.[3]

9. **Content Standard:** Understanding music in relation to history and culture
Achievement Standard, Proficient:
Students

    a. classify by genre or style and by historical period or culture unfamiliar but representative aural examples of music and explain the reasoning behind their classifications.

    b. identify sources of American music genres[4], trace the evolution of those genres, and cite well-known musicians associated with them.

    c. identify various roles[5] that musicians perform, cite representative individuals who have functioned in each role, and describe their activities and achievements.

Achievement Standard, Advanced:
Students

    d. identify and explain the stylistic features of a given musical work that serve to define its aesthetic tradition and its historical or cultural context.

    e. identify and describe music genres or styles that show the influence of two or more cultural traditions, identify the cultural source of each influence, and trace the historical conditions that produced the synthesis of influences.

Terms identified by an asterisk (*) are explained further in the glossary of *National Standards for Arts Education,* published by Music Educators National Conference, © 1994.

1. E.g., fugal entrances, chromatic modulations, developmental devices
2. E.g., language arts: compare the ability of music and literature to convey images, feeling and meanings; physics: describe the physical basis of tone production in string, wind, percussion and electronic instruments and the human voice and of the transmission and perception of sound
3. E.g., creators: painters, composers, choreographers, playwrights; performers: instrumentalists, singers, dancers, actors; others: conductors, costumers, directors, lighting designers
4. E.g., swing, Broadway musical, blues
5. E.g., entertainer, teacher, transmitter of cultural tradition

INTRODUCTION

Experiencing Choral Music is a four-level series designed to build music literacy and promote vocal development for all students and voice categories in grades 6–12. The series is a multitextbook program supported with print materials and audio listening components that enable students to develop music skills and conceptual understanding, and provides teachers with a flexible, integrated program.

Experiencing Choral Music presents beginning, intermediate, proficient and advanced literature for various voice groupings: unison, 2-part/3-part, mixed, treble, and tenor/bass. All selections in *Experiencing Choral Music* are recorded three ways: full performance with voices, accompaniment only, and individual part-dominant recordings. The program also includes companion *Sight-Singing* textbooks that present a sequential approach to musical literacy and is directly correlated to the literature books. This comprehensive choral music program includes student texts, teacher wraparound editions, teacher resource binders, and rehearsal and performance audio recordings designed to enhance student learning while reducing teacher preparation time.

Experiencing Choral Music is a curriculum that provides your students with a meaningful, motivating choral music experience, and will help you and your students build choral music knowledge and skills. For example:

Experiencing Choral Music connects to . . . the National Standards

The National Standards are correlated to each lesson for quick-and-easy identification and reference. The performance standards related to singing and reading notations are explicit in each lesson, and by using the extension activities, teachers can connect the musical elements through improvisation and composition. Analysis and evaluation are active and consistent components of lessons throughout the series. Additional student activities connect the lessons to the other arts, as well as provide a consistent historical and cultural context.

Experiencing Choral Music connects to . . . Skill Development

Through the Links to Learning exercises, students build vocal, theory and artistic expression skills necessary to perform each piece. Rhythmic, melodic and articulation skills are developed as needed for expressive interpretation. Students are encouraged to develop listening skills and use their perceptions to improve individual and group performance.

Experiencing Choral Music connects to . . . Creative Expression/Performance

Student performance provides opportunities for young musicians to demonstrate musical growth, to gain personal satisfaction from achievement, and to experience the joy of music making. To help develop skills, *Experiencing Choral Music* provides vocal, theory and artistic expression exercises, which help prepare students to successfully sing each piece. Conceptual understanding is built throughout the teaching/learning sequence, as the performance is prepared.

Experiencing Choral Music connects to . . . Historical and Cultural Heritage

Experiencing Choral Music provides a vehicle to help students gain knowledge and understanding of historical and cultural contexts across the curriculum. These concepts are presented in the Getting Started section of each lesson. Also, historical connections through art, history, time lines, performance practices and listening examples are made in Music & History.

Experiencing Choral Music connects to . . . the Arts and Other Curriculum Areas

Choral music provides a rich opportunity to connect the musical experience to other art disciplines (dance, visual arts, theater), and to enhance the learning in other subject areas.

PROGRAM PHILOSOPHY

Responding to New Trends in Choral Music Education

Experiencing Choral Music is consistent with current educational philosophy that suggests:

- Performance is a product that should be the end result of a sound educational process, building conceptual understanding and skills as the performance is prepared.
- Students are motivated through materials and concepts that are connected to their own lives and interests, and should be exposed to high-quality, challenging musical literature.
- Students learn best when they are active participants in their learning, and when they clearly understand and help set the goals and objectives of the learning outcome.
- Students understand concepts better when they have background information and skills that allow them to place their learning into a larger context.
- Students need to actively manipulate musical concepts and skills through improvisation and/or composition in order to fully assimilate and understand them.

- Students improve when they receive fair, honest and meaningful feedback on their success and failures.
- Students should be encouraged to assess themselves individually and as a group, learning to receive and process constructive criticism, leading to independent self-correction and decision making.

Scope and Depth of Music Literature

Most students are capable of performing more difficult material than they can sight-read. Therefore, the literature in *Experiencing Choral Music* is drawn from many periods and styles of music. The wide range of composers and publishers ensures variety, and allows for various skills and concepts to be developed as each new piece is encountered. The high standards set in *Experiencing Choral Music* provide selections that are inherently powerful and exciting for students. The *Sight-Singing* textbooks provide additional literature for sight-singing purposes. Written in a sequential manner, this component will present students with a developmental process for learning to read music.

Addressing the National Standards

The National Standards for Arts Education, published in 1994, launched a national effort to bring a new vision to arts education for all students. The National Standards provide a framework for achievement in music, with outcomes suggested for grades 4, 8, and 12. *Experiencing Choral Music* addresses the National Standards in several ways.

The most obvious and predominant National Standards addressed in choral ensemble are: (1) singing and (5) reading and notation. However, good performance requires musical understanding that only occurs when all aspects of musical experience are incorporated. The preparation of vocal performance is enriched and deepened by involvement in all nine of the National Standards.

As you teach with *Experiencing Choral Music*, there will be frequent opportunities to deepen or extend student learning through: (2) playing through creating accompaniments, (3) improvisation, (4) composition and arranging, (6) analyzing, (7) assessing, (8) linking with other arts and other academic disciplines, and (9) understanding historical and cultural contexts. The National Standards identified for each lesson and the Extension activities provided in the Teacher Wraparound Edition help you become aware of the National Standards, and the depth of learning that will occur as you implement this choral music program.

Promoting Music Literacy

Experiencing Choral Music promotes music literacy throughout the lessons. Literacy includes oral and aural aspects of music communication—reading, writing, singing and listening. Each lesson begins with Getting Started that (1)

connects the song to the student, and (2) frames the historical and cultural aspect of the music to be performed. From there the students are directed to the Links to Learning that is divided into three categories: Vocal, Theory and Artistic Expression. These exercises emphasize reading development and artistic expression. These may be rhythmic, melodic, harmonic or a combination thereof; and are directly related to the objectives of the lesson. The exercises lead directly into the musical selection. Students are encouraged to sight-sing in every lesson. Sight-singing is approached as a challenge and a means to musical independence for the student.

Literacy goes beyond simply reading pitch and rhythm, extending to the expressive elements of music and appropriate interpretation. Through Artistic Expression, students will be asked to explore interpretive aspects of music making, and are encouraged to suggest their own ideas for phrasing, dynamics, and so on. Through careful listening and constructive critique of their own work, they will gradually become more discriminating about the quality of performance and the impact of that performance on the audience.

Including Authentic Student Assessment

The assessment in *Experiencing Choral Music* is systematic, objective and authentic. There is ongoing informal assessment by teacher observation throughout the lessons. The text is written as a series of action steps for the student, so there are many opportunities for the director to hear and see the level of accomplishment.

Students will find objectives at the beginning of each lesson, and evaluation activities at the end. The Evaluation questions and activities are always related directly to the lesson objectives, and allow students to demonstrate their understanding. By answering the questions, and demonstrating as suggested, students are involved in *self-assessment*. Many times students are involved in their own assessment, constructing rubrics or critiquing their performance to determine what level of success has been achieved, and identifying the next challenge.

The *Teacher Wraparound Edition* includes lesson objectives, and each lesson is taught so the concepts and skills are experienced, labeled, practiced and reinforced, then measured through *formal assessment*. These assessment tasks match the lesson objectives, allowing students to demonstrate understanding of concepts and skills through performance, composition, or writing. Students are frequently required to produce audio- or videotapes. This authentic assessment keeps testing of rote learning to a minimum, and allows measurement of higher-level application of knowledge and skills. A portfolio can be constructed for individual students, groups, or the whole ensemble, demonstrating growth over time.

Connecting the Arts and Other Curriculum Areas

Lessons in *Experiencing Choral Music* integrate many appropriate aspects of musical endeavor into the preparation of a piece. Students compose, improvise, conduct, read, write, sing, play, listen/analyze and assess on an ongoing basis that builds understanding, as well as high standards. In this way, the many aspects of music are integrated for deeper learning.

As one of the arts, music can be linked to other arts through similarities and differences. Throughout the text, and particularly in the historical section, music is compared and contrasted with other arts to determine aspects of confluence and the unique features of each art.

As one way of knowing about the world, music can be compared with concepts and skills from other disciplines as seemingly different as science or mathematics. The integrations between music and other disciplines are kept at the conceptual level, to maintain the integrity of both music and the other subjects. For example, mathematical sets of 2, 3, 4, 5 and 6 might be explored as a link to pieces with changing meter; or the text of a piece might become a starting point for exploration of tone painting. In Music & History, a time line connects music to social studies, and a list of authors for each period provides a link to language and literature.

Providing a Variety of Student Activities

Experiencing Choral Music begins with the choral experience, and builds understanding through active participation in a range of activities including singing, playing, improvising, composing, arranging, moving, writing, listening, analyzing, assessing and connecting to cultures, periods or disciplines. Lessons are written with the heading "Direct students to . . ." so there is always an emphasis on learning by doing. In this way the teacher becomes a guide and places the responsibility for learning on the student. When students are engaged in meaningful and challenging activity, they are more likely to learn.

Fitting Your Classroom Needs

With *Experiencing Choral Music*, your students will be clear about purpose and direction, have multiple routes to success, and be involved in their own learning. The lessons will guide you and your students to share in the excitement of music making, and help you to grow together. The lessons are written the way you teach, and allow you to maintain and strengthen your routines, while adding flexibility, variety and depth.

ORGANIZATION AND FLEXIBILITY

Each *Experiencing Choral Music* text is divided into the following sections:
- Lessons
- Music & History
- Choral Library

Lessons

The Lessons are designed to be taught over a period of time. They are divided into three categories: Beginning of the Year, Mid-Winter, and Concert/Festival. Each lesson is developed around a piece of authentic and quality music literature. The lesson includes background information, vocal examples, sight-reading and rhythmic or melodic drills, all of which are directly related to preparation of the piece. Objectives are clearly stated, and a motivational opening activity or discussion is provided. The Teacher Wraparound Edition outlines a carefully sequenced approach to the piece and clear assessment opportunities to document achievement and growth.

Music & History

Music & History provides narrative and listening experiences for each of the five main historical periods. A *narrative lesson* provides a brief and interesting exposition of the main characteristics of the period outlining the achievements and new styles that emerged. A time line guides the student to place the musical characteristics into a larger historical and cultural context. The listening lesson includes both vocal and instrumental *listening selections* from the period, with a guide to student listening. A listing of the historical pieces to be sung from the period are cross-referenced from the Music & History divider page. Combined, these components give historical context of the period across the arts, then apply the context to musical literature.

Choral Library

The Choral Library provides the same comprehensive student lesson featured in the Lessons. The additional literature features multicultural selections, patriotic and seasonal selections, American folk music, African American spirituals, Broadway show tunes, and light concert pieces that can be used to enhance the repertoire of your choral music performance.

Overview of Lesson Objectives

Each lesson has objectives that emphasize and build conceptual understanding and skills across the lessons. The objectives in this book are:

LESSON OBJECTIVES	
Title	**Objective**
Let All Men Sing	• Sing harmony with major second intervals. • Identify and describe music related careers. • Describe and perform music representing the Contemporary period.
Annie Laurie	• Define and sing the interval of an octave. • Demonstrate musical artistry through phrasing. • Perform music representing the Scottish culture.
Cape Cod Girls	• Identify and correctly sing diphthongs. • Read and perform music with rhythmic accuracy. • Perform music representing the American sea chantey.
Gabi, Gabi	• Describe and perform call and response. • Perform music representing South African culture.
Tolite Hostias	• Perform music representing the Romantic oratorio. • Demonstrate musical artistry by singing maestoso. • Interpret music symbols referring to dynamics when performing.
Ose Shalom	• Perform music in a minor tonality. • Sing phrases expressively. • Perform music representing the Hebrew culture.
Pastores á Belén	• Read and perform music in compound meter. • Use correct diction when singing in Spanish. • Perform music representing the Puerto Rican culture.
Still, Still, Still	• Use standard terminology to describe suspension. • Identify the melody line and balance it against harmony parts when performing.
All Ye Who Music Love	• Perform with proper rhythmic clarity and good intonation. • Identify music written in contrapuntal and homophonic style. • Perform choral literature of the Renaissance.
Die Katze lässt das Mausen nicht	• Perform music representing the Baroque period. • Perform music with a German text. • Identify and perform homophony and counterpoint.
O Isis und Osiris, welche Wonne!	• Sing comfortably in falsetto range. • Perform music in the style of an opera chorus. • Describe and perform music representing the Classical period.
The Pasture	• Perform music with expressive phrasing. • Perform music with expressive word stress. • Understand the relationship between music and poetry.
Away From The Roll Of The Sea	• Sing music with legato phrases and staggered breathing. • Read and perform rhythm patterns with dotted notes and ties.

LESSON OBJECTIVES	
Title	**Objective**
Buffalo Gals	• Create rhythmic phrases using the swing style. • Define minstrel and discuss its role in American music history. • Perform music representing the American heritage.
Come To The Music	• Read and perform music that incorporates mixed meters. • Perform the interval of a perfect fifth. • Identify and describe the uses of music in society and culture.
Do You Hear The People Sing?	• Notate and perform triplets. • Relate music to history and culture. • Perform music representing the American musical theater.
Honey-Little 'Lize Medley	• Sing with accurate intonation. • Read and perform music notation in the key of B♭ major. • Perform music representing our American heritage.
Kalinka	• Define accelerando and crescendo. • Perform music representing the Russian culture.
Linden Lea	• Identify and demonstrate melodic contour. • Sing independently in small ensembles. • Perform music representing the British culture.
Loch Lomond	• Sing with accurate intonation and balance. • Sing with expressive phrasing. • Perform music representing the Scottish culture.
The Star-Spangled Banner	• Describe and sing an accidental accurately. • Read and perform rhythmic patterns that contain dotted rhythms. • Relate the music to history, to society and to culture.
Tears In Heaven	• Identify and describe uses of music in society and culture. • Perform and interpret expressively a varied repertoire of music. • Extend the vocal range with a smooth transition between registers.
Two Excerpts from *Liebeslieder Walzer*	• Perform and describe music from the Romantic period. • Extend the vocal range and demonstrate proper use of head voice. • Read and perform rhythmic notation in 3/4 meter.
Witness	• Identify call and response aurally and in notation. • Describe characteristics of the spiritual. • Perform music representing the African American spiritual.

STUDENT TEXT

The comprehensive student lessons are structured as follows:

- **FOCUS** . . . tells the student the main concepts and skills addressed in the lesson. By having only a few main goals, students and teacher will keep focused on these objectives as work progresses.

- **VOCABULARY** . . . gives the student an opportunity to build a musical vocabulary essential for clarity of thought in communicating about music to others.

- **LINKS TO LEARNING**

  Vocal . . . allows the student to explore the melodic and vocal skills that are directly related to some aspect of the upcoming musical selection. Also includes melodic sight-singing examples.

  Theory . . . builds rhythmic, theory and basic reading skills through exercises that are directly related to the musical selection about to be learned. Through sight-reading practice every day, students gain confidence and skills to become independent readers.

  Artistic Expression . . . provides interpretive aspects of music making, such as phrasing, dynamics, stylistic performance practices, movement, and artistic expression through drama, writing and the visual arts. Through interest and active participation, the student is then led logically into the piece.

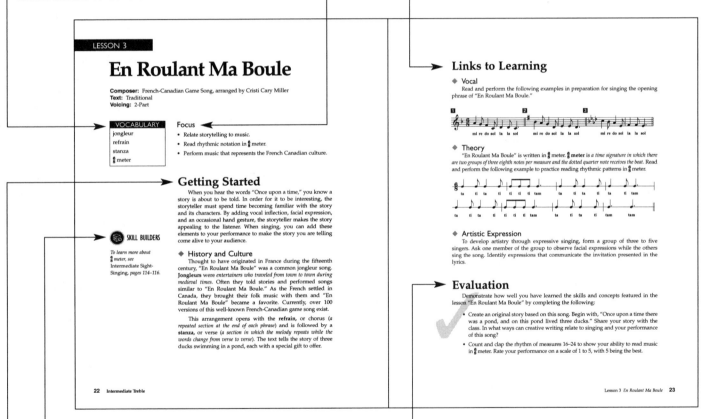

- **SIDEBAR REFERENCES** . . . provide additional information about the lesson through:
  Skill Builders . . . reference to *Sight-Singing* textbook
  Music & History . . . reference to the History section
  Spotlights . . . reference to a featured Spotlight page

- **GETTING STARTED.** . . provides a motivating introduction to the piece of music, related to the student's perspective. The History and Culture provides background information on the selection, the composer and/or the cultural context.

- **EVALUATION** . . . gives the student ways to assess accomplishment, growth and needs, for both self and group. Through careful listening and constructive critique of their own work, they will gradually become more discriminating about the quality of performance and the impact of that performance on the audience.

Lessons

The student lessons, through which students systematically build musical skills and conceptual understanding, comprise the first twelve selections of the text. They are presented in three general categories: Beginning of the Year, Mid-Winter, and Concert/Festival.

Music & History

The Historical section of the text provides a survey of Western music history through exploration of the culture and music of the five overarching periods: Renaissance, Baroque, Classical, Romantic and Contemporary. Each period is addressed in the following ways:

• **Historical Narrative Lesson** . . . provides a brief, student-oriented historical context of the period through visual art, architecture, historical events, musical developments, artistic characteristics, musical personalities and listening selections.

• **Historical Listening Lesson** . . . provides one choral and one instrumental listening selection to give students an aural experience with the styles, sounds and forms of the period. Recordings are provided to aid student learning.

Choral Library

The Choral Library maintains the same comprehensive lesson format of the Lessons and comprises the final twelve selections of the text. The additional literature features multicultural selections, patriotic and seasonal selections, American folk music, African American spirituals, Broadway show tunes and light concert pieces.

Glossary

The glossary provides brief, accurate definitions of musical terms used in the text.

TEACHER WRAPAROUND EDITION

National Standards Connections

Experiencing Choral Music affords multiple opportunities to address the National Standards. Correlations among lesson content, extension activities and bottom-page activities are listed to make obvious the relationship between lesson activities and the standards.

Suggested Teaching Sequence

Each lesson is organized to follow a logical progression from Getting Started through Evaluation, while providing maximum flexibility of use for your individual situation. Each lesson is linked to one musical selection, and provides learning opportunities based on the inherent concepts and skills required to understand and perform the piece. The lessons of the Teacher Wraparound Edition are structured as follows.

• **Overview** . . . Gives the teacher a brief analysis of the music being taught, including composer, text, voicing, key, meter, form, style, accompaniment, programming ideas and vocal ranges for each voice part.

• **Objectives** . . . Two or three concrete, measurable objectives form the skeletal structure for the lesson, allowing an interconnected approach to lesson segments.

• **Vocabulary** . . . Vocabulary terms are those used during the lesson and music terms used in the music to build understanding and skills.

• **Links to Learning** . . . The Links to Learning of the lesson includes exercises that focus on vocal, theory and artistic expression elements of the upcoming song. It provides rhythm and vocal, as well as sight-singing exercises. They are designed to sequentially develop vocal and sight-singing skills, and lead directly into the upcoming piece. These exercises may all be done before the piece is introduced, or they may be presented cumulatively, one each day, and concurrent with developing understanding of the piece.

• **The Lesson Plan: Suggested Teaching Sequence** . . . The Suggested Teaching Sequence is divided into three sections: Introduce, Rehearse, and Refine. At the end of each section, Progress Checkpoints are provided for quick informal assessment of the materials covered to that point. Introduce often refers to the Links to Learning exercises on the student page and provides meaningful ways to introduce a new song to students. Rehearse includes a list of recommended steps to teach the piece through a variety of teaching techniques. Refine puts it all together and prepares the students for performance of the piece. The Performance Tips provide teachers with the polishing nuances that transform the notes on the page into an expressive performance experience.

Informal Assessment, Student Self-Assessment, and Individual and Group Performance Evaluation

Informal Assessment is done by teacher observation during the lesson. Each objective is observable, and the text indicates the checkpoint for teacher assessment.

Student Self-Assessment is accomplished through student evaluation of their individual performance based on an established set of criteria.

Individual and Group Performance Evaluation requires the student to demonstrate a skill or understanding through individual or group evaluation. This is directly related to the Evaluation found in the student lesson. Individual and Group Performance Evaluation can be done by the teacher, student, peers or a combination thereof. Frequent audio- or videotaping is suggested as an effective means of evaluation. The tapes may be compiled into a portfolio that shows growth and developing understanding over time.

Bottom-Page Activities

Bottom-page activities in each lesson afford a plethora of background information, teaching strategies and enrichment opportunities.

- *Teacher 2 Teacher* provides a brief description of the main features of the lesson.
- *Enrichment activities* provide musical activities that go beyond the basic lesson, including composition, improvisation, and so forth.
- *Extension activities* expand the lesson to the other arts or other disciplines.
- *Teaching strategies* reinforce concepts or skills presented in the lesson, or elaborate on classroom management techniques.
- *More about* boxes provide background historical, cultural, and/or biographical information.
- *Curriculum connections* provide strategies to help students build bridges between music and other disciplines.
- *Vocal development strategies* give detailed information about specific techniques that facilitate vocal production and style.
- *Music literacy strategies* help students expand their ability to read and analyze music.
- *Cultural connections* provide cultural information related to the lesson.
- *Connecting to the arts* boxes provide strategies to help students connect music to the other arts.
- *Community connections* provide activities that extend into the community.
- *Careers in music* boxes provide information about career opportunities in music.
- *Online* directs students and teachers to **music.glencoe.com**, the Web site for *Experiencing Choral Music*.

TEACHER RESOURCE BINDER

The *Teacher Resource Binder* contains teaching materials designed to reduce teacher preparation time and maximize students' learning. The following categories are provided to assist with meeting the individual needs and interests of your students.

- **Teaching Masters.** The *Teaching Masters* support, extend and enhance the musical concepts and skills presented in the text lessons. Included are strategied focusing on composing, arranging, evaluating, analyzing, writing, multi-arts, culture and language pronunciation guides.
- **Evaluation Masters.** The *Evaluation Masters* provide performance assessment criteria, rubrics and other pages to help teachers and students with individual group, and ensemble assessment.
- **Music & History.** The *Music & History Masters* include full-color overhead transparencies of the visual art pieces introduced in each of the historical sections. They also include characteristics of the period, biographies of composers and other teaching strategies.
- **Vocal Development Masters.** The *Vocal Development Masters* provide important information about the voice. Included are numerous warm-up exercises that may be used throughout the year. Each exercise is recorded and included on the *Sight-Singing CD*.
- **Skill Builders Masters.** The *Skill Builders Masters* reinforce the development of fundamental skills, knowledge and understanding in areas such as rhythm, notation, music symbols, conducting patterns, improvisation, Kodály hand signs, time signatures and meter.
- **Sight-Singing Masters.** The *Sight-Singing Masters* are directly correlated to the *Sight-Singing* textbooks. They provide reproducible evaluation activity sheets for assessment and review.
- **Kodály, Dalcroze, Interdisciplinary.** Teaching strategies with a focus on Kodály, Dalcroze and Interdisciplinary are presented in this section.
- **Reference Resources.** The *Reference Resource Masters* serve as a resource bank for the teacher and provides a library of resource materials useful in supporting instruction.
- **Listening Selections CD.** The *Listening Selections CD* provides full recordings of the vocal and instrumental historical listening lessons from the student text. The CD also includes the accompaniment track to the vocal warm-up exercises in the Vocal Development section.
- **Sight-Singing CD.** The *Sight-Singing CD* provides a piano accompaniment track for practice songs found in the student text of *Experiencing Choral Music: Sight-Singing*.

EFFECTIVE TEACHING CHECKLIST

Teaching can be a rewarding as well as a challenging experience. The following is a compilation of suggestions and tips from experienced teachers. Review this list often.

Preparation

- Good planning leads to a successful rehearsal.
- Establish high expectations from the start—students want to succeed.
- Establish a routine and basic standards of behavior—and stick to it!
- Follow your planned routine every rehearsal (e.g., opening cue that rehearsal has begun, warm-up, sight-reading, repertoire, evaluation). Younger choirs in particular respond well to structure in a rehearsal.
- Plan, plan, plan.
- Develop long-range planning (the entire year's goals and activities, the semester, the month) and short-range planning (weekly plans and the daily lesson as they fit within the entire year's goals).
- Vary teaching strategies: modeling, peer coaching, large group, small group, cooperative learning, individual instruction, student conductors, independent practice and so forth.
- Study the score well. Anticipate problem areas.
- Be able to sing any one part while playing another.
- Know the vocal ranges of each member of the chorus.
- Select appropriate music to fit those vocal ranges.
- Remember: out-of-range results in out-of-tune singing.
- Select music of appropriate difficulty for the group.
- Plan evaluation techniques in advance.
- Have all necessary supplies and equipment ready (music in folders or ready to pass out, tapes cued, director's folder handy, recording equipment set, and so forth.) before the lesson begins.
- Plan to make beautiful music at least once during every rehearsal.

Presentation

- Begin each lesson with singing rather than talking.
- Make all parts of the lesson musical—including warm-ups and sight-reading.
- Rehearse a cappella. Use the piano as little as possible.
- Remember: Delivering information is not necessarily teaching.
- Display a positive attitude.
- Communicate effectively and concisely.
- Enthusiasm is essential.
- Make learning an enjoyable experience.
- Respect legitimate effort on the part of every student.
- Be the best musician you can be.
- Laugh often.

Pacing

- Be 30 seconds mentally ahead of the class at all times.
- Know where the lesson is going before it happens.
- Vary activities and standing/sitting positions.
- Plan a smooth transition from one activity to the next.
- Avoid "lag" time.
- If a "teachable" moment occurs, make the most of it.
- Avoid belaboring any one exercise, phrase or activity—come back to it at another time.
- Always give students a reason for repeating a section.
- Provide at least one successful musical experience in every rehearsal.

Evaluation

- Assess student learning in every lesson (formally or informally).
- Vary the assessment activities.
- Consider evaluating individual as well as group effort.
- Tape the rehearsals often (audio and/or video).
- Study the rehearsal tapes: (1) to discover where overlooked errors occur, (2) to assist in planning the next rehearsal, or (3) to share findings with the students.
- Provide students with opportunities to evaluate themselves.
- Teach critical listening to the students by asking specific students or a group of students to listen for a specific thing (balance of parts in the polyphonic section, a correct uniform vowel sound on a particular word or words, rise and fall of phrase, and so forth).
- Constantly evaluate what's really happening. (We often hear what we want to hear!)
- Listen, listen, listen.

Experiencing Choral Music

TEACHER WRAPAROUND EDITION

PROFICIENT

TENOR/BASS

Developed by

HAL•LEONARD® CORPORATION

Mc Graw Hill **Glencoe**

New York, New York   Columbus, Ohio   Chicago, Illinois   Peoria, Illinois   Woodland Hills, California

The portions of the National Standards for Music Education included here are reprinted from *National Standards for Arts Education* with permission from MENC—The National Association for Music Education. All rights reserved. Copyright © 1994 by MENC. The complete National Standards and additional materials relating to the Standards are available from MENC, 1806 Robert Fulton Drive, Reston, VA 20191 (telephone 800-336-3768).

A portion of the sales of this material goes to support music education programs through programs of MENC—The National Association for Music Education.

Glencoe

The *McGraw-Hill* Companies

Copyright © 2005 by Glencoe/McGraw-Hill, a division of The McGraw-Hill Companies. All rights reserved. Except as permitted under the United States Copyright Act, no part of this publication may be reproduced or distributed in any form or by any means, or stored in a database or retrieval system, without prior written permission from the publisher.

Printed in the United States of America.

Send all inquiries to:
Glencoe/McGraw-Hill
21600 Oxnard Street, Suite 500
Woodland Hills, CA 91367

ISBN 0-07-861125-3 (Student Edition)
ISBN 0-07-861126-1 (Teacher Wraparound Edition)

2 3 4 5 6 7 8 9   045   09 08 07 06 05

Credits

LEAD AUTHORS

Emily Crocker
Vice President of Choral Publications
Hal Leonard Corporation, Milwaukee, Wisconsin
Founder and Artistic Director, Milwaukee Children's Choir

Michael Jothen
Professor of Music, Program Director of Graduate Music Education
Chairperson of Music Education
Towson University, Towson, Maryland

Jan Juneau
Choral Director
Klein Collins High School
Spring, Texas

Henry H. Leck
Associate Professor and Director of Choral Activities
Butler University, Indianapolis, Indiana .
Founder and Artistic Director, Indianapolis Children's Choir

Michael O'Hern
Choral Director
Lake Highlands High School
Richardson, Texas

Audrey Snyder
Composer
Eugene, Oregon

Mollie Tower
Coordinator of Choral and General Music, K-12, Retired
Austin, Texas

AUTHORS

Anne Denbow
Voice Instructor, Professional Singer/Actress
Director of Music, Holy Cross Episcopal Church
Simpsonville, South Carolina

Rollo A. Dilworth
Director of Choral Activities and Music
    Education
North Park University, Chicago, Illinois

Deidre Douglas
Choral Director
Aragon Middle School, Houston, Texas

Ruth E. Dwyer
Associate Director and Director of Education
Indianapolis Children's Choir
Indianapolis, Indiana

Norma Freeman
Choral Director
Saline High School, Saline, Michigan

Cynthia I. Gonzales
Music Theorist
Greenville, South Carolina

Michael Mendoza
Professor of Choral Activities
New Jersey State University
Trenton, New Jersey

Thomas Parente
Associate Professor
Westminster Choir College of Rider University
Princeton, New Jersey

Barry Talley
Director of Fine Arts and Choral Director
Deer Park ISD, Deer Park, Texas

CONTRIBUTING AUTHORS

Debbie Daniel
Choral Director, Webb Middle School
Garland, Texas

Roger Emerson
Composer/Arranger
Mount Shasta, California

Kari Gilbertson
Choral Director, Forest Meadow Junior High
Richardson, Texas

Tim McDonald
Creative Director, Music Theatre International
New York, New York

Christopher W. Peterson
Assistant Professor of Music Education (Choral)
University of Wisconsin-Milwaukee
Milwaukee, Wisconsin

Kirby Shaw
Composer/Arranger
Ashland, Oregon

Stephen Zegree
Professor of Music
Western Michigan State University
Kalamazoo, Michigan

EDITORIAL

Linda Rann
Senior Editor
Hal Leonard Corporation
Milwaukee, Wisconsin

Stacey Nordmeyer
Choral Editor
Hal Leonard Corporation
Milwaukee, Wisconsin

Table of Contents

Music & History

Choral Library

TO THE STUDENT

Welcome to choir!

By singing in the choir, you have chosen to be a part of an exciting and rewarding adventure. The benefits of being in choir are many. Basically, singing is fun. It provides an expressive way of sharing your feelings and emotions. Through choir, you will have friends that share a common interest with you. You will experience the joy of making beautiful music together. Choir provides the opportunity to develop your interpersonal skills. It takes teamwork and cooperation to sing together, and you must learn how to work with others. As you critique your individual and group performances, you can improve your ability to analyze and communicate your thoughts clearly.

Even if you do not pursue a music career, music can be an important part of your life. There are many avocational opportunities in music. **Avocational** means *not related to a job or career*. Singing as a hobby can provide you with personal enjoyment, enrich your life, and teach you life skills. Singing is something you can do for the rest of your life.

In this course, you will be presented with the basic skills of vocal production and music literacy. You will be exposed to songs from different cultures, songs in many different styles and languages, and songs from various historical periods. You will discover connections between music and the other arts. Guidelines for becoming a better singer and choir member include:

- Come to class prepared to learn.
- Respect the efforts of others.
- Work daily to improve your sight-singing skills.
- Sing expressively at all times.
- Have fun singing.

This book was written to provide you with a meaningful choral experience. Take advantage of the knowledge and opportunities offered here. Your exciting adventure of experiencing choral music is about to begin!

Lessons

Lessons for the Beginning of the Year

Lessons for Mid-Winter

Lessons for Concert/Festival

Let All Men Sing

OVERVIEW

Composer: Keith Christopher
Text: Keith Christopher
Voicing: TTBB
Key: Bb major, G major, Ab major, Bb major, G major
Meter: 4/4
Form: ABABAB with introduction
Style: Contemporary American Anthem
Accompaniment: Piano
Programming: Festival

Vocal Ranges:

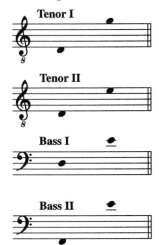

OBJECTIVES

After completing this lesson, students will be able to:

• Demonstrate accurate intonation and fundamental skills while performing.
• Identify music-related vocations within the community.
• Perform music representing the Contemporary period.

VOCABULARY

Have students review vocabulary in student lesson. Introduce terms found in the music. A complete glossary of terms is found on page 246 of the student book.

2

Let All Men Sing

Composer: Keith Christopher
Text: Keith Christopher
Voicing: TTBB

VOCABULARY

glee
avocation
Contemporary period
major second
diction

MUSIC & HISTORY

To learn more about the Contemporary period, see page 126.

Focus

• Sing harmony with intervals of a major second.
• Identify and describe music-related careers.
• Describe and perform music representing the Contemporary period.

Getting Started

Let All Men Sing!

Are there any football players in your choir? Soccer players? Do any of the singers in your choir want to be engineers? Teachers? Lawyers? All men certainly can sing!

Founded in 1859, the all-male Harvard University Glee Club is the oldest college chorus in America. The Glee Club has performed male chorus music, college songs and **glees** (*unaccompanied and homophonic vocal music in three or four parts*) for audiences around the world. Any male singer at Harvard can audition for the Glee Club. The chorus consists of students studying liberal arts, engineering, business, or any major offered at Harvard. The Glee Club is a good example of music **avocation** (*not related to a job or career*). Singing as a hobby can provide you with personal enjoyment, and it is something you can do for the rest of your life.

Sometimes students find that music study leads them to a vocation. If you have an interest in music education, performance, industry, composing, or other venues, music can provide countless opportunities for a rewarding career.

◆ History and Culture

Written in 1997, "Let All Men Sing" is a good illustration of choral music from the **Contemporary period** (*1900–present*). The frequent use of a **major second** (*two notes a whole step apart*) in the harmony is one characteristic of contemporary music. How many major seconds can you find in the harmonies of "Let All Men Sing"?

2   Proficient Tenor/Bass

RESOURCES

Proficient Sight-Singing

Sight-Singing in G Major, pages 71–73
Sight-Singing in Ab Major, pages 71–73
Sight-Singing in Bb Major, page 153

Teacher Resource Binder

Teaching Master 1, *All About Auditions*
Teaching Master 2, *Excitement Through Diction*
Skill Builder 1, *Chords and Harmony*
Vocal Development 9, *Diction*
Music and History 21, *Keith Christopher, a Contemporary Composer*

For additional resources, see TRB Table of Contents.

Links to Learning

◆ **Vocal**

The major seconds in "Let All Men Sing" give the harmony a stirring and colorful sound. To become familiar with the sound of a major second, you can sing two scales at the same time that are a major second apart. With a classmate, practice both scale fragments shown below and then sing them together.

F	G	A	B♭	C
do	re	mi	fa	sol

G	A	B	C	D
do	re	mi	fa	sol

◆ **Theory**

Another technique composer Keith Christopher uses to give "Let All Men Sing" harmonic excitement is to move from a unison melody to four-part harmony. This first occurs in measures 18–19. Use solfège syllables and practice the following patterns until you can confidently sing your part. In a TTBB quartet, sing the measures together to demonstrate moving from a unison melody to four-part harmony.

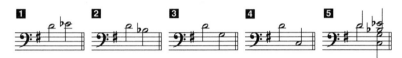

◆ **Artistic Expression**

• Clear **diction,** *the pronunciation of words while singing,* is necessary for an effective performance of "Let All Men Sing." Explode the consonants and go directly to tall vowel sounds. The diction must be crisp and clean.

Evaluation

Demonstrate how well you have learned the skills and concepts featured in the lesson "Let All Men Sing" by completing the following:

• In a TTBB quartet, sing measures 60–70 to demonstrate your ability to sing harmony with major seconds. Evaluate how well you were able to stay on your part and exhibit accurate intonation.

• Describe three types of music careers available to young people today.

Vocal

The Vocal section is designed to prepare students to sing major seconds.

Have students:

• Sing each example separately.

• Sing each example together, paying close attention to intonation.

Theory

The Theory section is designed to prepare students to sing in four-part harmony.

Have students:

• Sing examples 1–4.

• Sing example 5 when all pitches from the previous examples are secure.

Artistic Expression

The Artistic Expression section is designed to prepare students to sing with clear diction.

Have students remember to over-emphasize the consonants and focus on tall-vowel sounds as they learn this song.

RESOURCES

Proficient Tenor/Bass Rehearsal/Performance CD

CD 1:1 Voices

CD 1:2 Accompaniment Only

CD 3:1 Vocal Practice Track—Tenor I

CD 4:1 Vocal Practice Track—Tenor II

CD 5:1 Vocal Practice Track—Baritone

CD 6:1 Vocal Practice Track—Bass

National Standards

1. Singing, alone and with others, a varied repertoire of music. **(a, b, c)**

5. Reading and notating music. **(a)**

9. Understanding music in relation to history and culture. **(a)**

LESSON PLAN

Suggested Teaching Sequence and Performance Tips

1. Introduce

Direct students to:

- Read and discuss the information found in the Getting Started section on student page 2.
- Practice the examples found in the Vocal section.
- Practice the examples found in the Theory section.
- Review and discuss the importance of clear diction as stated in the Artistic Expression section.
- Introduce the opening fanfare in measures 1–8 and also in measures 60–end.

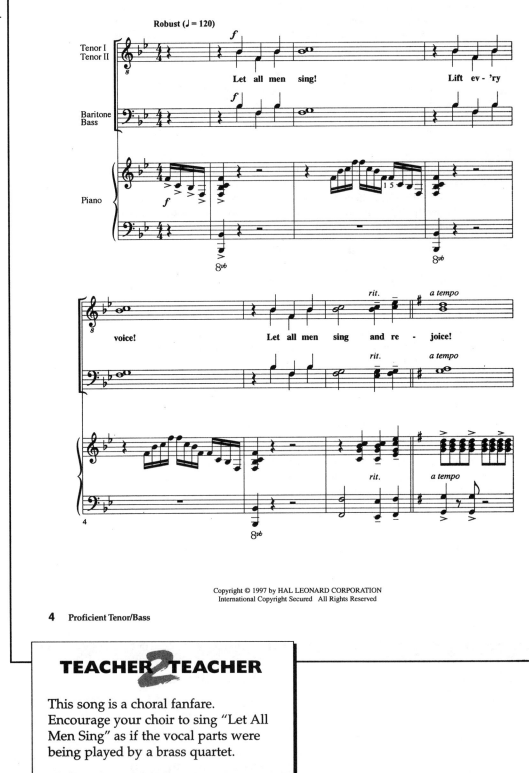

For Bill Stroud

Let All Men Sing

For TTBB and Piano

Words and Music by
KEITH CHRISTOPHER

Copyright © 1997 by HAL LEONARD CORPORATION
International Copyright Secured   All Rights Reserved

4   Proficient Tenor/Bass

TEACHER2TEACHER

This song is a choral fanfare. Encourage your choir to sing "Let All Men Sing" as if the vocal parts were being played by a brass quartet.

Progress Checkpoints

Observe students' progress in:

✓ Their ability to sing major seconds comfortably and in tune.

✓ Their ability to sing in four-part harmony.

✓ Their understanding of clear diction.

✓ Their understanding of the type of sound needed to sing this piece, a brass quartet fanfare.

CONNECTIONS

Fanfares

To learn more about fanfares, have your class listen to your school band or to a recording of a band play a fanfare. Discuss its musical characteristics and name other choral songs that use the singing style of a fanfare.

2. Rehearse

Direct students to:

- Rehearse measures 2–8 separately, paying attention to accurate intonation.
- Combine all four parts when all pitches and rhythms are secure.
- Continue to rehearse the piece in sections as above to the end of the piece. Suggested sections are: measures 11–26, measures 27–42, measures 43–59 and 60–73.
- Focus on any problem spots and drill until secure.
- Sing the entire piece, once all parts are secure.

Progress Checkpoints

Observe students' progress in:

- ✓ Their ability to read all rhythms correctly.
- ✓ Their ability to sing all pitches accurately and in tune.
- ✓ Singing with clear diction.

6   Proficient Tenor/Bass

Encourage your students to expore **music.glencoe.com**, the Web site for *Experiencing Choral Music*. You may wish to preview the rich content before directing your students online. Options available on the Web site include:

- Web Link Exercises
- Interactive Projects
- Audio Samples

3. Refine

Direct students to:

- Go to the beginning and sing the song again, focusing on all dynamic and expressive markings.
- Show a contrast between legato singing and a bouncy, more rhythmic style of singing, based on the requirements of the music.

Progress Checkpoints

Observe students' progress in:

✓ Their correct use of dynamics and expression.

✓ Performing an audible contrast between legato and rhythmic singing.

ASSESSMENT
Creating an Assessment Rubric

Have students:

1. Discuss the characteristics of a desirable performance of this piece, using all their knowledge of performance techniques.
2. Identify the criteria by which they think an adjudicator might assess the performance of this piece.
3. For each criterion, decide what characteristics will comprise an adequate, good, very good, and excellent performance.
4. Create a rubric chart.
5. Use the rubric to assess quartets or small ensembles performing all or part of this song.

ASSESSMENT

Informal Assessment

In this lesson, students showed the ability to:

- Sing major seconds in harmony.
- Identify and describe music-related careers.
- Describe and perform Contemporary music.

TEACHING STRATEGY

Reading Changing Meters

The only way to get comfortable with changing meters is to encounter them daily. To help your students in this area, have them;

- Compose short rhythms for each other to read, using at least two meters.
- Use different constants; for example, try 2/8, 3/8, 4/8, 5/8 and 6/8, with the eighth notes as the steady beat.
- Make up changing meter dances that have accents or stomps on the strong beat of each measure, so students are able to internalize each meter change.

Student Self-Assessment

Have students evaluate their individual performances based on the following:

• Diction
• Expressive Singing
• Phrasing
• Accurate Rhythms
• Intonation

Have each student rate his/her performance of this song in the areas above on a scale of 1–5, 5 being the best.

COMMUNITY CONNECTIONS

Contemporary Composers

To expose your students to more music from the Contemporary period, consider contacting a local arts agency to learn the names of any composers in the community.

• Invite a local composer to visit your classroom. (You will need to screen choices for appropriateness.)

• Plan questions to ask about the art of composing music. Listen to some compositions by the composer.

• Plan a performance using music by the composer.

Individual and Group Performance Evaluation

To further measure growth of musical skills presented in this lesson, direct students to complete the Evaluation section on page 3.

- Have students form TTBB quartets and sing measures 60–70, focusing on the major seconds in the passage. Help them evaluate their performance.

- Discuss music-related careers with your choir and help them identify various careers available to them.

ENRICHMENT

Composing Music

When composing music, a writer must take into consideration both melody and rhythm. Sometimes a composer will start with a rhythmic idea, while at other times he or she will start with a melody. Direct students to:

1. Select a meter:
- simple meter (2/4, 2/4, 4/4)
- compound meter (6/9, 9/8, 3/8)
- asymmetric meter (5/8, 7/8)
2. Write a four-measure simple or complex rhythmic pattern in that meter.
3. Select a key (major, minor, pentatonic, modal).
4. Using the newly composed rhythmic pattern, write a melody based on the selected key.
5. Exchange compositions with a classmate. Check each other's work for rhythmic and melodic accuracy.
6. Make changes and corrections as necessary.
7. Read and perform their compositions for the class.

TEACHING STRATEGY

Large-Ensemble Techniques

Videotape a class performance of "Let All Men Sing" Listen not only for choral blend and balance, clear diction and well-tuned singing, but also for shared communication and expression of the text. Critique the performance based on these large-ensemble performance techniques. Repeat this process based on a videotaped performance of a formal concert of the same song. Compare the two performances.

SPOTLIGHT

Posture & Breath Management

There are some basic techniques to help you sing higher, lower, louder, softer and for longer periods of time without tiring. First, a singer needs to have proper posture. Try the following exercise:

1. Stand with your feet shoulder width apart and your knees unlocked.
2. Balance your head effortlessly on the top of your spine.
3. Exhale all of your air.
4. Raise your arms up over your head.
5. Take in a deep breath as if you were sipping through a straw.
6. Slowly lower your arms down to your sides.
7. Let out your air on a breathy "pah" without letting your chest drop.

Now that you have discovered proper posture, try this for discovering how a singer should breathe and manage the breath:

1. Place your hands on your waist at the bottom of your ribcage.
2. Take in an easy breath without lifting your chest or shoulders.
3. Feel your waist and ribcage expand all the way around like an inflating inner tube.
4. Let your breath out slowly on "sss," feeling your inner tube deflating as if it has a slow leak.
5. Remember to keep your chest up the entire time.
6. Take in another easy breath over four counts before your inner tube has completely deflated, then let your air out on "sss" for eight counts.
7. Repeat this step several times, taking in an easy breath over four counts and gradually increasing the number of release counts to sixteen.
8. Once you have reached sixteen counts, try to see how many times you can repeat it without getting tired.

Practice this every day, gradually working up to five minutes of repetition. If you become lightheaded, you are taking in too much air for the number of counts you are exhaling.

A "catch breath," which is required when you don't have much time to breathe, should feel like the kind of breath you take when you are pleasantly surprised or see something lovely for the first time. It must be silent, though!

Spotlight *Posture & Breath Management* **11**

RESOURCES

Teacher Resource Binder

Vocal Development 1–6, *Keep the Joy in Singing!*
Vocal Development 13, *Posture and Breathing*
Reference 16, *Describing: Expanding a Musical Vocabulary*

National Standards

1. Singing, alone and with others. **(b)**

POSTURE & BREATH MANAGEMENT

Objectives

- Demonstrate basic performance techniques including proper singing posture.

Suggested Teaching Sequence

Direct students to:

- Read the Spotlight On Posture & Breath Management on student page 11 and identify the importance of proper posture in singing.
- Perform the exercise for developing posture as presented on page 11.
- Perform the exercise for breathing as presented on page 11.
- Compare the concept of proper posture to basic performance techniques and the effect posture has on breath support, tone quality and overall stage presence.

Progress Checkpoints

Observe students' progress in:

✓ Their ability to stand in correct singing posture.
✓ Their ability to breathe using correct breath management.
✓ Their ability to explain the importance of proper posture in singing.

Annie Laurie

OVERVIEW

Composer: Lady John Scott, arranged by Victor Johnson
Text: William Douglas
Voicing: TTB
Key: C major, D major
Meter: 4/4
Form: Strophic
Style: Scottish Folk Song
Accompaniment: Piano
Programming: Seasonal Concert

Vocal Ranges:

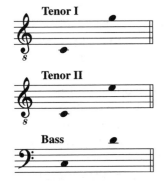

OBJECTIVES

After completing this lesson, students will be able to:

- Demonstrate accurate intonation and fundamental skills while performing.
- Interpret music terms (e.g., phrasing) referring to articulation during performances.
- Perform music representing the Scottish culture.

VOCABULARY

Have students review vocabulary in student lesson. Introduce terms found in the music. A complete glossary of terms is found on page 246 of the student book.

Annie Laurie

Composer: Lady John Scott, arranged by Victor Johnson
Text: William Douglas
Voicing: TTB

VOCABULARY

octave
interval
intonation
major scale
phrase

🔺 **SPOTLIGHT**

To learn more about the physiology of the voice, see page 21.

Focus

- Define and sing the interval of an octave.
- Demonstrate musical artistry through phrasing.
- Perform music representing the Scottish culture.

Getting Started

What pop song is number one this week? Do you know any of these former number one hits?

"My Heart Will Go On" (1999)
"Let It Be" (1972)
"Hound Dog" (1956)
"God Bless America" (1938)

Why do some songs stay popular for years and years? "Annie Laurie" has stood the test of time. It has been sung for more than 200 years.

◆ History and Culture

Annie Laurie (1682–1761) was the daughter of Sir Robert Laurie, the first Baronet of the Maxwelton family of Scotland. It is believed that one of Annie's suitors, William Douglas, wrote this poem to express his devoted feelings for her. Annie's father, however, did not accept William, and the two were never married.

In 1835 Lady John Scott, born Alicia Anne Spottiswoode (1810–1900) in Berwickshire, Scotland, set an adapted version of the poem to music. Lady John Scott was a very accomplished songwriter and left a great gift to homesick soldiers. "Annie Laurie" was a favorite song of the Scottish soldiers during the Crimean War (1854–1856) and then during World War I (1914–1918).

Here are the definitions for several Scottish words in "Annie Laurie:"

braes—the steep bank along a river
bonnie—good looking, pretty
fa's—falls (descends)
downe and dee—down and die
ee—eye

12 Proficient Tenor/Bass

RESOURCES

Proficient Sight-Singing
Reading in C Major, pages 13, 26–27, 34–35
Reading in D Major, pages 104–106

Teacher Resource Binder
Evaluation Master 1, *Accuracy in Performance*
Evaluation Master 4, *Checking Out Phrasing*
Skill Builder 20, *Naming Intervals*
Skill Builder 22, *Pitch Challenge in Major*
Reference 16, *Expanding a Musical Vocabulary*
For additional resources, see TRB Table of Contents.

Links to Learning

◆ Vocal

One of the most identifiable features of "Annie Laurie" is the **octave** *(two notes that are eight notes apart)* skip in the opening melody. Perform the following example to practice singing a large **interval** *(the distance between two notes)* with accurate **intonation** *(the accuracy of pitch)*. Sing cleanly without sliding from the first pitch to the second pitch.

mi   re   do   do   do   ti   ti   la_____

◆ Theory

This arrangement of "Annie Laurie" uses two major scales, C and D. A **major scale** is *a scale that has* do *as its keynote, or home tone.* Sing both scales using solfège syllables.

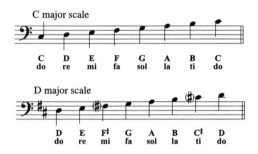

C major scale

C	D	E	F	G	A	B	C
do	re	mi	fa	sol	la	ti	do

D major scale

D	E	F♯	G	A	B	C♯	D
do	re	mi	fa	sol	la	ti	do

◆ Artistic Expression

"Annie Laurie" is known for its beautiful melodic line and long, smooth phrases. A **phrase** is *a musical idea with a beginning and end.* Sing the phrase in measures 4–8 and 9–12, while drawing an arch in the air with your arm. Shape the phrase by beginning softly. Your phrase should be the loudest at the highest point of your arch and the softest at its lowest point.

Evaluation

Demonstrate how well you have learned the skills and concepts featured in the lesson" Annie Laurie" by completing the following:

* Define the term *octave*. Individually sing the opening phrase, measures 4–8, to show that you can accurately sing the interval of an octave without sliding between the two pitches. Evaluate how well you were able to sing both pitches accurately.

* Perform measures 21–29 in small groups to show your understanding of phrases. Discuss how well your group was able to demonstrate the shaping of the phrase.

Lesson 2 *Annie Laurie* **13**

LINKS TO LEARNING

Vocal

The Vocal section is designed to prepare students to sing the interval of an octave.

Have students

* Sing the example using solfège syllables.
* Ensure that they do not slide from note to note.

Theory

The Theory section is designed to prepare students to sing the C major and D major scales.

Have students sing both scales using note names or solfège syllables.

Artistic Expression

The Artistic Expression section is designed to prepare students to sing phrases correctly.

Have students:

* Sing each phrase in the measures indicated.
* Use their arms to visually trace the phrase as they sing.

RESOURCES

Proficient Tenor/Bass Rehearsal/Performance CD

CD 1:3 Voices

CD 1:4 Accompaniment Only

CD 3:2 Vocal Practice Track—Tenor I

CD 4:2 Vocal Practice Track—Tenor II

CD 6:2 Vocal Practice Track—Bass

National Standards

1. Sing, alone and with others, a varied repertoire of music. **(a, b, c)**

5. Reading and notating music. **(a)**

6. Listening to, analyzing and describing music. **(c)**

9. Understanding music in relation to history and culture. **(a)**

LESSON PLAN

Suggested Teaching Sequence and Performance Tips

1. Introduce

Direct students to:

- Read and discuss the information found in the Getting Started section on student page 12.
- Practice the example in the Vocal section.
- Locate and identify the octaves that occur in the score in measures 4–12. *(measures 5 and 9)*
- Identify the key signature and clarify the pitch that is *do*. Have students locate and identify *do* in the melodic line by singing only the *do's* while you play the entire melodic line on the keyboard.
- Repeat measures 4–12 using solfège syllables.
- Add text and accompaniment measures in 4–12 when all pitches and rhythms are secure.

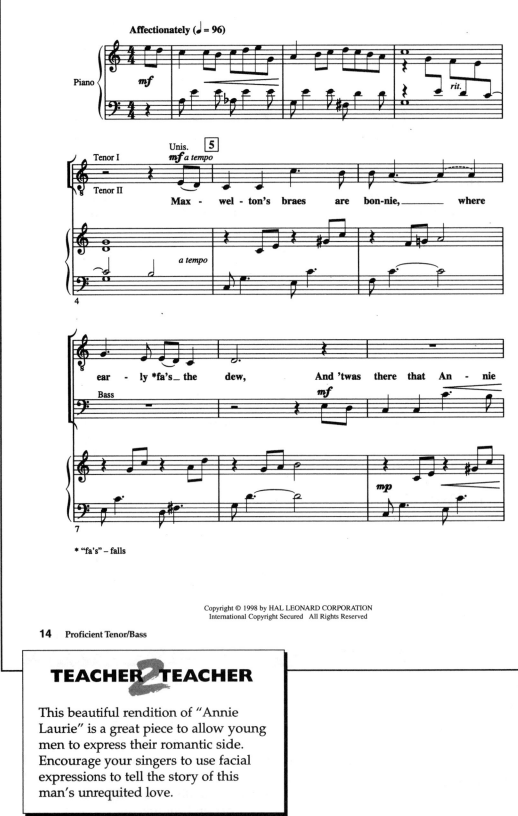

Annie Laurie

For TTB and Piano

Arranged by
VICTOR JOHNSON

Words by WILLIAM DOUGLAS
Music by LADY JOHN SCOTT

* "fa's" – falls

Copyright © 1998 by HAL LEONARD CORPORATION
International Copyright Secured   All Rights Reserved

14   Proficient Tenor/Bass

TEACHER 2 TEACHER

This beautiful rendition of "Annie Laurie" is a great piece to allow young men to express their romantic side. Encourage your singers to use facial expressions to tell the story of this man's unrequited love.

Lau-rie _____ gave me her prom - ise true; Gave_

me her prom - ise true, where_ ne'er for-got 'twill be, and for

bon - nie An - nie Lau-rie, _____ I will lay _ me *doon and dee.

* "doon and dee" – down and die

- Locate and identify octaves in the Bass part in measures 13–20. (measure 19)
- Sight-sing the Bass part in measures 13–20 on a neutral syllable while the Tenors locate the octaves in their own part. (measure 19)
- Sight-sing the Tenor part in the manner above.
- Add text and accompaniment in this section when all pitches and rhythms are secure.
- Review all parts from the beginning with text and accompaniment. Clarify any unknown text and define.

Progress Checkpoints

Observe students' progress in:
✓ Their ability to locate and recognize the octave skips in the music.
✓ Their ability to sing octaves correctly and without sliding from note to note.

TEACHING STRATEGY

Performance Techniques

Have students:

1. Identify appropriate performance techniques to be used in the performance of this song.
2. Either in small ensembles or with the entire choir (large ensemble), perform the song exhibiting these performance techniques.
3. Describe the performance techniques experienced during the performance.
4. Critique the performance based on the observed performance techniques.
5. Repeat this process often in both informal and formal concert settings.

2. Rehearse

Direct students to:

- Locate and identify which part has the melodic line in measures 22–37. *(Tenor I)*
- Sight-sing the first Tenor part in measures 22–37, with the text, while the Tenor IIs and Basses sight-sing their parts on a hum. Play all parts on the piano while your choir does this.
- Use rhythmic syllables and read the Tenor II part in the same section. Follow dynamic markings as written. Have the Basses and Tenor I section follow along and "score" their parts, planning their usage of dynamics.
- Sing both the Tenor parts with text and dynamics when all pitches and rhythms are secure.
- Sight-sing the Bass part in this section with text and dynamics.
- As a choir, sing all parts together in measures 22–37 with text with keyboard support (if necessary). Emphasize allowing the melody to come through.
- Review song from the beginning through measure 37.

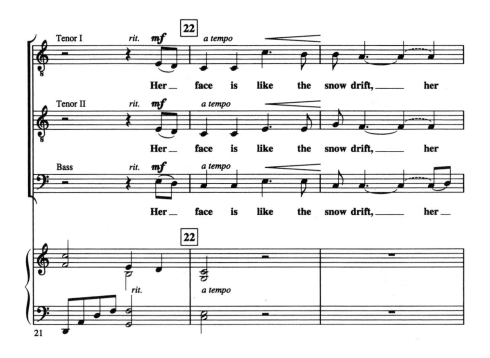

16   Proficient Tenor/Bass

CURRICULAR CONNECTIONS

Scottish Poetry

Have students form teams of two or three and research Scottish poets and/or Scottish ballad repertoire. Research should include basic knowledge of the author or composer, the time period or era in which the writer lived, and the major political or social issues of both Scotland and England in said time period. Students could also include a comparison of what was happening in the United States during the time they choose. Have each team present their research to the class.

fair-est _____ that e'er the sun shone on; That

fair-est _____ that e'er the sun _ shone on;

fair-est _____ that e'er the sun shone on;

27

- Locate and identify the key change. *(measures 38–39)*
- Identify *do* in the new key. *(D)*
- Sight-sing measures 39–46 using solfège syllables. Then review with text.
- Sight-sing measures 47–end with text, all parts.
- Practice moving from the D major chord to the A major chord, using solfège syllables or letter names.
- Sing the chords in measures 48–49 in the manner above.
- Review all parts in measures 47–49 and continue to read again to the end of the piece.
- Work parts as needed in measures 54–end. Be sure that singers end the piece "tenderly," not blasting the final phrase.

Progress Checkpoints
Observe students' progress in:
- ✓ Their ability to read all rhythms correctly.
- ✓ Their ability to sing all pitches accurately and in tune.
- ✓ Their ability to balance chords.
- ✓ Their effective use of dynamics.

e'er the sun shone on, and dark blue is her

Oo _____ sun shone on, _____ oo

Oo _____ sun shone on, _____ oo

30

TEACHING STRATEGY

Performing from Memory
Have students:
1. Memorize this piece by learning shorter phrases at a time.
2. Perform it from memory on a program or in competition.
3. Further develop memorization skills by memorizing other songs and solos to perform for the class informally or at formal concerts.

3. Refine

Direct students to:

- Sing measures 22–28 a cappella. Review the Bass line with an emphasis on tuning the many half steps in this line.
- Review from the beginning and work toward memorization.
- Watch the conductor for tempo changes.
- Listen for clean, accurate rhythmic and lyric articulation. Be sure the triplets in measures 24 and 32 are evenly spaced.

Progress Checkpoints

Observe students' progress in:

- ✓ Their ability to create a healthy balance in the a cappella section in measures 22–28. (Do the harmonic parts support the melody?)
- ✓ Their correct usage of the expressive markings to tell the story of the text.
- ✓ Their use of facial expressions to tell the story of the piece.
- ✓ Their ability to memorize the piece.

TEACHING STRATEGY

Concert Etiquette

Have students:

1. Identify appropriate concert etiquette in a variety of settings (formal concerts, informal concerts, large concert halls, small concert halls, and so forth).
2. Attend a variety of live performances.
3. Discuss the appropriate and inappropriate concert behaviors observed.
4. Write a short analysis of appropriate concert etiquette.

* "fa' " – fall

Lesson 2 *Annie Laurie* **19**

Informal Assessment

In this lesson, students showed the ability to:

- Define and sing octaves.
- Use phrasing to demonstrate artistry.
- Perform music representing the Scottish culture.

Student Self-Assessment

Have students evaluate their individual performances based on the following:

- Diction
- Expressive Singing
- Phrasing
- Breath Management
- Correct Part-Singing

Have each student rate his/her performance of this song in the areas above on a scale of 1–5, 5 being the best.

MORE ABOUT...

Expressive Elements of Music

In language, expression is used to communicate mood. The expressive elements of tempo, dynamics, tone color, pitch, articulation and intensity help to convey mood. These same expressive elements are available in performing music, and help the performer establish and communicate the intended mood. It is up to the performer to understand and interpret the intentions of the composer and arranger. In a large group, the conductor frequently helps the group make these decisions, so the entire group is interpreting the piece the same way.

Individual and Group Performance Evaluation

To further measure growth of musical skills presented in this lesson, direct students to complete the Evaluation section on page 13.

• Have students define the term octave. Direct them to individually sing the phrase in measures 4–8, to show they can sing an octave without sliding from note to note. Help them evaluate how they did.

• Have students get into small groups and perform measures 21–29 to show how well they can create phrases. Assist them in evaluating their performance.

ENRICHMENT

Analyzing Form

Form relates to the structure or musical design of a composition. If students can identify and analyze the form of a composition, they are able to perform with greater comprehension and understanding. Direct students to:

• Identify the form of "Annie Laurie" as strophic.

• Show where each verse begins. (Verse 1 measure 5; Verse 2 measure 22; Verse 3 measure 39)

• Analyze the form and discuss how each verse is treated differently. Have students discuss the elements of texture, harmony, placement of melody, dynamics, tempo and so forth.

20   Proficient Tenor/Bass

Additional National Standards

The following National Standards are addressed through the Assessment, Extension, Enrichment and bottom-page activities:

7. Evaluate music and music performances. **(a, b)**

8. Understanding relationships between music, the other arts and disciplines outside the arts. **(c)**

SPOTLIGHT

Physiology Of The Voice

Physiology is a branch of biology that deals with living organisms and their parts. It is interesting to see how the parts of the human body work together to produce vocal sound. Vocal production requires the following elements:

The Actuators

The actuators are parts of the body involved in the breathing process. The parts of the airway include (1) head airways (the nose and mouth), (2) pharynx (throat tube), (3) larynx (voice box), (4) trachea (windpipe), (5) bronchi (two branches of trachea that lead into the lungs), and (6) lungs. The muscles used in breathing include (1) the abdominals (belly muscles), (2) intercostals (muscles attached to the ribs), and (3) diaphragm (a horizontal, dome-shaped muscle separating the chest and abdominal cavities).

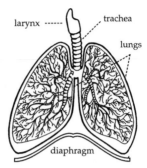

The Vibrators

The vocal folds (or "vocal cords") are housed in the larynx (the voice box) at the top of the trachea and vibrate when air from the lungs passes between them.

The Resonators

The sound waves produced by the vocal folds are enhanced and amplified by the resonators or natural cavities located in the pharynx, larynx, mouth, nasal passages and sinus passages.

The Articulators

The articulators are the parts of the body used in speech; namely, the lips, teeth, tongue, jaw and soft palate. To find the soft palate, place the tip of your tongue on the roof of your mouth and slide it toward your throat just past the bony ridge of your hard palate.

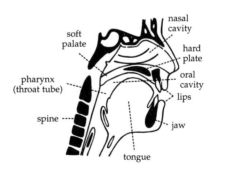

Spotlight *Physiology Of The Voice* **21**

RESOURCES

Teacher Resource Binder

Vocal Development 1–6, *Keep the Joy in Singing!*
Reference 16, *Expanding a Musical Vocabulary*
Reference 22, *Monitoring My Voice*

National Standards

1. Singing, alone and with others. **(b)**
8. Understanding relationships between music, the other arts, and disciplines outside the arts. **(a, b)**

PHYSIOLOGY OF THE VOICE

Objectives

• Define the relationship between the content of other subjects and those of music.
• Demonstrate knowledge and awareness of vocal physiology as important to musical vocal performance.

Suggested Teaching Sequence

Direct students to:

• Read the Spotlight On The Physiology Of The Voice on student page 21 and identify the four main elements of vocal production and the parts of the body used for speech.
• Listen and observe as teacher demonstrates various pitches on a stringed instrument—guitar, violin, and so forth.
• Comment on the correlation between string length, thickness as it affects pitch and tone color.
• Draw parallels between the human voice and musical instruments as it relates to pitch, timbre and tone color
• Relate the information about physiology of the parts of the voice to what they have studied in science class.

Progress Checkpoints

Observe students' progress in:

✓ Their ability to identify the parts of the body used for singing.
✓ Knowing the importance of how the voice works in relationship to how they sing.

Cape Cod Girls
OVERVIEW

Composer: Traditional Sea Chantey, arranged by Emily Crocker

Text: Traditional

Voicing: TTBB

Key: E major

Meter: 4/4

Form: AA¹BA² Coda

Style: Sea Chantey

Accompaniment: Piano

Programming: Americana Program, Thematic programming on songs of the sea

Vocal Ranges:

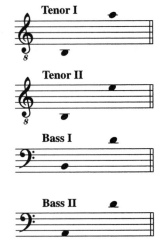

OBJECTIVES

After completing this lesson, students will be able to:

- Exhibit accurate fundamental skills while performing.
- Demonstrate accurate rhythm while performing.
- Perform music representing the American sea chantey.

VOCABULARY

Have students review vocabulary in student lesson. Introduce terms found in the music. A complete glossary of terms is found on page 246 of the student book.

22

Cape Cod Girls

Composer: Traditional Sea Chantey, arranged by Emily Crocker

Text: Traditional

Voicing: TTBB

VOCABULARY

sea chantey

diphthong

syllabic stress

Focus

- Identify and correctly sing diphthongs.
- Read and perform music with rhythmic accuracy.
- Perform music representing the American sea chantey.

Getting Started

When it comes to cleaning your room at home, which description best fits you?

1. You love to clean and go right to work.
2. You do not enjoy cleaning, but if you play music or sing, the work gets done.

If you relate to the second statement, you have something in common with eighteenth-century sailors. "Cape Cod Girls" is a **sea chantey,** or *a song sung by sailors in the rhythm of their work.*

◆ History and Culture

The work aboard early sailing ships included pulling the ropes, hoisting the sails and raising the anchor. The work was often repetitive and took a long time to complete. Sometimes the sailors created upbeat chanteys with improvised, humorous verses to pass the time. A Yankee sailor on his way to Australia is believed to have written "Cape Cod Girls."

Cape Cod, Massachusetts, has a rich maritime heritage. The Atlantic Ocean surrounds this tiny peninsula and has dominated Cape Cod's culture and economy ever since the arrival of the pilgrims in 1620. During the mid-nineteenth century, most of the captains of the tall ships that transported the world's goods were from Cape Cod. In addition, fishing and whaling were major industries in the area.

After you learn "Cape Cod Girls," you might want to sing it while you clean your room!

 SPOTLIGHT

To learn more about vowels, see page 99.

22 Proficient Tenor/Bass

RESOURCES

Proficient Sight-Singing

Reading in E Major, page 155

Reading Sixteenth and Eighth Note Combinations, pages 63–64, 76

Teacher Resource Binder

Teaching Master 4, *Text Emphasis in "Cape Cod Girls"*

Evaluation Master 6, *Diction Checkup*

Skill Builder 26, *Rhythm Challenge in Duple Meter*

Vocal Development 9, *Diction*

Reference 21, *Vocal: Diphthong Guide*

For additional resources, see TRB Table of Contents.

Links to Learning

◆ **Vocal**

The refrain in "Cape Cod Girls" presents several challenges for choral singers. First, the *ou* vowel sound in *bound* is a **diphthong** *(a combination of two vowel sounds)* and consists of the two sounds *ah* and *oo*. When you sing diphthongs, maintain tall vowels at all times. Another challenge is proper **syllabic stress** *(the stressing of one syllable over another)*. When you sing the word *Australia*, emphasize the second syllable and sing the final syllable very lightly (Aus-TRAL-ia). Finally, it is a challenge to sing the *r* in *for* very lightly or not at all. Practice these techniques in the following example.

Bound for   Aus - tral - ia!

◆ **Theory**

- Read and perform the following example to practice rhythmic patterns found in "Cape Cod Girls."

tim ka ti ti ti ka ti ka ti ti ka tam   ti ka ta - a   tim ka ti ti ti ka ti ka ti ti ka ti ta ti ta ta

Evaluation

Demonstrate how well you have learned the skills and concepts featured in the lesson "Cape Cod Girls" by completing the following:

- Perform measures 34–41 individually to show your ability to sing complex rhythmic patterns accurately. Evaluate how well you were able to perform the rhythms correctly.
- Sing measures 34–41 to demonstrate your understanding of diphthongs, syllabic stress and the final consonant *r*. Were you able to sing the first vowel of the diphthong longer than the second? Did you place the stress on the second syllable in the word *Australia*? Was the final consonant *r* performed lightly?

LINKS TO LEARNING

Vocal

The Vocal section is designed to prepare students to:
- Sing diphthongs correctly.
- Use correct syllabic stress while singing.

Have students:
- Sing the example as written.
- Focus on the first vowel in the diphthong and remember to stay on that vowel for as long as possible.
- Place the syllabic stress on the second syllable of Australia.

Theory

The Theory section is designed to prepare students to read sixteenth- and eighth-note combinations and dotted eighth note rhythms.

Have students:
- Tap or clap the quarter-note pulse.
- Speak the exercise while tapping the quarter-note pulse.
- Speak the exercise while feeling the quarter-note pulse inside.

RESOURCES

Proficient Tenor/Bass Rehearsal/Performance CD

CD 1:5 Voices
CD 1:6 Accompaniment Only
CD 3:3 Vocal Practice Track—Tenor I
CD 4:3 Vocal Practice Track—Tenor II
CD 5:2 Vocal Practice Track—Bass I
CD 6:3 Vocal Practice Track—Bass II

National Standards

1. Singing, alone and with others, a varied repertoire of music. **(a, b, c)**
5. Reading and notating music. **(a)**
9. Understanding music in relation to history and culture. **(b, c)**

LESSON PLAN

Suggested Teaching Sequence and Performance Tips

1. Introduce

Direct students to:

- Read and discuss the information found in the Getting Started section on student page 22.
- Listen to the recording of this song and discuss the character of the music.
- Practice the example in the Vocal section on page 23.
- Practice the example in the Theory section. You can vary this activity by having your students either clap or step the rhythms, or both.

Progress Checkpoints

Observe students' progress in:

✓ Their understanding of the social and cultural background from which this music arises. How could this type of "buoyant" music uplift the sailors' spirits as they performed their everyday work?

✓ Their ability to sing the phrase in the Vocal section with the correct usage of the diphthong and syllabic stress.

✓ Their rhythmic precision regarding the reading and clapping of the rhythm in the Theory section. The movement should be at the very least regular and mechanically correct at this point.

Cape Cod Girls

For TTBB and Piano

Arranged by EMILY CROCKER

Sea Chantey

Copyright © 1998 by HAL LEONARD CORPORATION
International Copyright Secured   All Rights Reserved

24   Proficient Tenor/Bass

This setting of a popular maritime chantey is muscular, energetic and is sure to appeal to your male singers. The tessitura calls upon your high Tenors to show off their upper range; however, the lower parts are quite manageable. It is mainly diatonic but rhythmically challenging. "Cape Cod Girls" provides a marvelous opportunity for your students to vocally project the energy of sailors at sea.

Heave a-way my bul-ly bul-ly boys, heave a-way, heave a-way.

Heave a-way and don't you make a noise, we are bound for Aus-tral-ia!

Way hey! Way hey!

Way hey! Way hey!

2. Rehearse

Direct students to:

- Clap and/or step the example in the Theory section. It is vital at this time that the rhythm becomes internalized, flowing and expressive in movement.

- Use rhythm sticks to perform the rhythms on page 23. As the rhythms become more secure, gradually increase the tempo to the performance speed. (Use a metronome to help keep tempos even.) As students progress, you should notice the rhythms becoming lighter and more buoyant. Repeat this over and over until students have internalized this rhythm.

- Sing measures 19–20 while playing the rhythm on rhythm sticks. Step the beat. Follow this procedure for all three parts.

Progress Checkpoints

Observe students' progress in:

✓ Their joyful response to moving.

✓ Their ability to perform the rhythms accurately. In order for the maritime-like energy of this to be captured, it is essential that the students' movements be free and uninhibited. Help them with this by making this activity challenging and fun.

Lesson 3 *Cape Cod Girls* **25**

3. Refine

Direct students to:

- Sing entire song one part at a time while stepping the basic pulse. Try singing the entire piece while: (1) stepping the pulse; (2) stepping the half note. (Be sure the step is approximately twice as large as that of the quarter note.)

- Divide into two groups and do both ways simultaneously. For this you will need to have your class form two circles—one for the "pulse" steppers and one for the "half" steppers. So both groups can kinesthetically and musically benefit from the other, have the "pulse" steppers form the outside circle.

Progress Checkpoints

Observe students' progress in:

- ✓ Their ability to perform all rhythms correctly.
- ✓ Their ability to maintain perfect focus and concentration in the midst of the other parts.
- ✓ Their ability to experience the mood of the music while playing the rhythms.
- ✓ Understanding perfect spatial relations—when playing the rhythm sticks the quarter-note step should twice as big as the eighth note that should be twice as big as the sixteenth etc.

26   Proficient Tenor/Bass

MORE ABOUT

Sea Chanteys

Sea chanteys were songs sung by sailors. They had many functions, usually related to the chores done while on board the ship. There were capstan chanteys for turning the capstan, long-haul chanteys for hauling the anchor, and so on. Have students research chanteys to find out what types there were, and sing some of these sailor songs.

Heave a - way and don't you make a noise, we are bound for Aus - tral - ia.

Bound for Aus - tral - ia!   Way hey!

Bound for Aus - tral - ia!   Way hey!

Way hey!

Bound for Aus - tral - ia!   molto rit.

Bound for Aus - tral - ia!   molto rit.

molto rit.

ASSESSMENT

Informal Assessment

In this lesson, students showed the ability to:

- Define and correctly sing diphthongs.
- Read and perform music with rhythmic accuracy.
- Perform music representing the American sea chantey.

Student Self-Assessment

Have students evaluate their individual performances based on the following:

- Correct Rhythms
- Expressive Singing
- Diction
- Intonation
- Correct Part-Singing

Have each student rate his/her performance of this song in the areas above on a scale of 1–5, 5 being the best.

TEACHING STRATEGY

Analyzing Form

Form relates to the structure or musical design of a composition. If students can identify and analyze the form of a composition, they are able to perform with greater comprehension and understanding. Direct students to:

- Identify the form of "Cape Cod Girls" as strophic.
- Show where each verse begins. (Verse 1 measure 5; Verse 2 measure 15; Verse 3 measure 27)
- Analyze form and discuss how each verse is treated differently. Have students discuss the elements of texture, harmony, placement of melody, dynamics, tempo and so forth.

Individual and Group Performance Evaluation

To further measure growth of musical skills presented in this lesson, direct students to complete the Evaluation section on page 23.

- Have students individually read the rhythms in measures 34–41, focusing on singing the complex rhythms accurately. Assist them in evaluating their performances.

- Direct students to sing the above passage, using correct technique for singing diphthongs and proper syllabic stress. Help them evaluate their own performances.

TEACHING STRATEGY

Compare and Contrast Form

The form used in "Annie Laurie" and "Cape Cod Girls" is strophic—a form in which the melody repeats while the words change from verse to verse. Have students:

- Identify the form of "Cape Cod Girls" and "Annie Laurie" as strophic.
- Show where each verse begins.
- Analyze form and discuss how each verse is treated differently.
- Compare and contrast the strophic form used in both songs. How are they similar? How are they different? Compare and contrast the elements of texture, harmony, placement of melody, dynamics, tempo and so forth.

way, heave a-way.   Heave   a-way and don't you make a noise, we are

Unis.

bound for Aus-tral - ia!   Bound   for   Aus -

ff   *Shout!*

tral   -   ia!   Heave a-way!

ff   *Shout!*

ff

Additional National Standards

The following National Standards are addressed through the Assessment, Extension, Enrichment and bottom-page activities:

3. Improvising melodies, variations and accompaniments. **(b)**

4. Composing and arranging music within specific guidelines. **(a)**

6. Listening to, analyzing and describing music. **(b, c)**

7. Evaluating music and music performances. **(a, b)**

8. Understanding relationships between music, the other arts and disciplines outside the arts. **(c)**

EXTENSION

Music and Movement

Experience the fun of this music while having a "tug of war." This is accomplished in the following way: One group sings and pulls the other group (with a real or imagined rope) while singing the words "Cape Cod Girls they have no combs." The other group then does the same while singing "Heave away, heave away." Continue in the same manner for every measure (this will create two-measure phrases).

ENRICHMENT

Improvisation and Composition

Consider the following activities:

- Improvise gestures that coincide with the words or rhythms to clap and/or step to go with the music.
- Compose a rhythmic phrase of 4–6 measures in length using values that have been learned. Have students notate clap and step their compositions.

Online

Encourage your students to expore **music.glencoe.com**, the Web site for *Experiencing Choral Music*. You may wish to preview the rich content before directing your students online. Options available on the Web site include:

- Web Link Exercises
- Interactive Projects
- Audio Samples

29

Gabi, Gabi

OVERVIEW

Composer: South African Praise Song, arranged by William C. Powell

Text: Zulu Praise Song

Voicing: TTBB

Key: A♭ Major

Meter: 4/4

Form: AAABBA' coda

Style: South African Praise Song

Accompaniment: A cappella

Programming: Concert

Vocal Ranges:

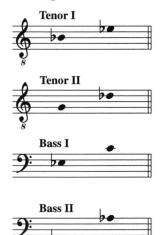

OBJECTIVES

After completing this lesson, students will be able to:

- Demonstrate basic performance techniques (e.g., call and response) while performing.
- Perform music representing the South African culture.

VOCABULARY

Have students review vocabulary in student lesson. Introduce terms found in the music. A complete glossary of terms is found on page 246 of the student book.

Gabi, Gabi

Composer: South African Praise Song, arranged by William C. Powell

Text: Zulu Praise Song

Voicing: TTBB

VOCABULARY

call and response

ostinato

chord

Focus

- Describe and perform call and response.
- Perform music representing South African culture.

 SPOTLIGHT

To learn more about improvisation, see page 145.

Getting Started

You come to choir class to sing, but you don't always sing in English. "Gabi, Gabi" is written in Zulu, the most common spoken language of South Africa. This song was used at gatherings to express political change. Can you name other songs that have been used for political change, such as the civil rights movement?

◆ History and Culture

Nelson Mandela (b. 1918), the first democratically elected State President of South Africa from 1994–99, has spent his entire life fighting for human rights. The song "Gabi, Gabi" was often sung at gatherings led by Mandela and, later, by others who were relentless in their fight for equality and freedom for all people.

The traditional music of South Africa often features **call and response,** *a style in which a leader or group sings a phrase (call) followed by a response of the same phrase by another group.* The musical phrases are typically short and repeated many times to a changing text. In addition, percussion instruments often accompany the voices using a repeated **ostinato** pattern *(a rhythmic or melodic passage that is repeated continuously).*

Arranger William C. Powell adapts these stylistic features to "Gabi, Gabi." The first Tenor section functions as the soloist, to which the remaining sections respond. The musical phrases are four measures long and contain within them repetitions of both music and text. Furthermore, the four percussion instruments repeat their own rhythmic pattern in each phrase.

RESOURCES

Proficient Sight-Singing

Reading in A♭ Major, page 153

Reading Rhythms with Syncopation, pages 85–85

Teacher Resource Binder

Teaching Master 5, *Pronunciation Guide for "Gabi, Gabi"*

Teaching Master 6, *African Influence on Music*

Skill Builder 1, *Building Harmony*

Skill Builder 14, *Improvising Melodies*

Vocal Development 16, *Warm-up: Part Singing*

For additional resources, see TRB Table of Contents.

Links to Learning

◆ **Vocal**

Read and perform the following example to practice singing chords found in "Gabi, Gabi." A **chord** is *three or more pitches sounded simultaneously.*

◆ **Artistic Expression**

Movement can enhance the interpretation or character of a song. Step in place in this manner: Step with the right foot, then lightly tap with your left heel. Step with the left foot, then lightly tap with your right heel. This should be a subtle step-touch pattern.

Evaluation

Demonstrate how well you have learned the skills and concepts featured in the lesson "Gabi, Gabi" by completing the following:

- In quartets with one singer per part, sing measures 1–5 to show your understanding of call and response. Which voice part sings the call and which part sings the response?

- With the assistance of your teacher, videotape your class performing "Gabi, Gabi" as described in the Artistic Expression section above. View the video and evaluate your interpretation of the song. Discuss ways to improve your performance.

LINKS TO LEARNING

Vocal

The Vocal section is designed to prepare students to sing a harmonic progression of chords that are found in "Gabi, Gabi."

Have students:

- Sing each part separately.
- Combine all parts when each pitch is secure.

Artistic Expression

The Artistic Expression section is designed to prepare students to:

- Use movement to enhance their interpretation of "Gabi, Gabi."
- Discover which syllables are stressed based on their movement.

Have students:

- Form two or three circles in the room.
- Walk to the beat of a drum and step the beat.
- Sing the opening sections and notice what words or syllables fall on the beat. These are the syllables that should be stressed as they perform this song.

RESOURCES

Proficient Tenor/Bass Rehearsal/Performance CD

CD 1:7 Voices

CD 1:8 Accompaniment Only

CD 3:4 Vocal Practice Track—Tenor I

CD 4:4 Vocal Practice Track—Tenor II

CD 5:3 Vocal Practice Track—Baritone

CD 6:4 Vocal Practice Track—Bass

National Standards

1. Singing, alone and with others, a varied repertoire of music. **(a, b, c)**
5. Reading and notating music. **(a)**
6. Listening to, analyzing and describing music. **(c)**
9. Understanding music in relation to history and culture. **(a)**

LESSON PLAN

Suggested Teaching Sequence and Performance Tips

1. Introduce

Direct students to:

- Read and discuss the information found in the Getting Started section on student page 30.
- Practice the example in the Vocal section.

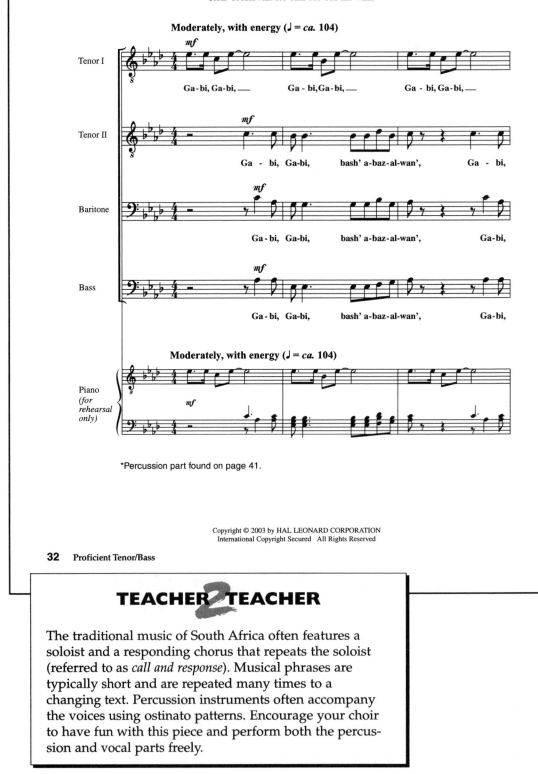

Gabi, Gabi

For TTBB, a cappella with Optional Percussion*

Arranged by
WILLIAM C. POWELL

South African Praise Song

Pronunciation Guide:
Gabi, Gabi: gah-bee, gah-bee,
bash' abazalwan': bahsh ah-bahz-ahl-wahn
Siyoshiywa khona: see-yohsh-ee-wah koh-nah
Sidal' ubuzalwan: see-dahl oob-ooz-ahl-wahn

*Percussion part found on page 41.

Copyright © 2003 by HAL LEONARD CORPORATION
International Copyright Secured All Rights Reserved

32   Proficient Tenor/Bass

TEACHER 2 TEACHER

The traditional music of South Africa often features a soloist and a responding chorus that repeats the soloist (referred to as *call and response*). Musical phrases are typically short and are repeated many times to a changing text. Percussion instruments often accompany the voices using ostinato patterns. Encourage your choir to have fun with this piece and perform both the percussion and vocal parts freely.

Observe students' progress in:
- ✓ Their ability to sing chords correctly and in tune.
- ✓ Their production of a good choral tone.

TEACHING STRATEGY

Musical Elements of Style

The combination of musical elements determines the style of a piece.
Have students:

1. Compile a list of musical elements that might affect style.

2. Share the lists to compile one master list.

3. Sing known songs, trying out different styles, and then try to describe the musical elements that are characteristic of that style. (For example, try salsa, opera, Broadway, rock, military, lullaby, and so forth.)

4. Select appropriate literature for a particular style.

2. Rehearse

Direct students to:

- Speak the text in rhythm in measures 1–9.
- Sing each part separately on a neutral syllable.
- Sing with the text when all pitches and rhythms are secure. Use the piano for support as needed.
- Sing the Tenor I and Bass lines together for the entire piece.
- Sing the Tenor II and Bass lines together from measure 17 to the end.
- Sing the Tenor I and Baritone lines together in the following measures: 7–9, 13–17, 21–25, 29–32 and 41 to the end.
- Combine all parts when secure.

TEACHING STRATEGY

Performance Techniques

Have students:

1. Identify appropriate performance techniques to be used in the performance of this song.
2. Either in small ensembles or with the entire choir (large ensemble), perform the song exhibiting these performance techniques.
3. Describe the performance techniques experienced during the performance.
4. Critique the performance based on the observed performance techniques.
5. Repeat this process often in both informal and formal concert settings.

Progress Checkpoints

Observe students' progress in:

✓ Properly pronouncing the text.

✓ Their correct usage of word stress.

✓ Their ability to read all rhythms correctly.

✓ Their ability to sing all pitches accurately and in tune.

CONNECTING THE ARTS

Multicultural Dances

Have students research African dances using books and recordings or resources in the community. Direct them to learn some of the dances and compare the movements and musical characteristics to those found in "Gabi, Gabi."

3. Refine

Direct students to:

- Go back to the beginning and sing the piece, observing all dynamic and expressive markings.
- Notice the use of tenuto over the syllable *kho* in the word *khona* and also over *cap* in the word *captives*.
- Begin to memorize "Gabi, Gabi." (This should be easy, since your choir will only have a few measures to learn.
- Locate the percussion part at the end of the song and use it to enhance their performance.

ENRICHMENT

Improvisation

The arranger of "Gabi, Gabi" notes on the percussion page of the music that the rhythms notated can either be played as written, or they can be used as suggestions. Encourage your choir to improvise their own rhythmic accompaniments as their comfort level with the piece grows.

Praise the Fa-ther! He frees all the cap - tives and gives the hun-gry

Fa-ther, Lib-er - a - tor, Lord! He frees all the cap - tives and gives the hun-gry

Fa-ther, Lib-er - a - tor, Lord! He frees all the cap - tives and gives the hun-gry

Fa-ther, Lib-er - a - tor, Lord! He frees all the cap - tives and gives the hun-gry

28

bread. He frees all the cap - tives and gives the hun - gry,

bread. He frees all the cap - tives and gives the hun - gry

bread. He frees all the cap - tives and gives the hun - gry

bread. He frees all the cap - tives and gives the hun - gry

31

Progress Checkpoints

Observe students' progress in:

✓ Their ability to sing all dynamics, expressive and tenuto markings.

✓ Memorizing the piece.

✓ Their use of percussion to enhance their performance.

ASSESSMENT

Informal Assessment

In this lesson, students showed the ability to:
- Define and perform call and response.
- Perform music representing the South African culture.

Encourage your students to expore **music.glencoe.com**, the Web site for *Experiencing Choral Music*. You may wish to preview the rich content before directing your students online. Options available on the Web site include:
- Web Link Exercises
- Interactive Projects
- Audio Samples

Student Self-Assessment

Have students evaluate their individual performances based on the following:

- Diction
- Expressive Singing
- Foreign Language
- Accurate Rhythms
- Correct Part-Singing

Have each student rate his/her performance of this song in the areas above on a scale of 1–5, 5 being the best.

TEACHING STRATEGY

Musical Form

To help your students understand the concept of form and how it relates to this piece, consider having them create a visual representation of the form of "Gabi, Gabi." Encourage them to use mediums such as coloring, painting, drawing, computer graphic design, sculpture, etc. Have them share their art with the class and explain why they chose the particular medium and how it relates to the song.

Individual and Group Performance Evaluation

To further measure growth of musical skills presented in this lesson, direct students to complete the Evaluation section on page 31.

- Have students get into quartets and sing the opening measures of the song. Which part has the call? *(Tenor I)* Which parts have the response? *(Tenor II, Baritone and Bass)*

- Videotape the choir performing this song and help them evaluate their performance.

Additional National Standards

The following National Standards are addressed through the Assessment, Extension, Enrichment and bottom-page activities:

3. Improvising melodies, variations and accompaniments. **(b)**

7. Evaluate music and music performances. **(a, b)**

8. Understanding relationships between music, the other arts and disciplines outside the arts. **(a)**

Gabi, Gabi

South African Praise Song
Arranged by
WILLIAM C. POWELL

PERCUSSION*
(Claves, Shekere, Conga, Djembe)

*Rhythms and instruments are suggestions; other instruments may be added, omitted or substituted as needed.

Lesson 4 *Gabi, Gabi* **41**

TEACHING STRATEGY

Small-Ensemble Techniques

Invite a local group that specializes in African fold music to come perform for the class. Ask students to share what they observed and learned from the experience. Then, have students prepare a performance of "Gabi, Gabi," exhibiting the techniques they observed. Critique their performances based on the small-ensemble techniques of balance of parts, energized singing inthe style of an African praise song, and in tune singing.

EXTENSIONS

The Music of South Africa

Listen to other vocal music from South Africa performed by South Africans, such as Ladysmith Black Mambazo. Look for features of South African folk music discussed in this lesson.

ENRICHMENT

Composing Music

When composing music, a writer must take into consideration both melody and rhythm. Sometimes a composer will start with a rhythmic idea, while at other times he or she will start with a melody. Direct students to:

1. Select a meter:
   • simple meter (2/4, 2/4, 4/4)
   • compound meter (6/9, 9/8, 3/8)
   • asymmetric meter (5/8, 7/8)
2. Write a four-measure simple or complex rhythmic pattern in that meter.
3. Select a key (major, minor, pentatonic, modal).
4. Using the newly composed rhythmic pattern, write a melody based on the selected key.
5. Exchange compositions with a classmate. Check each other's work for rhythmic and melodic accuracy.
6. Make changes and corrections as necessary.
7. Read and perform their compositions for the class.

41

Tolite Hostias

OVERVIEW

Composer: Camille Saint-Saëns (1835–1921), arranged by Roger Emerson
Text: Biblical
Voicing: TTBB
Key: C major
Meter: 4/4
Form: ABA'
Style: Romantic French Oratorio
Accompaniment: Piano
Programming: Sacred, Christmas

Vocal Ranges:

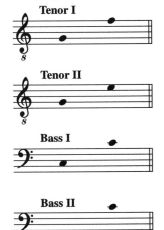

OBJECTIVES

After completing this lesson, students will be able to:

- Perform music representing the Romantic oratorio.
- Demonstrate musical artistry by singing *maestoso*.
- Interpret musical symbols referring to dynamics while performing.

VOCABULARY

Have students review vocabulary in student lesson. Introduce terms found in the music. A complete glossary of terms is found on page 246 of the student book.

42

Tolite Hostias

Composer: Camille Saint-Saëns (1835–1921), arranged by Roger Emerson
Text: Biblical
Voicing: TTBB

VOCABULARY

Romantic period
oratorio
maestoso
motive
dynamics

Focus

- Perform music representing the Romantic oratorio.
- Demonstrate musical artistry by singing *maestoso*.
- Interpret music symbols referring to dynamics when performing.

Getting Started

What do these events have in common?

- Roller-skating was introduced in America.
- Eddie Cuthbert of the Philadelphia Keystones stole the first base in a baseball game.
- American automobile industrialist Henry Ford was born.
- President Lincoln issued the Emancipation Proclamation.

All of these events occurred in 1863, the same year Camille Saint-Saëns wrote "Praise Ye The Lord Of Hosts," or "Tolite Hostias," the original Latin title.

MUSIC & HISTORY

To learn more about the Romantic period, see page 122.

◆ History and Culture

French composer Camille Saint-Saëns (1835–1921) is sometimes compared to Mozart since both men were considered child prodigies. Saint-Saëns started piano lessons at age three and was dazzling Paris audiences with brilliant recitals by age ten. Saint-Saëns, a composer, organist and pianist, lived and worked in France during the late **Romantic period** *(1820–1900)*.

Saint-Saëns wrote *Oratorio de Noël (Christmas Oratorio)* in 1858, when he was just twenty-three. An **oratorio** is *a piece for solo voices, chorus and orchestra that is an expanded dramatic work on a literary or religious theme presented without theatrical action.* Oratorio de Noël was originally scored for five vocal soloists, chorus, harp, string quartet and organ. "Tolite Hostias" is the final movement of the oratorio and is in the style of an old French Christmas song. It is a hymn of praise.

In this arrangement, Roger Emerson has set the music for men's voices only. The melody line moves from voice part to voice part and should always be heard above the harmony.

42 Proficient Tenor/Bass

RESOURCES

Proficient Sight-Singing

Sight-Singing in C Major, pages 13, 26–27, 34–35

Reading Rhythms in 4/4 Meter, pages 2, 6

Teacher Resource Binder

Teaching Master 7, *Pronunciation Guide for "Tolite Hostias"*

Evaluation Master 8, *Evaluating Musical Expression*

Music and History 14, *Characteristics of Romantic Music: 1820–1900*

Music and History 16, *Camille Saint-Saëns, a Romantic Composer*

For additional resources, see TRB Table of Contents.

Links to Learning

◆ **Vocal**

Perform the following example that outlines the melody of the opening section. Sing **maestoso** *(a musical term meaning majestic)*. To create a majestic quality, sing legato, connecting each syllable to the next with a subtle crescendo.

◆ **Theory**

Perform the following example to practice singing the four-note "Alleluia" motive. A **motive** is *a short rhythmic or melodic idea that can serve as the basic element in a more complex composition.*

◆ **Artistic Expression**

Dynamics are *symbols used in music to tell a singer how loud or soft to sing.* Locate the dynamic markings in this song and sing the dynamic changes artistically.

Evaluation

Demonstrate how well you have learned the skills and concepts featured in the lesson "Tolite Hostias" by completing the following:

• Sing measures 32–39 to show your ability to sing in a *maestoso* style. Did you sing majestically? Did you sing in a smooth and legato style?

• Record yourself singing "Tolite Hostias." Listen to the recording and evaluate how well you were able to sing the dynamic changes. Re-record and reevaluate as necessary.

Vocal

The Vocal section is designed to prepare students to sing *maestoso*.

Have students:

• Sing the example on a neutral syllable.

• Sing the example using solfège syllables.

• Sing legato and with a subtle crescendo to create the majestic sound for this piece.

Theory

The Theory section is designed to prepare students to sing the "Alleluia" motive.

Have students:

• Sing each part separately.

• Combine when each part is secure.

Artistic Expression

The Artistic Expression section is designed to prepare students to use dynamics while singing.

Have students:

• Locate the dynamic markings in the music.

• Focus on these markings and following them as they learn this piece.

RESOURCES

Proficient Tenor/Bass Rehearsal/Performance CD

CD 1:9 Voices

CD 1:10 Accompaniment Only

CD 3:5 Vocal Practice Track—Tenor I

CD 4:5 Vocal Practice Track—Tenor II

CD 5:4 Vocal Practice Track—Baritone

CD 6:5 Vocal Practice Track—Bass

National Standards

1. Singing, alone and with others, a varied repertoire of music. **(a, b, c)**

5. Reading and notating music. **(a)**

9. Understanding music in relation to history and culture. **(a)**

LESSON PLAN

Suggested Teaching Sequence and Performance Tips

1. Introduce

Direct students to:

- Read and discuss the information found in the Getting Started section on student page 42.
- Sing the melody in the Vocal section to practice creating a *maestoso* articulation.
- Practice the "Alleluia" passage shown in the Theory section.
- Survey the score for dynamic marks. Discuss where dynamic levels change and how they change.

Progress Checkpoints

Observe students' progress in:

- ✓ Their ability to sing *maestoso*.
- ✓ Their ability to sing the "Alleluia" excerpt correctly.
- ✓ Their ability to identify various dynamic marks.

From ORATORIO de NOËL
Tolite Hostias
For TTBB and Piano

Edited and Arranged by
ROGER EMERSON

CAMILLE SAINT-SAËNS
(1835–1921)

Copyright © 2003 by HAL LEONARD CORPORATION
International Copyright Secured   All Rights Reserved

TEACHER 2 TEACHER

Roger Emerson's TTBB arrangement of a well-known SATB anthem makes this choral classic available to men's choruses. The harmonies will sound thick and rich in men's voices, particularly through the "Alleluia" passage.

2. Rehearse

Direct students to:

- Sight-sing the rhythms in each section: measures 5–12, 13–20, 21–31. Take notice of where all parts share the same rhythm.
- Sight-sing the pitches in each section on a neutral syllable. Review each part individually as needed and then sing all parts together.
- When pitches are secure, add the lyrics. Direct the choir to sing pure, round vowels.

Progress Checkpoints

Observe students' progress in:

- ✓ Their ability to perform correct rhythms and pitches.
- ✓ Their ability to contribute to accurately tuned chords throughout.
- ✓ Their ability to sing pure, round vowels.

MORE ABOUT...

The Christmas Oratorio

"Praise Ye the Lord of Hosts" is the final movement from Saint-Saëns's *Christmas Oratorio*. This work for SATB choir, soloists, string quartet, harp and organ contains nine movements, several of which are for the soloists. The size of this oratorio is significantly smaller than the most famous oratorio of all, Handel's *Messiah*. This classic contains at least 53 movements (it depends how they are counted) that are divided into three parts. The extraordinary length is due to the fact that the lyrics span not only the Christmas story but also the Easter story.

3. Refine

Direct students to:

- Sing *maestoso* throughout to carry the line forward with energy.
- Apply the dynamic markings to give artistic shape to the music.
- Sing the repeated "Alleluias" gracefully, without clipping or punching the final syllable.

Progress Checkpoints

Observe students' progress in:

✓ Their ability to sing *maestoso*.

✓ Their ability to make dynamic changes audible.

✓ Their ability to sing the "Alleluias" gracefully without accenting the final syllable.

46   Proficient Tenor/Bass

MUSIC AND HISTORY

The History of the Oratorio

An oratorio is a music drama on a religious topic. As a musical genre, the oratorio developed in the seventeenth century. The word *oratorio* came from the name of a building known as an *oratory*, a word from the Latin *oratio*, meaning "prayer." Oratories were buildings adjacent to churches where people met for informal lessons, prayers and music. Rectangular in shape, oratories usually seated 200–400 people and featured excellent acoustics, not only for the spoken word, but also for music. Thus, the musical genre oratorio took its name from the buildings, called oratories, in which they were first presented.

Additional National Standards

The following National Standards are addressed through the Assessment, Extension, Enrichment and bottom-page activities:

6. Listening to, analyzing and describing music. **(a, b)**

7. Evaluate music and music performances. **(a)**

8. Understanding relationships between music, the other arts and disciplines outside the arts. **(c)**

ASSESSMENT

Informal Assessment

In this lesson, students showed the ability to:

- Perform music representing the Romantic oratorio.
- Sing *maestoso*.
- Follow dynamics while performing.

Student Self-Assessment

Have students evaluate their individual performances based on the following:

- Phrasing
- Expressive Singing
- Foreign Language
- Vowels
- Correct Part-Singing

Have each student rate his/her performance of this song in the areas above on a scale of 1–5, 5 being the best.

Individual and Group Performance Evaluation

To further measure growth of musical skills presented in this lesson, direct students to complete the Evaluation section on page 43.

- Have students sing measures 32–39 to show they can sing in the *maestoso* style. Help them evaluate how they did.
- Record students singing this song. Play back the recording and help students determine if there was an audible difference between the contrasting dynamics.

Ose Shalom

OVERVIEW

Composer: John Leavitt
Text: Traditional Hebrew
Voicing: TTB
Key: E minor
Meter: 4/4
Form: ABB¹CC¹BB¹CC¹A¹
Style: Contemporary
Accompaniment: Piano/
Optional B♭ Clarinet
Programming: Multicultural
Concert

Vocal Ranges:

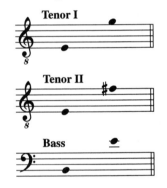

OBJECTIVES

After completing this lesson,
students will be able to:

- Identify minor tonality
  when performing music.
- Demonstrate musical artistry
  by singing phrases
  expressively.
- Perform music that represents the Hebrew culture.

Have students review
vocabulary in student lesson.
Introduce terms found in the
music. A complete glossary
of terms is found on page
246 of the student book.

Ose Shalom

Composer: John Leavitt
Text: Traditional Hebrew
Voicing: TTB

VOCABULARY

minor tonality
melodic minor scale
phrase

Focus

- Perform music in a minor tonality.
- Sing phrases expressively.
- Perform music representing the Hebrew culture.

Getting Started

Music has the power to call us to action. Songs of peace—or war—travel into our hearts and make us ask *why*. If the *why* is a call to arms, then we may be stirred by the sounds of a John Phillip Sousa march or our national anthem. On the other hand, if the *why* is a call to peace, we might sing "Let There Be Peace on Earth," "Dona Nobis Pacem," or "Imagine" in hopes of bringing peace to a troubled time. "Ose Shalom" is a traditional Hebrew prayer of peace. Whether we sing songs of war or songs of peace, the music connects our hearts and minds in a way that touches the human spirit.

◆ History and Culture

The English translation of the Hebrew text is as follows:

Ose shalom bimromav—The one who makes peace in the heavens

hu ya'ase shalom aleynu—may he make peace for us

veh'al kol Yisrael—and for all of Israel

veh'imru amen—and let us say, amen.

"Ose Shalom" is a liturgical prayer that is found in the order of the Jewish service and often used at weddings. Composer John Leavitt has set this traditional prayer of peace to a beautiful, haunting melody. He is currently the artistic director and conductor of the Master Arts Chorale and the Master Arts Youth Chorale in Wichita, Kansas.

SKILL BUILDERS

To learn more about the key of E minor, see Proficient Sight-Singing, page 78.

48 Proficient Tenor/Bass

RESOURCES

Proficient Sight-Singing

Sight-Singing in E Minor,
  pages 78–80, 86
Studying the Three Minor Scales,
  pages 37–38

Teacher Resource Binder

Teaching Master 8, *Pronunciation Guide for "Ose Shalom"*

Teaching Master 9, *Conducting "Ose Shalom"*

Evaluation Master 4, *Checking Out Musical Phrases*

Reference 26, *IPA Vowels*

For additional resources, see TRB Table of Contents.

Links to Learning

◆ **Theory**

"Ose Shalom" is in the key of E minor and is based on the E melodic minor scale. *A song that is based on a minor scale with* la *as its keynote, or home tone, is described as being* in **minor tonality.** A **melodic minor scale** is *a minor scale that uses raised sixth and seventh notes:* fi *raised from* fa, *and* si *raised from* sol. Often, these notes are raised in the ascending patterns but not in the descending patterns. To locate "E" on the piano, find any set of two black keys. "E" is the white key to the right. This scale uses the notes E, F#, G, A, B, C#, D#, E ascending, and D-natural and C-natural descending. Using the keyboard below as a guide, play the E melodic minor.

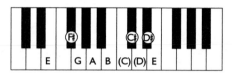

Sing the E melodic minor scale.

◆ **Artistic Expression**

Be the conductor! As the class sings measures 7–14 of "Ose Shalom," take turns being the conductor. Through your conducting gestures, outline the shape of the **phrase,** *a musical idea with a beginning and an end.*

Evaluation

Demonstrate how well you have learned the skills and concepts featured in the lesson "Ose Shalom" by completing the following:

• Write a 4-measure sight-singing melody that is based on the E melodic minor scale. Begin and end your piece on *la.* Trade compositions with a classmate, and sight-sing each other's melody. Check your work for pitch accuracy.

• Show that you can perform expressively by chanting the text and conducting the contour of the phrase. How did your conducting convey the shape of the phrase?

LINKS TO LEARNING

Theory

The Theory section is designed to prepare students to:

• Play the E melodic minor scale on a keyboard.

• Sing the E melodic minor scale.

Have students:

• Use the keyboard on the page as a guide to playing the scale.

• Sing the scale, ascending and descending.

Artistic Expression

The Artistic Expression section is designed to prepare students to visually outline the shapes of phrases through conducting.

Have students:

• Sing measures 7–14.

• Take turns conducting this section and shaping the phrase or phrases.

RESOURCES

Proficient Tenor/Bass Rehearsal/Performance CD

CD 1:11 Voices

CD 1:12 Accompaniment Only

CD 3:6 Vocal Practice Track—Tenor I

CD 4:6 Vocal Practice Track—Tenor II

CD 6:6 Vocal Practice Track—Bass

National Standards

1. Singing, alone and with others, a varied repertoire of music. **(a, b, c)**

5. Reading and notating music. **(a, b)**

9. Understanding music in relation to history and culture. **(a)**

LESSON PLAN

Suggested Teaching Sequence and Performance Tips

1. Introduce

Direct students to:

- Read and discuss the information found in the Getting Started section on student page 48.
- Practice playing and singing the E melodic minor scale found in the Theory section.
- Take turns conducting the phrasing as described in the Artistic Expression section. (If you have not taught the pronunciation of the piece at this point, consider having your students sing on a neutral syllable so they can focus on the phrasing.)

Progress Checkpoints

Observe students' progress in:

- ✓ Their ability to play and sing the E melodic minor scale correctly.
- ✓ Their conducting skills and shaping phrases.

For the 2002 KMEA Middle Level Choir
Dedicated to Dr. James L. Hardy for his 29 years of service as Kansas Music Review editor and as Director of Music Education at Wichita State University

Ose Shalom
(The One Who Makes Peace)

For TTB and Piano

Traditional Hebrew Text

Music by JOHN LEAVITT

Copyright © 2002 by HAL LEONARD CORPORATION
International Copyright Secured   All Rights Reserved

50   Proficient Tenor/Bass

TEACHER 2 TEACHER

This song gives the student the opportunity to learn about the different forms of the minor scale and how they relate to the major scale. It also gives the student the opportunity to experience music of a different culture.

2. Rehearse

Direct students to:

- Echo the Hebrew text as you say the words.
- Chant the text in rhythm once all pronunciation is secure.
- Sing the Tenor II part (melody) in measures 7–14.
- Add the other parts once the Tenor II part is secure.
- Break down the rest of the song into manageable sections and rehearse as above, working the part that has the melody first. (Suggested sections are: measures 15–22, 23–30, 38–45, 46–53, 54-end.)

Progress Checkpoints

Observe students' progress in:

✓ Their ability to perform correct rhythms and pitches.
✓ Their ability to sing the text correctly.

CURRICULUM CONNECTIONS

More Ways To Say "Peace"

"Ose Shalom" is a song about peace. Have students list the ways to say "peace" they already know. Then collect more from students who speak languages other than English, teachers of non-English languages, teachers of the hearing impaired, staff members and faculty who know languages, community members and parents. Make a large mural that includes all these words and their country of origin.

3. Refine

Direct students to:

- Sing the entire work with Hebrew text, using correct syllabic stress and vowels with attention and ability to listen and react to others.
- Sing with expressive phrasing.
- Observe all dynamic and expressive markings.

Progress Checkpoints

Observe students' progress in:

- ✓ Their ability to sing with correct syllabic stress and vowels.
- ✓ Their use of expressive phrasing.
- ✓ Their use of dynamics and expression.

TEACHING STRATEGY

Tonal Production

Here are some hints to help students with tonal production while singing "Ose Shalom." Have students:

- Sing the song on a neutral syllable, such as "mah," placing the tone forward to develop tonal focus.
- Take deep breaths for abdominal support to keep the tone free from strain.
- Sing with courage and determination to help negotiate the demanding pitches.

ASSESSMENT

Informal Assessment

In this lesson, students showed the ability to:

- Perform music in a minor key and sing and play the E melodic minor scale.
- Sing phrases with expression.
- Perform music that represents the Hebrew culture.

TEACHING STRATEGY

Interpreting Music Through Dynamics

To help your students make the most of the dynamic markings in this piece, have them:

- Review the music and look for all the dynamic markings.
- Identify the purpose behind each marking, such as phrasing, a certain meaning in the text, and so on.
- Sing the piece, paying special attention to the dynamics and phrasing for a more meaningful interpretation.

Student Self-Assessment

Have students evaluate their individual performances based on the following:

- Phrasing
- Expressive Singing
- Foreign Language
- Vowels
- Accurate Pitches

Have each student rate his/her performance of this song in the areas above on a scale of 1–5, 5 being the best.

Individual and Group Performance Evaluation

To further measure growth of musical skills presented in this lesson, direct students to complete the Evaluation section on page 49.

- Have students compose a four-measure sight-singing melody in the key of E minor. Trade with a classmate and sing each other's melody. Help them evaluate their own work for pitch accuracy.
- Select a section from the piece and have students conduct the phrasing and evaluate how well their gestures shaped the phrase.

54   Proficient Tenor/Bass

TEACHING STRATEGY

Solo and Small Ensemble Performances

Have students:

1. Prepare solos and small ensembles for performance or competition.
2. Interpret music symbols and terms referring to dynamics, tempo, and articulation during the performance.
3. Critique and analyze the quality of the performance using standard terminology.

ENRICHMENT

Have students identify and describe the small-ensemble performance techniques appropriate for "Ose Shalom" such as balance between parts, accurate intonation and expressive singing. Have students divide into small ensembles. While performing in small ensembles for a formal concert or competition, have students evaluate how well each ensemble demonstrated these performance techniques."

Encourage your students to expore **music.glencoe.com**, the Web site for *Experiencing Choral Music.* You may wish to preview the rich content before directing your students online. Options available on the Web site include:
• Web Link Exercises
• Interactive Projects
• Audio Samples

Additional National Standards

The following National Standards are addressed through the Assessment, Extension, Enrichment and bottom-page activities:

4. Composing and arranging music within specific guidelines. **(c)**

6. Listening to, analyzing and describing music. **(b)**

7. Evaluating music and music performances. **(a, b)**

8. Understanding relationships between music, the other arts and disciplines outside the arts. **(a, b)**

Pastores á Belén

OVERVIEW

Composer: Traditional Puerto Rican Carol, arranged by Emily Crocker

Text: Traditional Spanish text, adapted by Jaime Pérez

Voicing: TTB

Key: F major

Meter: 6/8

Form: Through-composed

Style: Traditional Puerto Rican Carol

Accompaniment: A cappella

Programming: Holiday, Multi-cultural, Concert

Vocal Ranges:

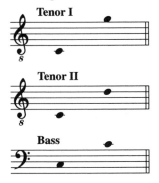

OBJECTIVES

After completing this lesson, students will be able to:

• Demonstrate, independently and in ensembles, accurate rhythm and fundamental skills while performing.

• Perform expressively a varied repertoire of music representing styles from diverse cultures.

VOCABULARY

Have students review vocabulary in student lesson. Introduce terms found in the music. A complete glossary of terms is found on page 246 of the student book.

56

Pastores á Belén

Composer: Traditional Puerto Rican Carol, arranged by Emily Crocker

Text: Traditional Spanish text, adapted by Jaime Pérez

Voicing: TTB

VOCABULARY

coda

parallel thirds

interval

compound meter

SPOTLIGHT

To learn more about arranging, see page 73.

Focus

• Read and perform music in compound meter.

• Use correct diction when singing in Spanish.

• Perform music representing the Puerto Rican culture.

Getting Started

"Pastores á Belén" is a Christmas carol from Puerto Rico. The Christmas season in Puerto Rico is long, extending from early December until January 6, or even longer. It is a time of delicious food, great music and merrymaking. One custom is a *parranda*, or a small group of friends who gather to make a surprise visit to another friend. The group gathers quietly at the front door and then begins singing carols and playing musical instruments. The host invites the group in for refreshments. The *parranda* grows as it moves from house to house. The party sometimes lasts until dawn.

◆ History and Culture

This arrangement of "Pastores á Belén" is set for men's voices. To follow the melody line throughout, it is necessary to shift from one voice part to another. Beginning with the pickup note to measure 5, the Tenor II section sings the melody through measure 20. At measure 21, the melody shifts to the Tenor I section for four measures. Then, the Basses have the melody in measures 25–28. The final section, measures 29–38, is a **coda**, *a concluding section to a song,* and has been added by the arranger, Emily Crocker.

A characteristic of Hispanic music found in this piece is the use of **parallel thirds,** *two notes that are three notes apart and move in like motion.* Find an example of parallel thirds in the music.

56 Proficient Tenor/Bass

RESOURCES

Proficient Sight-Singing

Sight-Singing in F Major, pages 45–46

Reading Rhythms in 6/8 Meter, pages 114, 117

Reading Spanish Text, page 65

Teacher Resource Binder

Teaching Master 11, *Pronunciation Guide for "Pastores á Belén"*

Evaluation Master 15, *Diction Check-up*

Skill Builder 25, *Rhythm Challenge in Compound Meter*

Skill Builder 30, *Solfège Hand Signs*

Dalcroze 13, *Moving in Triple and Duple Meters*

For additional resources, see TRB Table of Contents.

Links to Learning

◆ **Vocal**

An **interval** is *the distance between two notes.* Perform the examples below to practice singing the intervals between *sol, mi* and *la,* as well as the intervals between *do, sol* and *la.*

◆ **Theory**

⁶⁄₈ meter is an example of **compound meter,** *a time signature in which the dotted quarter note or three eight notes receive the beat.* In the example below, clap the rhythm while stepping the dotted quarter note beat. Then, clap the beat and step the rhythm.

◆ **Artistic Expression**

Spanish, like Italian and Latin, is a wonderful language to sing because it uses pure singing vowels. Practice speaking the Spanish text before singing. Create plenty of space inside the mouth for tall, rich vowel sounds.

Evaluation

Demonstrate how well you have learned the skills and concepts featured in the lesson "Pastores á Belén" by completing the following:

- To show your ability to read music notation in compound rhythm, sing measures 1–20. Decide which category best matches your performance: (1) I was able to read all of the rhythms correctly; (2) I was able to read most of the rhythms correctly; (3) I was able to read only a few of the rhythms correctly.

- Speak the Spanish text phrase by phrase into a recorder. Listen and evaluate how well you were able to speak with tall, pure vowel sounds. Identify words that need improvement.

RESOURCES

Proficient Tenor/Bass Rehearsal/Performance CD

CD 1:13 Voices

CD 1:14 Accompaniment Only

CD 3:7 Vocal Practice Track—Tenor I

CD 4:7 Vocal Practice Track—Tenor II

CD 6:7 Vocal Practice Track—Bass

National Standards

1. Singing, alone and with others, a varied repertoire of music. **(a, c)**

5. Reading and notating music. **(a, b)**

9. Understanding music in relation to history and culture. **(a)**

LINKS TO LEARNING

Vocal

The Vocal section is designed to prepare students to:

- Understand interval.
- Sing the intervals most frequently used in this song.

Have students:

- Read the definition of interval.
- Sing the Vocal example in the tenor clef using the *sol, mi* and *la* solfège syllables.
- Sing the Vocal example in bass clef using the *do, sol* and *re* solfège syllables.

Theory

The Theory section is designed to prepare students to:

- Understand compound meter.
- Perform a rhythm in 6/8 meter.

Have students:

- Read the definition of compound meter.
- Step the dotted quarter note pulse while clapping the rhythm example.
- Clap the dotted quarter note pulse while stepping the rhythm example.

Artistic Expression

The Artistic Expression section is designed to prepare students to speak the Spanish text with accuracy and tall vowels.

Have students:

- Echo the teacher in speaking the Spanish text. A pronunciation guide can be found in the Teacher Resource Binder, Teacher Master 11. Go line by line until accurate.
- Speak the Spanish text in rhythm.

LESSON PLAN

Suggested Teaching Sequence and Performance Tips

1. Introduce

Direct students to:

- Read and discuss the information found in the Getting Started section on page 56.
- Find examples of parallel thirds in their music.
- Practice the interval example in the Vocal section on page 57.
- Practice reading rhythms in compound meter as found in the Theory section on page 57.
- Practice speaking the Spanish text. A pronunciation guide can be found in the Teacher Resource Binder, Teacher Master 11. When comfortable, speak in rhythm.

Progress Checkpoints

Observe students' progress in:

- ✓ Finding parallel thirds in their choral scores.
- ✓ Singing intervals with accurate intonation.
- ✓ Performing rhythms in compound meter.
- ✓ Speaking the Spanish text correctly.

Pastores á Belén

For TTB, a cappella

Spanish text adapted by JAIME PÉREZ
English text by EMILY CROCKER

Traditional Spanish Carol
Arranged by EMILY CROCKER

Copyright © 2005 by HAL LEONARD CORPORATION
International Copyright Secured   All Rights Reserved

TEACHER 2 TEACHER

"Pastores á Belén" is a way of introducing students to sing in a foreign language. Here is an accessible piece for young males that moves in a traditionally harmonic and repetitious fashion.

2. Rehearse

Direct students to:

- Sing the melody in the Tenor II part from pickup to measure 5 to measure 12. All parts should become familiar with the tune. Sing in Spanish if possible. If not, use a neutral syllable such as "doo" for now and add the Spanish when comfortable.

- Divide into sections and learn the accompanying parts (Tenor I and Bass) to the melody in measures 5–12. Note that measures 5–6 are repeated measures from the introduction (measures 1–4). Use piano as necessary.

- Find which parts sing the melody in measures 13–20. *(Tenor II in measures 13–14, Bass in measures 15–16, Tenor II in measures 17–18, Bass in measures 19–20)* Have all students sing the melody.

- Divide into sections and learn the accompanying parts in measures 13–20. Use piano as necessary.

- Sight-sing all three parts in measures 21–24, carefully tuning the parallel thirds in the Tenor I and II parts. Rehearse until all parts are comfortable and in tune.

- Sing the melody in the Bass part in measures 23–28. Have all students sing the melody.

MORE ABOUT...

Spanish Music in Your Community

Have students:

- Search for performances of Spanish music within your community.
- Explore recordings of Spanish music available in the record store.
- Make plans to attend a live performance of Spanish music.
- Invite a Spanish music performer, composer, or other artist from the community to come to the class and discuss Spanish music with them.

- Divide into sections and learn the accompanying parts in measures 23–28. Use piano as necessary.
- Sight-sing all parts in measures 29–end, noting in which part the melody lies. Use piano as necessary. Divide the Tenor II section in the last two measures.

Progress Checkpoints

Observe students' progress in:

✓ Locating and singing the melody in whatever part in occurs.

✓ Singing the accompanying parts without interfering with the melody.

✓ Singing the Spanish text correctly.

MORE ABOUT...

Developing Vocal Resonance

Resonance is the unique sound of a voice that identifies it and gives it a rich beauty. To get resonance, there must be large spaces. The head is your resonating chamber for sound and needs large spaces with firm walls (your facial bone structure) to ring and sound out. The resonance or tone placement of the voice is also called the *mask*. Have students:

- Focus the tone behind the nose, feeling a buzz or ring when singing an "ng."
- Keep the buzzing feeling in the mask on every sound to keep a continuous focus.
- Use a hum, and vocalize with "m" and "ng" sounds to create resonance, then add different vowels.

3. Refine

Direct students to:

- Find all dynamic and tempo marking throughout the piece. Note that dynamic levels are not the same for each section. The melody is always prominent.
- Sing through the piece observing all dynamic marking and tempo changes. Watch the director in measure 29 for the new temp and the cutoff on the fermata in measures 30 and 34. Carefully watch the director in the rubato section (measures 35 to end).
- Step to the dotted quarter note beat throughout, swaying from side to side to give the piece motion.
- Sing through the piece with expression to convey the meaning of the text and concentrating on singing the Spanish lyrics with tall vowels.

Progress Checkpoints

Observe students' progress in:

- ✓ Observing and performing all dynamic markings within their section.
- ✓ Watch the conductor for tempo changes, fermatas and the rubato section.
- ✓ Giving movement and expression to the piece.

TEACHING STRATEGY
Intervals and Chords

Have students:

- Locate where there are only two voice parts and where there are three.
- Distinguish between harmony created by two parts (intervals) and harmony created by three or more parts (chords).
- Determine if there is anything in the text that the composer was responding to in choosing intervals or chords. (*The intervals, the simpler sound is the call to the shepherds to wake up and come to see the baby. The chords are when the shepherds are entering the stall and will actually see the baby.*)
- In groups, compose melodies in two or three parts that sound good together, and use them as warmups.

ASSESSMENT

Informal Assessment

In this lesson, students showed the ability to:

- Sing Spanish text correctly with tall vowels.
- Sing parallel thirds in tune in the key of F major.
- Sing in compound meter in fluidity and motion.
- Watch the director for dynamic and tempo indication.

Student Self-Assessment

Have students evaluate their individual performances based on the following:

- Posture
- Spanish Pronunciation
- Tall Vowels
- Expressive Singing
- Correct Part-Singing

Have each student rate his/her performance of this song in the areas above on a scale of 1–5, 5 being the best.

62   Proficient Tenor/Bass

TEACHING STRATEGY

Interpreting the Piece Through Dynamics

Have students:

- Review the notation of "Pastores á Belén" for all dynamic markings.
- Identify the purpose behind each marking, such as phrasing, a certain meaning in the text, accompanying the melody and so on.
- Sing the piece, attending to the dynamics and phrasing for more meaningful interpretation.

Individual and Group Performance Assessment

To further measure growth of musical skills presented in this lesson, direct students to complete the Evaluation section on page 57.

- After each student has sung measures 1–20 on their own at home or in a practice room, they should evaluate their performance based on the scale given.
- After all students have recorded themselves speaking the Spanish text into a recorder, they should listen to the recording and evaluate their ability to speak with tall, pure vowels. Assist them in identifying any words that need improvement.

EXTENSION

Composition

Have each student write a short melodic passage in F major and in 6/8 meter. For greater challenge, have students create a complex rhythmic pattern in 6/8 meter to accompnay their melody. Have each student perform his/her piece for the rest of the class."

ENRICHMENT

Other Carols

Compare and contrast another carol in 6/8 meter of a different ethnic origin. What is similar? What is different?

Additional National Standards

The following National Standards are addressed through the Assessment, Extension, Enrichment and bottom-page activities:

4. Composing and arranging music within specific guidelines. **(a)**

5. Reading and notating music. **(a)**

7. Evaluating music and music performance. **(a, b)**

Still, Still, Still

OVERVIEW

Composer: Austrian Carol, arranged by Audrey Snyder

Text: Traditional Austrian Carol

Voicing: TTB

Key: F major, G major

Meter: 4/4

Form: Strophic with minor variations

Style: Traditional Austrian Carol

Accompaniment: Piano

Programming: Seasonal Concert

Vocal Ranges:

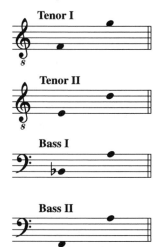

OBJECTIVES

After completing this lesson, students will be able to:

• Define the concepts of dissonant and consonant intervals.

• Identify melodic and harmonic parts when listening to and/or performing music.

VOCABULARY

Have students review vocabulary in student lesson. Introduce terms found in the music. A complete glossary of terms is found on page 246 of the student book.

Still, Still, Still

Composer: Austrian Carol, arranged by Audrey Snyder

Text: Traditional Austrian Carol

Voicing: TTB

VOCABULARY

carol

suspensions

Focus

• Use standard terminology to describe *suspension*.

• Identify the melody line and balance it against harmony parts when performing.

Getting Started

Can you match each carol with the correct country?

a. "Joy To The World"	**1.** Austria
b. "Carol of the Bells"	**2.** England
c. "Riu, Riu Chiu"	**3.** Ukraine
d. "Still, Still, Still"	**4.** Spain

The Austrian carol "Still, Still, Still" is also sung as a lullaby. As you learn this song, look for ways in which the melody and rhythms create a calm and soothing mood.

SKILL BUILDERS

To learn more about the key of F major, see Proficient Sight-Singing, *page 45.*

◆ History and Culture

A **carol** is *a song of English origin dating back to the Middle Ages with subject matter pertaining to the Virgin Mary or Christmas.* Christmas carols often were usually strophic in nature with a recurring refrain between verses. Similar songs existed in other cultures—*noël* in France and *Weihnachtlied* in Germany—although today all of these Christmas songs are referred to as carols.

In this arrangement, composer Audrey Snyder alternates the melody between the Tenor I and Tenor II parts. She also uses **suspensions** *(the holding over of one or more musical tones in a chord into the following chord producing a momentary discord)* in the harmony to emphasize the rocking motion of this lullaby. Enjoy learning "Still, Still, Still" with its familiar flowing melody that has been popular for years.

RESOURCES

Proficient Sight-Singing

Sight-Singing in F Major, pages 45–46

Sight-Singing in G Major, pages 71–73

Reading Rhythms in 4/4 Meter, pages 2–9

Reading Consonant and Dissonant Intervals, page 175

Teacher Resource Binder

Teaching Master 12, *Exploring Musical Expression*

Teaching Master 13, *Analyzing for Musical Contrast*

Skill Builder 21, *Pitch and Kodály*

Skill Builder 30, *Solfège Hand Signs*

For additional resources, see TRB Table of Contents.

Links to Learning

◆ **Vocal**

Suspension creates the effect of tension and release in music. Locate the suspensions in the following example. Which voice part sings the note that creates the suspension? Practice each suspension using solfège syllables. Emphasize the suspended note so it is the most prominent note of the chord.

◆ **Artistic Expression**

It is important that the melody line be heard above the harmony parts in ensemble singing. To hear the balance of the parts, form a circle of six singers with two singers to a part. Sing measures 7–20 and focus on bringing out the melody by having each section move one step into the circle when their part sings a phrase of the original carol melody. Step back into place when you have a harmonic supporting part.

Evaluation

Demonstrate how well you have learned the skills and concepts featured in the lesson "Still, Still, Still" by completing the following:

• Define *suspension*. With a group of nine singers, sing measures 2–6 to show your ability to sing suspensions accurately. Evaluate how well you did.

• Analyze your voice part. Decide in what measures you sing the melody and in what measures you sing the harmony.

Lesson 8 *Still, Still, Still* **65**

RESOURCES

Proficient Tenor/Bass Rehearsal/Performance CD

CD 1:15 Voices

CD 1:16 Accompaniment Only

CD 3:8 Vocal Practice Track—Tenor I

CD 4:8 Vocal Practice Track—Tenor II

CD 6:8 Vocal Practice Track—Bass

National Standards

1. Singing, alone and with others, a varied repertoire of music. **(a, c)**

6. Listening to, analyzing, and describing music. **(b)**

• Demonstrate independently and in ensembles accurate intonation and rhythm, fundamental skills, and basic performance techniques while performing moderately easy to moderately difficult literature.

LINKS TO LEARNING

Vocal

The Vocal section is designed to prepare students to:

• Understand suspensions and locate them in their music.

• Sing suspensions with accuracy and expression.

Have students:

• Locate the suspensions that occur in the Vocal example.

• Sing the example using solfège syllables, emphasizing the suspended note.

Artistic Expression

The Artistic Expression section is designed to prepare students to:

• Identify the melody line in ensemble singing.

• Bring out the melody line when their part is singing it.

Have students follow the instructions given for the activity to bring the melody forward when their part has it.

LESSON PLAN

Suggested Teaching Sequence and Performance Tips

1. Introduce

Direct students to:

- Read and discuss the information found in the Getting Started section on page 64. *("a" matches 2, "b" matches 3, "c" matches 4, "d" matches 1)*

- Practice the exercise on suspensions in the Vocal section on page 65. Locate these suspensions in their choral score.

- Locate and identify the initial key signature in the score. *(F major)*

- Locate and identify the key change in the score. *(G major, measure 37)*

- Actively listen to measures 7–18 with pencil in hand. Lightly circle the notes and text of the original carol melody as it switches from Tenor I to Tenor II. Teacher plays Tenor I in measures 7–8, Tenor II in measures 9–14, Tenor I in measures 15–16, Tenor II measures 17–18.

- Sing the original melody in unison measures 7–18.

Still, Still, Still

For TTB and Piano

Arranged by
AUDREY SNYDER

Austrian Carol

Copyright © 2002 by HAL LEONARD CORPORATION
International Copyright Secured   All Rights Reserved

TEACHER 2 TEACHER

This beautiful rendition of "Still, Still, Still" is a excellent piece to allow students to express their gentle side. Encourage your singers to use facial expressions that exhibit a peaceful quietness.

hear the ___ fall - ing snow. Oo. ____

hear the ___ fall - ing ___ snow. For all is __ hushed, the world is __ sleep-ing,

hear the fall - ing snow. Oo. ____

shin - ing ___ star its vig - il ___ keep - ing. Still, still, still, you can

Still, ___ still, ___ still, you can

Still, ___ still, ___ still, ____

- Listen to measures 1–36 of the CD recording. While listening, hum the melody in measures 7–18 and circle the phases that use the exact melody in measures 19–36, noting the phrases that use a melodic variant. *(Tenor I has melodic variant in measures 21–24, Tenor II has original melody in measures 25–29, Tenor I has melodic variant in measures 29–32)*
- Have Tenor I sing measures 21–24 and the rest of the ensemble join in the melody measures 25–29.
- Sight-read the melodic line in measures 37–48.

Progress Checkpoints

Observe students' progress in:
✓ Singing suspensions with accuracy and expression.
✓ Their ability to identify key signatures.
✓ Their ability to identify melodic and harmonic parts.

CONNECTING THE ARTS
Expression Through Color

People find many ways to express themselves with spoken language and body language. With text, pitch, body language and the expressive elements of music, the singer or ensemble paints a visual and aural picture for the audience. Direct the ensemble to experiment with the expression of "Still, Still, Still" through color. Ask them to try singing the song as if it were the color: (1) bright red, (2) rich, deep velvety purple, (3) sky blue. Let the students create expressive effects by choosing the color to imagine. Have the students evaluate and describe how the piece changes with each rendition and decide what mood or color they truly want to set for the audience.

2. Rehearse

Direct students to:

- Return to the beginning of the piece after locating and learning all of the melody lines and sing the harmony parts.
- Practice individual parts in sections with an emphasis on using the dynamic markings accurately. Have the nonsinging section listen to evaluate the singers' effective use of the dynamic markings.
- Sing the entire song on their own part. This time have singers stand when their section has the melody and sit when they sing harmony. Have singers make a continued conscious effort to use the dynamic markings.
- Locate all the suspension in their choral scores and note which part is singing the suspended note.
- Sing these suspensions with strength but without punching the attack.

Progress Checkpoints

Observe students' progress in:

- ✓ Their ability to effectively use dynamics and maintain accurate intonation and phrasing.
- ✓ Their ability to attack and release dissonant intervals without punching the attack.
- ✓ Their ability to effectively use attack and release of dissonant pitches yet maintain a strong legato sense of phrasing.
- ✓ Their ability to demonstrate accurate part singing and intonation within the ensemble.

MORE ABOUT...
Christmas Carols

Although today Christians associate Christmas with the birth of Jesus, in fact, no one really knows his birth date. We do know that late December marks the end of the winter solstice, a time to anticipate and prepare for the lengthening of days and the coming of spring. Since the days of the Roman Empire, the end of the winter solstice has been celebrated with festivals, and song has always been a part of celebrations. Like "Still, Still, Still," many of the Christmas carols sung today in America had their origins in European countries.

keep. The ___ night is peace-ful 'round you,

keep. The night is ___ peace-ful all a-round you.

keep. Night, 'round you,

sleep ___ sur-round you. Sleep, sleep, ___ sleep, ___ while

Close your eyes, let sleep sur-round you. Sleep, ___

sleep sur - round you. Sleep, ___ sleep, ___

3. Refine
Direct students to:
- Sing complete four-measure phrases with continued energy throughout the phrase, spinning the voice through long, sustained pitches.
- Listen for the melody and have singers adjust their dynamics to support with good vocal tone, but not cover the melodic line.
- Emphasize the calmness of the text through a dramatic use of the tempo markings.
- Articulate clear, precise diction.
- Keep the humming sections bright and forward, buzzing just behind the teeth and nose, but with the jaw dropped for resonance.

Progress Checkpoints
Observe students' progress in:
- ✓ Singing phrases with energy through the soft dynamics.
- ✓ Performing the dynamics as marked in the score.
- ✓ Performing the tempos as marked in the score.
- ✓ Attacking and releasing dissonant intervals effectively.
- ✓ Effectively communicating the text.

MUSIC LITERACY
Dynamics and Shaping Phrases
To help students expand their music literacy, have them:
- Review the parts of a phrase—beginning, peak, and end.
- Discuss how to shape phrases using dynamics, with a crescendo from the beginning to the peak, and then a release to the end.
- Recall that the dynamic marking at the beginning of a phrase may indicate the overall average dynamic for the entire phrase.

ASSESSMENT

Informal Assessment

In this lesson, students showed the ability to:

- Locate in the score dissonance; visually and aurally.
- Identify major key signatures.
- Sing in three parts accurately and in tune.
- Locate in the score the melodic line of the traditional carol and its composed variants.
- Identify melodic and harmonic parts.
- Apply tempo and dynamic markings.

Student Self-Assessment

Have students evaluate their individual performances based on the following:

- Expressive Singing
- Intonation
- Accurate Pitches
- Accurate Rhythms
- Correct Part-Singing

Have each student rate his/her performance of this song in the areas above on a scale of 1–5, 5 being the best.

70   Proficient Tenor/Bass

PERFORMANCE TIPS

Suspensions and Dissonances

There are suspensions and resolutions in this composition. You may want to rehearse these separately from the piece. The ending consonants should connect to the word that follows. Be careful not to close to the "l" on still. Students should be careful to drop the jaw and keep an open sound.

Individual and Group Performance Assessment

To further measure growth of musical skills presented in this lesson, direct students to complete the Evaluation section on page 65.

- After defining suspension, have a group of nine singers sing measures 2–6 for the rest of the class. Assist the class in evaluating by asking the following question, "Was this group able to sing suspensions accurately?"

- After each student has analyzed his/her part as to where he sings the melody, sing the piece again. Each student should stand when his/her part is singing the melody and sit when his/her part is singing the harmony. Evaluate whether each student has a grasp on where the melody lies.

TEACHING STRATEGY

Suspensions and Altered Tones

Have students:

- Identify the altered tones in their voice part, and practice them in isolation until they are familiar.

- Discuss how a suspension holds a pitch in one part while the other parts move to a new chord, thereby creating dissonance.

- Find places in their voice part where they have a suspended tone.

- Sing the piece again, listening to the effect of suspensions in keeping the tension of the piece constant, and moving the piece forward without rest until a cadence.

EXTENSION

Pitch Accuracy

Check the ensemble's pitch accuracy by having the students sing this piece a cappella. Challenge the group to sing with a well-supported tone and well-defined rhythms for a clean a cappella rendition.

Additional National Standards

The following National Standards are addressed through the Assessment, Extension, Enrichment and bottom-page activities:

7. Evaluating music and music performances. **(b)**

8. Understanding relationships between music, the other arts, and disciplines outside the arts. **(a)**

SPOTLIGHT

Arranging

When asked how he approaches choral arranging, composer and arranger Roger Emerson had this to say:

"Generally, an arranger takes the basic melody and accompaniment of a song and prepares it (arranges it) so that it may be performed by a group of instruments or voices. These are things that I take into consideration.

Key

Specifically, as a choral arranger, I begin by finding the best key for the melody. That means finding the scale to use that makes the song the most comfortable to sing. I look for the highest and lowest note of the song, and what ranges would work best for my group of singers.

Melody and Harmony

I then determine the best places for the singers to sing unison or where harmony would be most effective. Using the basic chord symbols as a guide, I like to make the song more interesting by substituting expanded or more colorful chords throughout the song. Depending on the group who will perform the song, I will then write out parts for Sopranos, Altos, Tenor and Baritone or Bass singers, using the melody and new chords that I have chosen. The next step is to create a piano accompaniment that supports and hopefully enhances the vocal parts.

Accompaniment

Particularly in 'pop' style arrangements, the left hand carries a bass line while the right hand plays chords.

Finishing the Arrangement

The final step is to add lyrics, dynamic and style markings.

There are books that provide guidelines for arranging such as chord voicings and comfortable ranges for each instrument or voice, but most 'arrangers' will tell you (like the commercial says) JUST DO IT! Then listen to the outcome and see if you like the way it sounds. We all began somewhere. Good luck!"

Contemporary composer Roger Emerson has over 500 titles in print and 15 million copies in circulation. He is one of the most widely performed choral composers in America today. After a twelve-year teaching career, he now devotes himself full-time to composing, arranging and consulting.

Spotlight *Arranging* **73**

RESOURCES

Teacher Resource Binder

Skill Builder 1, *Building Harmony*
Skill Builder 15, *Major and Minor Scales*
Reference 16, *Expanding a Musical Vocabulary*

National Standards

4. Composing and arranging music within specific guidelines. **(b)**

ARRANGING

Objectives

- Create and arrange music within specified guidelines.

Suggested Teaching Sequence

Direct students to:

- Read the Spotlight On Arranging on student page 73 and discuss the definition of an arrangement.
- Discuss the four elements of arranging presented by arranger Roger Emerson.
- What decisions must be made in creating an arrangement?
- Using the guidelines presented on this page, write a simple vocal arrangement to a familiar song.
- Perform the arrangement for the class.
- Find other familiar songs and write arrangements for those as well.

Progress Checkpoints

Observe students' progress in:

✓ Their ability to identify the techniques used in arranging.
✓ Their ability to write a simple arrangement of a familiar song.

All Ye Who Music Love
OVERVIEW

Composer: Baldassare Donato (c. 1525–1603), arranged by Sherri Porterfield

Text: Thomas Oliphant

Voicing: TTB

Key: G Major

Meter: 2/2, 3/4

Form: AABCAABC

Style: Italian Renaissance Madrigal

Accompaniment: A cappella

Programming: Concert, Contest, Festival, Madrigal Program, Appropriate for small ensembles

Vocal Ranges:

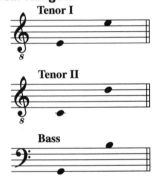

Tenor I

Tenor II

Bass

OBJECTIVES

After completing this lesson, students will be able to:

• Demonstrate in ensembles accurate intonation and rhythm while performing.

• Identify melodic and harmonic parts when listening and performing music.

• Perform expressively a varied repertoire of music representing styles from diverse periods including Renaissance.

VOCABULARY

Have students review vocabulary in student lesson. Introduce terms found in the music. A complete glossary of terms is found on page 246 of the student book.

All Ye Who Music Love

Composer: Baldassare Donato (c. 1525–1603), arranged by Sherri Porterfield

Text: Thomas Oliphant

Voicing: TTB

VOCABULARY

Renaissance period

motet

madrigal

homophony

polyphony

MUSIC & HISTORY

To learn more about the Renaissance period, see page 110.

Focus

• Perform with proper rhythmic clarity and good intonation.

• Identify music written in contrapuntal and homophonic style.

• Perform choral literature of the Renaissance.

Getting Started

If you were a singer during the **Renaissance period** *(c. 1430–1600)* in Italy, you would have had two basic choices for music—sacred or secular. Vocal music flourished during the Renaissance as an important part of religious services, pageants and daily life. The short pieces that composers wrote for singers fell into two major categories: **motets** *(short, sacred choral pieces with Latin texts that are used in religious services, but are not a part of the regular mass)* and **madrigals** *(short, secular choral pieces with texts in the common language)*. Today's music, like the Renaissance, is still categorized as sacred or secular, but we have many more choices in style: gospel, jazz, pop, chorale, oratorio, Broadway, rock, and so forth.

◆ History and Culture

Baldassare Donato (c. 1525–1603) lived his entire life in Venice, where he was choirmaster and composer for the prestigious St. Mark's Cathedral. He is most known for his light, secular music. During the Renaissance, **homophony** *(a type of music in which there are two or more parts with similar or identical rhythms being sung at the same time)* and **polyphony** *(a type of music in which there are two or more different melodic lines being sung or played at the same time)* were used in music to create harmony. Examples of both may be found in "All Ye Who Music Love."

74 Proficient Tenor/Bass

RESOURCES

Proficient Sight-Singing

Sight-Singing in G Major, pages 71–73

Reading Rhythms in Cut Time, page 147

Reading Rhythms in 3/4 Meter, page 14

Reading Syncopations, page 85

Teacher Resource Binder

Teaching Master 14, *Musical Texture and Expression*

Evaluation Master 9, *Evaluating Rhythmic Accuracy*

Music and History 1, *Characteristics of Renaissance Music: 1430–1600*

Music and History 3, *Baldassare Donato, a Renaissance Composer*

For additional resources, see TRB Table of Contents.

Links to Learning

◆ Vocal

Perform the following example to practice singing homophony. Sing on the neutral syllable "pahm" to achieve rhythmic precision. Keep every note value staccato, and close to the "m" immediately.

◆ Theory

During the Renaissance, music was notated without barlines. The rhythm followed the flow of the words, sometimes creating irregular patterns. This technique is found in measures 14–21. To feel the irregular pattern in measures 14–21, chant the words in rhythm while maintaining a steady beat.

Evaluation

Demonstrate how well you have learned the skills and concepts featured in the lesson "All Ye Who Music Love" by completing the following:

- Divide the choir into trios with one singer on each part. Have each group sing measures 29–42 while the rest of the choir listens for clear articulation of diction, precise rhythms, and proper intonation.

- Demonstrate an understanding of *polyphony* and *homophony* by locating in the music all the occurrences of contrapuntal entrances and homophonic entrances.

Lesson 9 *All Ye Who Music Love* **75**

RESOURCES

Proficient Tenor/Bass Rehearsal/Performance CD

CD 1:17 Voices

CD 1:18 Accompaniment Only

CD 3:9 Vocal Practice Track—Tenor I

CD 4:9 Vocal Practice Track—Tenor II

CD 6:9 Vocal Practice Track—Bass

National Standards

1. Singing, alone and with others, a varied repertoire of music. **(a, c)**

6. Listening to analyzing, and describing music. **(b)**

9. Understanding music in relation to history and culture. **(a)**

LINKS TO LEARNING

Vocal

The Vocal section is designed to prepare students to:

- Understand homophony.
- Sing in a homophonic style with accuracy and rhythmic precision.

Have students:

- Sing each line independently on the syllable "pahm" concentrating on rhythmic precision.
- Divide into sections and sing all three lines together, keeping every note value staccato and closing to the "m" immediately.

Theory

The Theory section is designed to prepare students to:

- Understand the characteristics of Renaissance music.
- Perform irregular rhythm patterns found in the music.

Have students:

- Locate measures 14–21 in their choral scores.
- Explain the Renaissance concept of notation without barlines.
- Chant the words in measures 14–21 while maintaining a steady beat.

LESSON PLAN

Suggested Teaching Sequence and Performance Tips

1. Introduce

Direct students to:

- Read and discuss the information found in the Getting Started section on page 74.
- Practice the Vocal exercise on page 75 to achieve rhythmic precision in homophonic singing.
- Practice singing measures 29–42 as a warm-up exercise to reinforce homophonic singing.

Progress Checkpoints

Observe students' progress in:

✓ Understanding Renaissance madrigals.

✓ Singing a homophonic texture with rhythmic accuracy and good intonation.

All Ye Who Music Love

For TTB, a cappella

Arranged by
SHERRI PORTERFIELD

Words by THOMAS OLIPHANT
Music by BALDASSARE DONATO (c. 1525–1603)

Copyright © 1997 by HAL LEONARD CORPORATION
International Copyright Secured All Rights Reserved

TEACHER 2 TEACHER

Through this lesson the student will learn about the madrigal of the sixteenth century and the styles of composition the madrigal used.

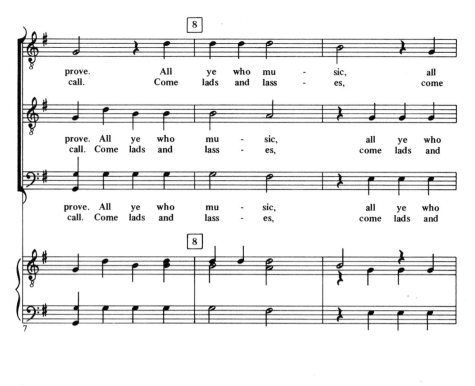

2. Rehearse

Direct students to:

- Sight-sing measures 1–13 at a slow but comfortable tempo in cut time. Rehearse parts individually if necessary until secure. Is this section homophonic or polyphonic? *(polyphonic)*
- Repeat the same procedure for measures 14–28. Is this section homophonic or polyphonic? *(polyphonic)*
- Repeat the same procedure for measures 29–42. Is this section homophonic or polyphonic? *(homophonic)*
- Increase tempo as notes and rhythms become secure.

Progress Checkpoints

Observe students' progress in:

✓ Their ability to decipher between homophony and polyphony.

✓ Singing their parts independently whether in the homophonic section or the polyphonic section.

✓ Their ability to sing each section in tune.

MORE ABOUT...

The Madrigal Style

Madrigals were composed mostly in Italy and England, and were secular vocal pieces, often with a theme of unrequited love. Many madrigals were polyphonic, with intricately interwoven melodic lines that had many scale-wise passages and fast-moving rhythms. The English madrigals often had couplets of rhymes, interspersed with refrains of *fa la* or the like. Madrigals were usually composed for individual voices on each part, to be sung with a light, quick style that enhanced the intricate weaving of the lines and quick rhythms. The dominant line was sung stronger, and each line came forward or receded to accommodate the most important melodic part. Help students identify characteristics of the madrigal in "All Ye Who Music Love."

3. Refine

Direct students to:

- Sing each section with attention to proper word accent.
- Sing each section with proper attention to open vowel sounds.
- Sing transition from measure 25 to measure 33 smoothly

Progress Checkpoints

Observe students' progress in:

✓ Singing with proper word accent and open vowel sounds.

✓ Their ability to sing a smooth transition from 2/2 to 3/4 meter.

ASSESSMENT

Informal Assessment

In this lesson, students showed the ability to:

- Recognize homophonic style verses contrapuntal style in a Renaissance madrigal.
- Sing accurately and with good intonation in the key of G major.
- Sing a smooth transition between 2/2 meter and 3/4 meter.
- Sing with proper syllabic stress and open vowel sounds.

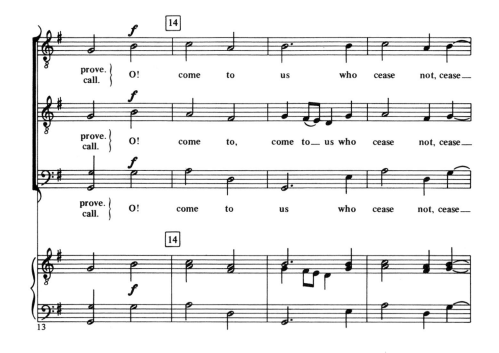

78 Proficient Tenor/Bass

MUSIC LITERACY

Alla Breve

Introduce or review alla breve meter. Explain that spirited, fast music demands less busy conducting. All note values are cut in half—two beats per measure with a half note equaling one beat, a quarter note equaling half of a beat and so forth.

Have students:

- Listen while they follow your movements on their octavo as you tap the beat and speak the rhythms of the song.
- Repeat the exercise, but this time have them speak the rhythms while you tap the beat.
- Repeat the exercise again, while you conduct in two.

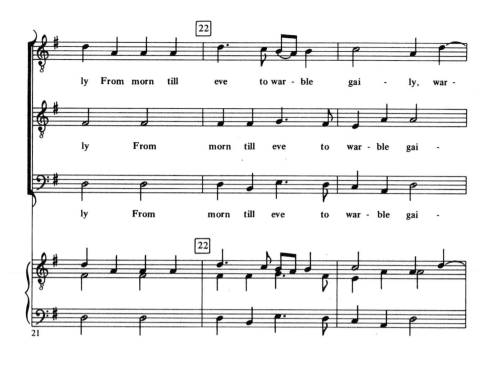

Student Self-Assessment

Have students evaluate their individual performances based on the following:

- Posture
- Diction
- Tall Vowels
- Intonation
- Correct Part-Singing

Have each student rate his/her performance of this song in the areas above on a scale of 1–5, 5 being the best.

Individual and Group Performance Evaluation

To further demonstrate musical growth, direct students to complete the Evaluation section on page 75.

- After each trio has sung measures 29–42 for the rest of the class, assist the class in evaluating the trio's ability to sing with clear diction, precise rhythms and proper intonation.
- Have each student mark their scores with a P over the polyphonic sections and an H over the homophonic sections. Have the students exchange books and evaluate each other's work.

TEACHING STRATEGY

Musical Elements of Style

The combination of musical elements determines the style of a piece.
Have students:

1. Compile a list of musical elements that might affect style.
2. Share the lists to compile one master list.
3. Sing known songs, trying out different styles, and then try to describe the musical elements that are characteristic of that style. (For example, try salsa, opera, Broadway, rock, military, lullaby, and so forth.)
4. Select appropriate literature for a particular style.

EXTENSION

Tempo

This piece can get away from a conductor, because the singers might begin to rush. Have students construct their own solutions for this problem of rushing, including conducting themselves as they sing and watching the conductor carefully.

ENRICHMENT

Improvisation

Some student may be reluctant to try improvisation. As a teacher, it is important to set up guidelines and to create a safe environment. Remind students that any effort is a worthy effort. Praise students often. Follow these steps to lead students to successful improvisation.

1. Play on a keyboard, guitar or some other instrument the I-IV-V-I chord progression. Play it several times until students become familiar with it.

2. Ask for volunteers to improvise a musical melody above the chord progression. Singers may use nonsense or scat syllables.

3. Have students analyze ways in which they can improve their skills in improvisation.

80 Proficient Tenor/Bass

MORE ABOUT...

Rubrics and Evaluation

The construction of a rubric is a good way to evaluate student understanding of the parameters of a good performance. In this piece, a good rubric would include all the characteristics worked on, and give criteria for what comprises an A, B, C, or D performance grade. The rubric is then written or typed, with spaces for checkmarks of accomplishment and a space for comments at the bottom of the page. As the students assess each other's performances, they will demonstrate acute listening skills, which will affect their future performance.

ENRICHMENT

Compare and Contrast Form

The form used in "All Ye Love Music" is a madrigal. Have students identify and describe the characteristics of a madrigal. Then, have them read pages 112–113 to learn more about the form of a motet. Have students identify and describe the characteristics of a motet. Listen to a recording of the motet "O Magnum Mysterium" by Victoria as found on page 113. Finally, have students compare and contrast the form of the madrigal "All Ye Love Music" and the motet "O Magnum Mysterium." How are they similar? How are they different? Compare and contrast the elements of texture (polyphonic or homophonic), harmony, dynamics, tempo, text and so forth.

Small-Ensemble Techniques

"All Ye Who Love Music" works well when performed by a small ensemble. Have students identify and describe the small-ensemble techniques appropriate for this madrigal such as balance of parts, precise rhythms, a light tone and tall vowels. While performing in small ensembles for a formal concert or competition, evaluate how well each ensemble demonstrates these performance techniques.

Additional National Standards

The following National Standards are addressed through the Assessment, Extension, Enrichment and bottom-page activities:

6. Listening to, analyzing, and describing music. **(a, b, c)**

7. Evaluating music and music performances **(a, b)**

Die Katze lässt das Mausen nicht

OVERVIEW

Composer: Johann Sebastian Bach (1685–1750), arranged by Michael Spresser

Text: Christian Friedrich Henrici (Picander), English text by J. Mark Baker

Voicing: TTB

Key: G major, B minor, E minor

Meter: Cut time (alla breve)

Form: Da capo (ABA)

Style: German Baroque Chorale

Accompaniment: Piano

Programming: Concert, Contest, Festival, appropriate for large or small ensembles

Vocal Ranges:

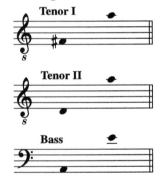

OBJECTIVES

After completing this lesson, students will be able to:

- Perform expressively a varied repertoire of music representing styles from diverse periods including Baroque.

- Demonstrate basic fundamental skills while performing.

VOCABULARY

Have students review vocabulary in student lesson. Introduce terms found in the music. A complete glossary of terms is found on page 246 of the student book.

82

Die Katze lässt das Mausen nicht

Composer: Johann Sebastian Bach (1685–1750), arranged by Michael Spresser
Text: Christian Friedrich Henrici (Picander), English text by J. Mark Baker
Voicing: TTB

VOCABULARY

Collegium musicum

Baroque period

cantata

homophony

counterpoint

MUSIC & HISTORY

To learn more about the Baroque period, see page 114.

Focus

- Perform music representing the Baroque period.
- Perform music with a German text.
- Identify and perform homophony and counterpoint.

Getting Started

It's Friday at 6:00 p.m. The young woman behind the counter relays the customers' orders to her capable staff, who serve coffee and pastries. A group of animated students enjoy their coffee while studying at the large table near the front window.

This scene could be at a Starbucks® in any college town. You may be surprised to learn, however, that the setting is Zimmerman's Coffee House in Leipzig, Germany, and the year is 1732.

◆ History and Culture

By the middle of the eighteenth century, coffeehouses had sprung up across Europe. The students were members of the Leipzig **Collegium musicum** *(a student musical group that performs serious music).* They rehearsed or performed every Friday night at Zimmerman's. Their director was none other than the greatest composer of the **Baroque period** *(1600–1750),* Johann Sebastian Bach (1685–1750). Although his musical genius is undisputed, there was a practical reason for almost everything he wrote. Bach's primary job was to compose a sacred **cantata** *(a musical piece made up of several movements for singers and instrumentalists)* for each Sunday service of the Lutheran church year. However, his fondness for Zimmerman's and the Collegium musicum may have been the motivation for using the sacred cantata form for a comic piece about the German coffee craze. The trio, "Die Katze lässt das Mausen nicht," is the lively conclusion to the secular cantata *Schweigt stille, plaudert nicht.*

82   Proficient Tenor/Bass

RESOURCES

Proficient Sight-Singing

Sight-Singing in G Major, pages 71–73

Sight-Singing in E Minor, pages 78–80

Reading Rhythms in Cut Time, page 147

Teacher Resource Binder

Teaching Master 14, *Pronunciation Guide for "Die Katze Lässt das Mausen nicht"*

Teaching Master 16, *Exploring Musical Texture*

Evaluation Master 15, *Diction Check-up*

Music and History 8, *Johann Sebastian Bach, a "Baroque" Composer*

For additional resources, see TRB Table of Contents.

Links to Learning

◆ **Theory**

Look at the two phrases shown below. Example 1 is **homophony,** *a type of music in which there are two or more parts with similar or identical rhythms being sung or played at the same time.* Example 2 is **counterpoint,** *the combination of two or more melodic lines where the parts move independently while harmony is created.* Sing both examples using solfège syllables, and then the words.

◆ **Artistic Expression**

To effectively convey the meaning of music with a foreign-language text, singers must know the translation of the words. In German, nouns are always capitalized. Find the definitions of these German words: (1) *die Katze,* (2) *die Mutter,* (3) *das Mausern,* (4) *die Grossmama,* (5) *die Jungfern,* (6) *die Töchter.*

Evaluation

Demonstrate how well you have learned the skills and concepts featured in the lesson "Die Katze lässt das Mausen nicht" by completing the following:

• Identify the following phrases as homophony or counterpoint: **(1)** measures 36–42, **(2)** measures 55–61, **(3)** measures 78–84, **(4)** measures 48–54, **(5)** measures 72–77, **(6)** measures 85–93. Check your answers with a classmate.

• Write each of the following German phrases on a slip of paper: *Die Katze lässt das Mausern nicht; Die Mutter liebt den Coffee brauch;* and *Auf die Töchter lastern.* Place the slips in a coffee mug. Ask a classmate to draw one slip from the mug and sing all occurrences of the phrase. Evaluate his performance for correct pitches, rhythm and pronunciation. Switch roles.

Lesson 10 *Die Katze lässt das Mausen nicht* **83**

RESOURCES

Proficient Tenor/Bass Rehearsal/Performance CD

CD 1:19 Voices

CD 1:20 Accompaniment Only

CD 3:10 Vocal Practice Track—Tenor I

CD 4:10 Vocal Practice Track—Tenor II

CD 6:10 Vocal Practice Track—Bass

National Standards

1. Singing, alone and with others, a varied repertoire of music. **(a, b, c)**

6. Listening to, analyzing, and describing music. **(b)**

9. Understanding music in relation to history and culture. **(a)**

• Identify melodic and harmonic parts when listening to and performing music.

LINKS TO LEARNING

Theory

The Theory section is designed to prepare students to:

• Understand homophony and counterpoint.

• Sing the homophonic and contrapuntal sections in this song.

Have students:

• Sing example 1 on solfège syllables concentrating on accurate intervals to demonstrate homophony.

• Sing example 1 on the text, then locate this phrase in their choral scores.

• Sing example 2 on solfège syllable concentrating on independence of lines to demonstrate counterpoint.

• Sing example 2 on the text, then locate this phrase in their choral scores.

Artistic Expression

The Artistic Expression section is designed to prepare students to understand the meaning of the German text.

Have students research and define the terms listed. (*die Katze*—cat; *das Mausen*—mice; *die Jungfern*—maidens; *die Töchter*—daughters)

LESSON PLAN

Suggested Teaching Sequence and Performance Tips

1. Introduce

Direct students to:

- Read and discuss the ideas presented in the Getting Started section on page 82. (a) Discuss the coffee culture of today. (b) Share any information they may know about Johann Sebastian Bach or the Baroque period.

- Complete the activities presented in Links to Learning. (a) Listen to other pieces by Bach or other Baroque music. (i.e. 2/3 part inventions, fugues, sacred choruses) (b) Distinguish between the homophonic and polyphonic phrases. (c) Translate the German text by using the assistance of a dictionary, German teacher or students fluent in German. (d) Practice speaking the text with correct German pronunciation.

- Sing the G major and E minor scales using solfège.

- As a class, sing the Tenor I part measures 24–30 with solfège syllables. Do the same with the Tenor II and Bass parts in measures 24–30.

Die Katze lässt das Mausen nicht

final trio from
Schweigt stille, plaudert nicht
(Coffee Cantata, BWV 211, #10)

For TTB and Piano

Arranged by MICHAEL SPRESSER
English text by J. MARK BAKER

Words by PICANDER
JOHANN SEBASTIAN BACH (1685–1750)

Copyright © 2005 by HAL LEONARD CORPORATION
International Copyright Secured   All Rights Reserved

84   Proficient Tenor/Bass

TEACHER 2 TEACHER

This chorus is an adaptation of the concluding trio for *Schweigt stille, plaudert nicht (Be quiet, do not chat)* BWV 211, which is often referred to as the *Coffee Cantata*. Three characters, Herr Schlendrian (the father), Lieschen (his daughter), and the narrator sing the entire cantata.

- Count off by threes. Sing measures 24–30 all together with the one's singing the Tenor I part, the twos singing the Tenor II part and the threes singing the Bass part. Sing again and switch parts (i.e., the twos sing Tenor I, the threes sing Tenor II and the threes sing Bass). Sing again and switch parts once more.

- Form trios and practice measures 24–30 with one singer on each part. Sing for the class and critique each other's performances.

- Work in sectional groups and learn the solfège syllables for the remaining phrases: measures 31–36, 37–42, 43–48, 49–57. As sections, sing for the class and critique each other's performances.

- Form new trios (TTB) or double trios, and rehearse the entire piece on solfège. Sing for the class and critique each other's performances.

Progress Checkpoints

Observe students' progress in:

✓ Their ability to accurately sing the chromatically altered pitches (i.e., "tay" in measure 27 and "di" in measure 38).

✓ Their ability to accurately sing rhythm patterns and maintain a steady beat.

CONNECTING THE ARTS

Style: Comparing and Contrasting

Have students:

- Find examples of other artwork or art forms from the Baroque period, describing how they exhibit the characteristics of the period. (Choose from visual art, architecture, dance, drama, poetry or literature.)
- Discuss how these examples are similar to and different from music, taking into consideration the roles of artists, performers and audience.
- Find another example from the same art category, but from a different style, period or culture.
- Discuss similarities and differences between the examples.

2. Rehearse

Direct students to:

- Count-sing (see Teaching Strategy Box on page 92) all the phrases at a slow, but steady tempo.

- Count-sing all three parts at the same time.

- Recite or chant the German text in rhythm.

- Return to sectional groups and rehearse their voice part with the German text. Sing for the class and critique each other's performances.

- Bring a coffee mug from home with their name clearly labeled on the bottom (see the Evaluation section in the Student Edition). (a) Find 4–6 difficult measures in their voice part and copy each measure onto a slip of staff paper. (b) Put the measure slips in the coffee mug. (c) Work in groups of 2–4 (all students on the same voice part). Choose a slip from each other's mug. Locate the measure in the music and sing it correctly with solfège syllables and then with the German text. (d) Repeat until all measure slips have been sung accurately.

- As a class, sing the entire piece with the German text.

86 Proficient Tenor/Bass

TEACHING STRATEGY

Concert Etiquette

Have students:

1. Identify appropriate concert etiquette in a variety of settings (formal concerts, informal concerts, large concert halls, small concert halls, and so forth).

2. Attend a variety of live performances.

3. Discuss the appropriate and inappropriate concert behaviors observed.

4. Write a short analysis of appropriate concert etiquette for each setting.

Cof - fee - schwes - tern.
cof - fee sis - ters.

Progress Checkpoints

Observe students' progress in:

✓ Correctly pronouncing the German text.

✓ Their ability to read musical notation.

✓ Their ability to sing with a supported tone throughout each phrase.

✓ Their ability to listen and match tone with each other.

ASSESSMENT

Evaluating the Quality of a Performance

Have students:

1. Watch a video or listen to an audio recording of this piece as performed by the choir.

2. Compare this performance to exemplary models such as other recordings or other live performances of the piece.

3. Develop constructive suggestions for improvement based on the comparison.

3. Refine

Direct students to:

- Read the translated libretto of the complete cantata.
- Work in the trios formed in the Introduce section of the Suggested Teaching Sequence. Create a short skit of the dramatic action that occurs prior to this chorus. (a) The Tenor I will be the narrator, the Tenor II will be Lieschen and the Bass will be Schlendrian. (b) Students can bring in one prop for each character (i.e., feather quill pen—narrator, apron—Lieschen, spectacles—Schlendrian). Students should also use their coffee mugs in the skit. (c) Present skits for the class.
- As a full ensemble, sing the entire chorus in German, observing all expressive markings and phrase contours.

TEACHING STRATEGY

Solo and Small Ensemble Performances

Have students:

1. Prepare solos and small ensembles for performance or competition.
2. Interpret music symbols and terms referring to dynamics, tempo and articulation during the performance.
3. Critique and analyze the quality of the performance using standard terminology.

Progress Checkpoints

Observe students' progress in:

✓ Their ability to sing with a free and relaxed head tone especially throughout the large interval skips and long phrases.

✓ Their ability to express the mood of the piece through facial expression.

Lesson 10 *Die Katze lässt das Mausen nicht* **89**

CONNECTING THE ARTS

Processes in the Arts

Have students:

1. Find examples of artwork or art forms from the Baroque period, describing how they exhibit the characteristics of the period. (Choose from visual art, architecture, dance, drama, poetry or literature.)

2. Discuss how the processes used in the other areas are the same and different from music, taking into consideration the roles of artists, performers and audience.

3. Find other examples from the same art category, but from a different style, period or culture.

4. Discuss similarities and differences between the examples.

ASSESSMENT

Informal Assessment

In this lesson, students showed the ability to:

- Work in student-led sectionals to learn correct notes, rhythms and German pronunciation.
- Develop an accurate character interpretation for a vocal line.
- Identify and perform homophonic and polyphonic phrases.
- Sing independently in a trio.
- Sing with correct German pronunciation.

Student Self-Assessment

Have students evaluate their individual performances based on the following:

- Diction
- German Language
- Expressive Singing
- Accurate Pitches
- Accurate Rhythms

Have each student rate his/her performance of this song in the areas above on a scale of 1–5, 5 being the best.

MORE ABOUT...

Schweigt stille, plaudert nicht

There are just three characters in this secular cantata, which can almost be considered a miniature comic opera. Herr Schlendrian, the father, is a bass. His daughter, Lieschen, is a soprano. There is also a Narrator, sung by a tenor. Herr Schlendrian, an old curmudgeon, is trying to convince Lieschen to give up coffee, which he feels is an evil drink. He threatens to take away many of her privileges and luxuries, but she refuses to give in saying, "Coffee is more delicious than a thousand kisses and sweeter than muscatel wine." Only when Schlendrian refuses to allow her to marry does Lieschen relent. As Schlendrian goes off to find her a husband, Lieschen reveals, however, that she will include in her marriage contract the stipulation that her husband must allow her three cups of coffee a day!

To further measure growth of musical skills presented in this lesson, direct students to complete the Evaluation section on page 83.

- After students have identified the given measures as homophony or counterpoint, they should exchange their work with a classmate. They should check each other's answers. Assist them in the evaluation. [*Answers: (1) measures 36–42—homophony, (2) measures 55–61—homophony, (3) measures 78–84—homophony, (4) measures 48–54—counterpoint, (5) measures 72–77—counterpoint, (6) measures 85–93—counterpoint*]

- Follow the directions in the Evaluation section and have selected students draw slips of paper and perform all occurrences of the phrase selected. Have the class or one other individual evaluate their performances.

EXTENSION

Important Baroque Events

The life of Johann Sebastian Bach (1685–1750) coincides with the most active years of the Baroque period in classical music. Make a chart that highlights the important political, artistic, musical, literary, scientific and religious events that occurred during Bach's lifetime.

TRANSLATION

"Die Katze lässt das Mausen nicht"

Die Katze lässt das Mausen nicht,
Die Jungfern bleiben Coffeeschwestern.
Die Mutter liebt den Coffeebrauch,
Die Grossmama trank solchen auch,
Wer will nun auf die Töchter lästern!

A cat won't stop catching mice,
and maidens remain faithful to their coffee.
The mother holds her coffee dear,
the grandmother drank it also,
who can thus rebuke the daughters!

ENRICHMENT

Large-Ensemble Performance Techniques

Have students view a video-taped performance of "Die Katze lasst das Mausen nicht." As they view the video, have them describe an dlist the performance techniques they observed that are appropriate to the Baroque period. These might include singing with pitch accuracy, especially in chromatic sections, keeping a steady, unrelenting pulse, precision of the dotted rhythms, and balancing the main theme over the accompanying parts. Then, have the choir perform the song again, demonstrating their understanding of the performance techniques of the Baroque period. Have the choir critique their performance based on these identified techniques.

TEACHING STRATEGY

Count-Singing

Count-singing is a rehearsal technique developed by Robert Shaw to achieve rhythmic accuracy and a constant pulse throughout a piece of choral music. To count-sing, the students sing the subdivisions of the beat on the correct pitches. For example, in a measure of 4/4, the students sing 1+2+3+4+ on the correct pitches. In 3/4, students sing 1+2+3+. For rests, students maintain the subdivisions at a whisper.

EXTENSION

More Activities

- Have students write an eight-measure phrase for the choir in G major or E minor with a German text. Set some words with one pitch per syllable (syllabic) and other words with several pitches per syllable (melismatic).

- Have students follow a translated libretto and listen to the entire cantata, *Schweigt stille, plaudert nicht.*

- Have students learn a section of one of the Narrator's or Schlendrian's arias from *Schweigt stille, plaudert nicht* and perform it for your class.

- Have students listen to sections of other Bach cantatas (secular or sacred) and discuss whether a particular text is set in a homophonic or polyphonic style.

Encourage your students to expore **music.glencoe.com**, the Web site for *Experiencing Choral Music.* You may wish to preview the rich content before directing your students online. Options available on the Web site include:

- Web Link Exercises
- Interactive Projects
- Audio Samples

Additional National Standards

The following National Standards are addressed through the Assessment, Extension, Enrichment and bottom-page activities:

4. Composing and arranging music within specific guidelines. **(a)**

5. Reading and notating music. **(a)**

8. Understanding relationship between music, the other arts, and disciplines outside the arts. **(c)**

O Isis und Osiris, welche Wonne!

OVERVIEW

Composer: Wolfgang Amadeus Mozart (1757–1791), edited by Stacey Nordmeyer

Text: Emanuel Schikaneder, English text by J. Mark Baker

Voicing: TTB

Key: D Major

Meter: Cut time, (alla breve)

Form: Through-composed

Style: Classical Opera Chorus

Accompaniment: Piano

Programming: Contest, Festival, Honor Chorus

Vocal Ranges:

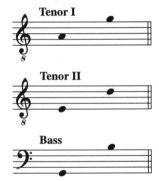

OBJECTIVES

After completing this lesson, students will be able to:

- Demonstrate fundamental skills such as singing comfortably in falsetto range while performing.

- Perform expressively a varied repertoire of music representing styles from diverse periods including Classical and from diverse genres including opera choruses.

VOCABULARY

Have students review vocabulary in student lesson. Introduce terms found in the music. A complete glossary of terms is found on page 246 of the student book.

O Isis und Osiris, welche Wonne!

Composer: Wolfgang Amadeus Mozart (1756–1791), edited by Stacey Nordmeyer
Text: Emanuel Schikaneder, English text by J. Mark Baker
Voicing: TTB

VOCABULARY

grand opera

Classical period

singspiel

falsetto

adagio

Focus

- Sing comfortably in falsetto range.
- Perform music in the style of an opera chorus.
- Describe and perform music representing the Classical period.

Getting Started

With what occasion do you associate this famous tune? Grand ceremonies are often accompanied by musical pomp and circumstance.

Some people think that **grand opera** (*opera on a large scale*) is stuffy pomp and circumstance from curtain to curtain. This is not the case with the masterful *Die Zauberflöte (The Magic Flute)* by Wolfgang Amadeus Mozart (1756–1791), the greatest composer of the **Classical period** (*1750–1820*). *Die Zauberflöte* is actually a **singspiel** (*a light German opera with spoken dialogue*). First presented in 1791, it has been enjoyed by children and adults for over 200 years.

◆ History and Culture

"O Isis und Osiris, welche Wonne!" is a stately chorus sung by an ensemble of solemn priests. Sarastro, the head priest, intends to admit Prince Tamino into his consecrated band, but first Tamino must prove himself worthy by successfully completing the trials of steadfastness, constancy and courage. In this chorus, the priests sing of their support for Tamino.

In addition to *Die Zauberflöte*, Mozart wrote other brillant operas, including *The Marriage of Figaro* (1786), *Don Giovanni* (1787) and *Cosi Fan Tutti* (1790).

MUSIC & HISTORY

To learn more about the Classical period, see page 118.

94 Proficient Tenor/Bass

RESOURCES

Proficient Sight-Singing

Sight-Singing in D Major, pages 100–106

Reading Rhythms in Cut Time, page 147

Reading Dotted Half and Dotted Quarter Notes, page 51

Teacher Resource Binder

Teaching Master 17, *Pronunciation Guide for "O Isis und Osiris, welche Wonne!"*

Teaching Master 18, *Let's Imagine: An Opera Moment*

Evaluation Master 10, *Focus on Stage Presence*

Music and History 11, *Wolfgang Amadeus Mozart, a Classical Composer*

For additional resources, see TRB Table of Contents.

Links to Learning

◆ Vocal

Singing in your **falsetto** voice *(a high voice used for notes that lie above normal register)* will help you achieve the smooth and unforced tone quality necessary for the **adagio** *(slow)* phrases of this chorus. Starting with your falsetto voice, sing the D major scale as shown below. Keep the same light tone quality as you change registers.

◆ Artistic Expression

Below is a list of the principal characters in *Die Zauberflöte*. Research the names and match them with the correct description. How might this information improve your performance?

1. Magic Flute	**a.** a bird catcher
2. Tamino	**b.** the High Priest of Isis and Osiris
3. Pamina	**c.** a heartless ruler with evil power
4. Papageno	**d.** a talisman given for protection by the Three Ladies
5. Queen of the Night	**e.** an Egyptian Prince
6. Sarastro	**f.** the daughter of the Queen of the Night

Evaluation

Demonstrate how well you have learned the skills and concepts featured in the lesson "O Isis und Osiris, welche Wonne!" by completing the following:

- Sing measures 1–6 as written, and then again in your falsetto voice one octave higher. Were you able to sing with a free, unforced tone?

- With a small group of classmates, choose two students to be Sarastro and Tamino. Position the other singers around the characters and perform the chorus as the scene might appear on the opera stage. Evaluate how well your group was able to stay in character while singing and expressing the dramatic meaning of the story.

Lesson 11 O Isis und Osiris, welche Wonne! **95**

RESOURCES

Proficient Tenor/Bass Rehearsal/Performance CD

CD 1:21 Voices

CD 1:22 Accompaniment Only

CD 3:11 Vocal Practice Track—Tenor I

CD 4:11 Vocal Practice Track—Tenor II

CD 6:11 Vocal Practice Track—Bass

National Standards

1. Singing, alone and with others, a varied repertoire of music. **(a, c, f)**

9. Understanding music in relation to history and culture. **(a, d)**

LINKS TO LEARNING

Vocal

The Vocal section is designed to prepare students to:

- Understand falsetto and adagio.
- Sing comfortably in their falsetto range for use in this piece.

Have students:

- Sing the D major scale on "loo," beginning in their falsetto range and keeping the same light tone quality as they move downward.
- Sing the D major scale on solfège syllables the same way.
- Locate notes in the choral score that will require them to use their falsetto range.

Artistic Expression

The Artistic Expression section is designed to prepare students to become familiar with the libretto of *Die Zauberflöte* so the chorus can be sung with contextual meaning.

Have students:

- Research the names listed on page 95 and match them with the correct description. *(1=d, 2=e, 3=f, 4=a, 5=c, 6=b)*
- Discuss how this information might improve their performance.

LESSON PLAN

Suggest Teaching Sequence and Performance Tips

1. Introduce

Direct students to:

- Read and discuss the ideas presented in the Getting Started section on page 94. *(song is "Pomp and Circumstance" by Edward Elgar)*
- Practice the D major scale in the Vocal section on page 95. When the students finish the first octave, have half of the choir turn around and ascend while the other half continues downward.
- Use solfège and learn measures 1–6 in three parts. Then divide into three small choirs and assign one choir measures 7–18, one choir measures 20–28, and the last choir measures 29–42. Have each choir perform for the class. Then divide into sections and teach each other the three phrases.

Progress Checkpoints

Observe students' progress in:

✓ Accurately singing the skip of a ninth in the Bass part in measures 4–5.

✓ Singing the correct solfège syllables on the chromatic pitches.

O Isis und Osiris, welche Wonne!

from *Die Zauberflöte*

For TTB and Piano

Edited by STACEY NORDMEYER
English text by J. MARK BAKER

Words by EMANUEL SCHIKANEDER (1751–1812)
Music by WOLFGANG AMADEUS MOZART
(1756–1791)

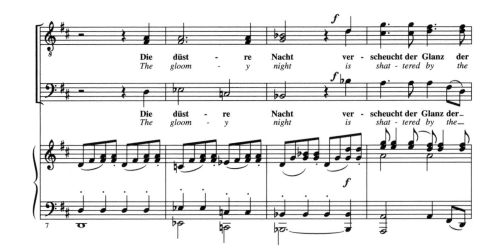

Copyright © 2005 by HAL LEONARD CORPORATION
International Copyright Secured   All Rights Reserved

 **TEACHER 2 TEACHER**

In the opera world, there is an ongoing discussion as to whether opera should be sung in the vernacular or the original language. Is it better to hear a compromised translation or the libretto as the composer intended? Because of its tempo and length, encourage the students to sing this chorus slowly, majestically and in German!

CONNECTIONS

- Research the tale of the Egyptian gods Isis and Osiris and write a short synopsis for the program.
- Watch a performance of *Die Zauberflöte* on videotape or DVD and write a short critique of the performance.

2. Rehearse

Direct students to:

- Learn the pronunciation for the German text. A pronunciation guide can be found in the Teacher Resource Binder, Teaching Master 17.
- Research one German word that is assigned to each singer and ask him/her to find the definition of the word. Put the definitions on the wall in music order with the German text written above.
- Sing the chorus while following the "wall text." Return to sectionals and rehearse with the German text.
- Observe the dynamics marching band style. While singing, turn away from the director for "mp" and "p," but turn toward the director for "mf," "f" and "sf."

Progress Checkpoints

Observe students' progress in:

✓ Singing with proper vowel sounds and unique consonants in the German pronunciation.

✓ Observing the dynamics throughout.

3. Refine

Direct students to:

- Sing the Tenor II part all together in unison falsetto. Work for a smooth, light, floating tone.
- Practice the chorus with the German text, long phrases, stress syllables and dramatic contrasts in dynamics.

Progress Checkpoints

Observe students' progress in:

✓ Singing with a free and relaxed falsetto tone supported with lots of deep breaths.

ASSESSMENT

Informal Assessment

In this lesson, students showed the ability to:

- Sing in the falsetto range.
- Sing a German text with correct pronunciation and syllabic stress.

Student Self-Assessment

Have students evaluate their individual performances based on the following:

- Breath Management
- Phrasing
- German Language
- Expressive Singing
- Intonation
- Correct Part-Singing

Have each student rate his/her performance of this song in the areas above on a scale of 1–5, 5 being the best.

Individual and Group Performance Evaluation

To further measure growth of musical skills presented in this lesson, direct students to complete the Evaluation section on page 95.

- Have each student sing measures 1–6 as written and then an octave higher in their falsetto range. Evaluate whether they were able to sing falsetto with a free, unforced tone.
- Evaluate each group's ability to stay in character while singing.
- Divide into two equal choirs. As one choir sings the chorus, the other students complete a written critique regarding the German pronunciation, vocal tone quality and dynamic contrast.

Additional National Standards

The following National Standards are addressed through the Assessment, Extension, Enrichment and bottom-page activities:

6. Listening to, analyzing, and describing music **(a, b, c, d, e, f)**
7. Evaluating music and music performances **(a, c)**
8. Understanding relationships between music, the other arts, and disciplines outside the arts **(a)**

SPOTLIGHT

Vowels

The style of a given piece of music dictates how we should pronounce the words. If we are singing a more formal, classical piece, then we need to form taller vowels as in very proper English. If we are singing in a jazz or pop style, then we should pronounce the words in a more relaxed, conversational way. To get the feeling of taller vowels for classical singing, do the following:

- Let your jaw gently drop down and back as if it were on a hinge.
- Place your hands on your cheeks beside the corners of your mouth.
- Sigh on an *ah* [ɑ] vowel sound, but do not spread the corners of your mouth.
- Now sigh on other vowel sounds—*eh* [ɛ], *ee* [i], *oh* [o] and *oo* [u]—keeping the back of the tongue relaxed.
- As your voice goes from higher notes to lower notes, think of gently opening a tiny umbrella inside your mouth.

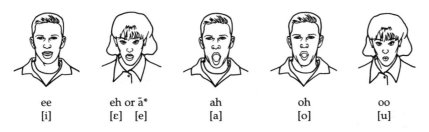

| ee | eh or ā* | ah | oh | oo |
| [i] | [ɛ] [e] | [a] | [o] | [u] |

Other vowel sounds used in singing are diphthongs. A **diphthong** is *a combination of two vowel sounds.* For example, the vowel *ay* consists of two sounds: *eh* [E] and *ee* [i]. To sing a diphthong correctly, stay on the first vowel sound for the entire length of the note, only lightly adding the second vowel sound as you move to another note or lift off the note.

I = *ah*_____(ee) [ɑi]

boy = *oh*_____(ee) [oi]

down = *ah*_____(oo) [ɑu]

*Note: This is an Italian "ā," which is one sound, and not an American "ā," which is a diphthong, or two sounds.

RESOURCES

Teacher Resource Binder

Vocal Development 10, *Diphthongs*
Vocal Development 15, *Vowels*
Reference 29, *IPA Vowels*

National Standards

1. Singing, alone and with others. **(b)**

VOWELS

Objectives

- Demonstrate basic performance techniques through proper use of vowels.

Suggested Teaching Sequence

Direct students to:

- Read the Spotlight On Vowels on student page 99 and identify the importance of uniform vowels in singing.
- Practice the exercise as presented on page 99.
- Identify the five basic vowels. Practice speaking and singing each.
- Define diphthong and demonstrate the proper and improper way to sing a diphthong.
- Find examples of each of the five basic vowels and diphthongs in music they are currently studying.
- Compare the concept of uniform vowels to appropriate large- and small-ensemble performance techniques.

Progress Checkpoints

Observe students' progress in:

✓ Their ability to speak the five basic vowels properly and uniformly.

✓ Their ability to define diphthong, find examples in the music and sing them properly.

✓ Their ability to relate the importance of uniform vowels in ensemble singing.

The Pasture

OVERVIEW

Composer: Randall Thompson (1899–1984)
Text: Robert Frost (1874–1963)
Voicing: TBB
Key: F major
Meter: 6/8 and 4/4
Form: IntroAA'Coda
Style: American Art Song
Accompaniment: Piano
Programming: Concert, Americana, Contest

Vocal Ranges:

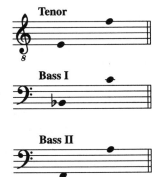

OBJECTIVES

After completing this lesson, students will be able to:

• Perform expressively from phrasing.

• Define the relationships between the concepts of other fine arts and those of music.

VOCABULARY

Have students review vocabulary in student lesson. Introduce terms found in the music. A complete glossary of terms is found on page 246 of the student book.

The Pasture

Composer: Randall Thompson (1899–1984)
Text: Robert Frost (1874–1963)
Voicing: TBB

VOCABULARY

legato
crescendo
diminuendo
word stress

SPOTLIGHT

To learn more about posture and breath management, see page 11.

Focus

• Perform music with expressive phrasing.

• Perform music with expressive word stress.

• Understand the relationship between music and poetry.

Getting Started

What grabs your attention first when you learn a song? Is it the music, the words, or both? The renowned German recital singer, Dietrich Fischer-Dieskau made this observation:

Words are the marriage of sound and expression, and both should thus enjoy equal importance in the elevated language of song. If either is neglected, the result tends either towards instrumental music or towards pure speech.

While learning "The Pasture," you will be treated to the fusion of poetry and music by two distinguished American artists, poet Robert Frost (1874–1963) and composer Randall Thompson (1899–1984). Both men wrote in a clear and direct style. When joined together, the words and the music of "The Pasture" complement each other perfectly.

◆ History and Culture

In selecting a text, composer Randall Thompson (1899–1984) chose poetry by Robert Frost (1874–1963), the most highly esteemed American poet of the twentieth century. The poem "The Pasture" is from an early collection of Frost's poetry entitled *North of Boston* (1914). For the most part, Robert Frost wrote about the ordinary events, the people and the natural landscapes of New England. His poetry speaks about life's simple pleasures and helps us see the beauty and wonder of nature. "The Road Not Taken" and "Stopping By The Woods On A Snowy Evening" are among the best-known of his many poems.

Randall Thompson composed "The Pasture" in 1958 as part of a commissioned work entitled *Frostiana*. It is a collection of songs based on poems by Robert Frost and is considered one of the jewels in American choral music.

RESOURCES

Proficient Sight-Singing

Sight-Singing in F Major, pages 45–46, 54

Reading Rhythms in 6/8 Meter, pages 114, 117

Reading Rhythms in 4/4 Meter, pages 2, 6

Reading Eighth Notes and Eighth Rests, pages 23–24

Teacher Resource Binder

Teaching Master 19, *Robert Frost: American Poet*

Teaching Master 20, *Text Emphasis in "The Pasture"*

Evaluation Master 8, *Evaluating Musical Expression*

Reference 16, *Expanding a Musical Vocabulary*

For additional resources, see TRB Table of Contents.

Links to Learning

◆ Vocal

Perform the following example in **legato** (*a connected and sustained style of singing*) style. Use correct breath management to connect each pitch to the next, and keep your airflow moving forward steadily throughout each phrase. Shape the phrase with a gentle **crescendo** (*a dynamic marking that indicates to gradually sing louder*) and **diminuendo** (*a dynamic marking that indicates to gradually sing softer*).

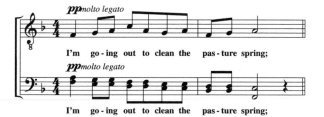

◆ Artistic Expression

In the following example, chant the words giving particular attention to **word stress** (*singing the important parts of the text in a more accented style than the other parts*). Each eighth note should not receive the same stress.

Evaluation

Demonstrate how well you have learned the skills and concepts featured in the lesson "The Pasture" by completing the following:

• Form a trio to sing measures 28–37 to demonstrate your ability to sing this passage *legato*. Evaluate how well you did.

• Identify the words in measures 10–13 that you think should be stressed. Sing the passage. Evaluate how well you were able to show the difference between the stressed and unstressed words.

LINKS TO LEARNING

Vocal

The Vocal section is designed to prepare students to:
• Sing in a legato style.
• Perform a phrase with dynamics.

Have students:
• Sing the exercise with legato articulation in one breath.
• Add dynamics with a slight crescendo initially and ending with a diminuendo.

Artistic Expression

The Artistic Expression section is designed to prepare students to sing a passage with proper word stress.

Have students:
• Sing each part using solfège syllables.
• Sing each part with lyrics and observe the dynamic markings.
• Chant the lyrics in rhythm using proper word stress for each syllable.
• Sing the lyrics with proper word stress.

RESOURCES

Proficient Tenor/Bass Rehearsal/Performance CD

CD 1:23 Voices
CD 1:24 Accompaniment Only
CD 3:12 Vocal Practice Track—Tenor
CD 5:5 Vocal Practice Track—Bass I
CD 6:12 Vocal Practice Track—Bass II

National Standards

1. Singing, alone and with others, a varied repertoire of music. **(a)**
8. Understanding relationships between music, the other arts, and disciplines outside the arts. **(c)**

LESSON PLAN

Suggested Teaching Sequence and Performance Tips

1. Introduce

Direct students to:

- Read and discuss the information found in the Getting Started section on page 100.
- Practice singing the phrase in the Vocal section on page 101. Relate to the first phrase of the piece. *(measures 10–11)*
- Practice singing the three-part passage in the Artistic Expression section on page 101. Work on proper word stress when singing the syllables. Find this section in the score. *(measures 13–17)*

Progress Checkpoints

Observe students' progress in:

- ✓ Singing a phrase in one breath in a legato style.
- ✓ Singing a phrase with proper dynamics.
- ✓ Using the correct word stress for the text.

To the townspeople of Amherst, Massachusetts, 1759-1959

The Pasture

For TBB and Piano

Words by ROBERT FROST*

RANDALL THOMPSON (1899–1984)

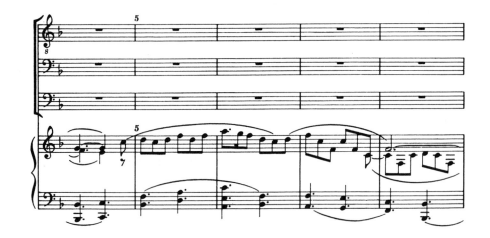

*Text from You Come Too by Robert Frost, Copyright 1916, 1921, 1923, 1947, © 1959,
by Henry Holt and Company, Inc. Copyright 1942, 1944, 1951 by Robert Frost, and used with their permission.
© Copyright 1959 and 1960 by E.C. Schirmer Music Company, Inc., a division of ECS Publishing, Boston Massachusetts.
All Rights Reserved   Made in U.S.A.

102   Proficient Tenor/Bass

TEACHER2TEACHER

This song, a favorite of directors and singers alike, is part of the Randall Thompson work *Frostiana*. The simple, but expressive, text is full of words seldom used by us today—so take the time to explain the text and each word's meaning.

2. Rehearse

Direct students to:

- Sing the song using solfège syllables.

- Transfer to a neutral syllable once pitch is secure—using a "loo" or "loh" to enhance the legato feel.

- Have one or more read the poem for the class and explain what they feel the text is saying.

- Underline the stress syllables in each phrase.

- Sing a descending scale on syllables. Then use a "hmm" or "loo." Finally, have the choir sing the Baritone/Bass descending lines (measure 10, measure 28) and sing in tune.

Progress Checkpoints

Observe students' progress in:

✓ Good intonation at all landing spots (cadences).

✓ Singing the correct pitches.

✓ Their ability to identify correct syllabic stress.

✓ Their ability to sing descending line in tune.

✓ Their ability to keep a constant eighth-note feeling throughout.

Lesson 12 *The Pasture* **103**

MORE ABOUT...
Poet Robert Frost

Robert Frost was awarded 44 honorary degrees, a Congressional Medal of Honor, and an appointment as honorary consultant to the Library of Congress. He also received an invitation from John F. Kennedy to recite a poem at Kennedy's presidential inauguration. Frost was awarded the Pulitzer Prize for poetry four times (1924, 1931, 1937 and 1943).

3. Refine

Direct students to:

- Sing in a nice head voice quality in the upper range for the Tenors (measures 14–15, 32–33).
- Have students pulse the eighth note by tapping with their hands or by pulsing with their voices as they sing.
- Work for long phrases.

Progress Checkpoints

Observe students' progress in:

✓ Their ability to keep a consistent eighth-note feeling throughout.

✓ Their ability to sing the upper register in tune and within the dynamics indicated.

✓ Their ability to sing four-measure phrases.

104   Proficient Tenor/Bass

CONNECTING THE ARTS

Visual Arts

Have students:

- Describe the characteristics of the singer who is telling the story and the visual setting of "The Pasture."
- Discuss images, concrete or abstract, that might represent each of the characteristics or images mentioned in the piece. (This might include creating some art, using fine art from local or national museum, taking photographs, and so on.)
- Plan a slide show to accompany the performance of the piece at concert time.

ASSESSMENT

Informal Assessment

In this lesson, students showed the ability to:

- Recognize correct syllabic stress.
- Sing expressively.
- Maintain an eight-note pulse to help drive phrases and keep phrase motion moving forward.

TEACHING STRATEGY
Legato Articulation

Have students:

- Pretend to play the beginning of "The Pasture" on a violin, using legato bowing.
- Discuss the need for longer bowing action on longer notes.
- Discuss the change in bowing direction on shorter notes, which creates a slight stress.
- Sing the piece, using these clues to help the legato articulation, and think about the bowing action as they sing.
- Discuss how this piece would be differently played by a trumpet, and whether a trumpet or a violin is more appropriate.

Student Self-Assessment

Have students evaluate their individual performances based on the following:

- Breath Management
- Phrasing
- Expressive Singing
- Intonation
- Correct Part-Singing

Have each student rate his/her performance of this song in the areas above on a scale of 1–5, 5 being the best.

Individual and Group Performance Evaluation

To further measure growth of musical skills presented in this lesson, direct students to complete the Evaluation section on page 101.

- After singing measures 28–37 as a quartet, evaluate each performance by asking, "How legato was the singing? Which section(s) needs to sing in a more legato fashion?"
- After identifying the words in measures 10–13 that should be stressed, compare the answers with a class-mate from the same section. Sing those measures with the syllabic stress that was identified. Switch roles.

VOCAL DEVELOPMENT

Have students:

- Demonstrate good vocal tune by singing tall vowels and alter (or modify) the vowel sounds when necessary.
- Energize the ascending chords with increased breath support.
- Energize sustained tones by increasing the breath support and dynamic level.
- Sustain phrases by staggering the breathing through the four-bar phrases.
- Increase intensity on repeated notes to feel forward movement.
- Listen for the diphthong in "away."
- Identify melodic and harmonic intervals between the parts and tune them.

ENRICHMENT

Ensemble Performance Techniques

- Videotape a class performance of "The Pasture." Have students describe the performance techniques observed such as choral blend and balance, well-tuned singing, and expressive legato singing. Critique the performance based on these performance techniques. Repeat this process using a videotaped performance of a formal concert of the same song. Compare the two performances. Ask students to identify the choral techniques that need improvement.

- "The Pasture" can also be performed as a small-ensemble with two or three singers on a part. Ask two members from each voice part to come forard and perform "The Pasture." Ask the rest of the class to describe the performance techniques they observed during the performance These techniques may include the following elements of good singing: tall vowels, dynamic contrasts, expressive singing, and clear diction. Which techniques were performed well? Which techniques needed improvement?"

MORE ABOUT...
Composer Randall Thompson

American composer, Randall Thompson, was trained at Harvard where he eventually taught. Although he is best known for his choral works, he is also recognized for three symphonies, two string quartets and *A Trip to Nahanti*, which is a symphonic fantasy.

EXTENSION

Setting Poetry

Have students locate other examples of poems by Robert Frost or other favorite poems from the library or Internet. Depending on the ability of the students, have them write rhythmic patterns that could be used to chant the poems or simple melodies that could be sung with the poetry used as lyrics. If the students have studied harmony, they could set the melodies and add one or two parts for harmony. For more advanced students, they could write an accompaniment on the piano. If some of the compositions are successful, program the pieces on your next concert.

ENRICHMENT

Improvisation

Some student may be reluctant to try improvisation. As a teacher, it is important to set up guidelines and to create a safe environment. Remind students that any effort is a worthy effort. Praise students often. Follow these steps to lead students to successful improvisation.

1. Play on a keyboard, guitar or some other instrument the I-IV-V-I chord progression. Play it several times until students become familiar with it.

2. Ask for volunteers to improvise a musical melody above the chord progression. Singers may use nonsense or scat syllables.

3. Have students analyze ways in which they can improve their skills in improvisation.

15-16 • VI • '59

108   Proficient Tenor/Bass

Additional National Standards

The following National Standards are addressed through the Assessment, Extension, Enrichment and bottom-page activities:

1. Singing, alone and with others, a varied repertoire of music. **(c)**

4. Composing and arranging music within specific guidelines. **(a)**

5. Reading and notating music. **(b)**

7. Evaluating music and music performances. **(a)**

8. Understanding relationships between music, the other arts, and disciplines outside the arts. **(a)**

Music & History

Links to Music

RENAISSANCE

OVERVIEW

Objectives

After completing this lesson, students will be able to:

- Describe the Renaissance period, including important developments.
- Describe characteristics of Renaissance music.

VOCABULARY

Have students review vocabulary in student lesson. A complete glossary of terms is found on page 246 of the student book.

Introduce the Renaissance period through visual art. Analyze the painting by Leonardo da Vinci on page 110. Show Fine Art Transparency 1, *Ginevra de' Benci*, (from the Teacher Resource Binder) and direct students to discuss the costume of the day as depicted in the painting. Review the background information about Renaissance art as found on teacher page 112.

MUSIC & ART Italian painter Leonardo da Vinci (1452–1519) was a genius who showed great skill in everything he tried. In *Ginevra de' Benci*, he uses a blending of light and dark values. The subtle changes in the light make the sad face seem three-dimensional. Notice how the figure of the woman stands out dramatically against the dark background. It is interesting to speculate about who this woman is and why she is so sad.

Leonardo da Vinci. *Ginevra de' Benci.* c. 1474. Oil on panel. 38.1 x 37.0 cm (15 x 14 9/16"). National Gallery of Art, Washington, D. C. Ailsa Mellon Bruce Fund.

110 Proficient Tenor/Bass

RESOURCES

Teacher Resource Binder

Music and History 1, *Renaissance Music*

Music and History 3, *Baldassare Donato*

Fine Art Transparency 1, *Ginevra de' Benci*, Leonardo da Vinci

Music and History 4, *Fine Art Teaching Strategy—Renaissance*

For additional resources, see Music and History section.

Listening Selections CD

(found in the Teacher Resource Binder)

Track 1: "O Magnum Mysterium"

Track 2: "Canzon XV"

Focus

- Describe the Renaissance Period, including important developments.
- Describe characteristics of Renaissance music

The Renaissance— A Time of Discovery

Renaissance means "rebirth" or "renewal." The **Renaissance period** *(1430–1600)* was a time of rapid development in exploration, science, art and music. Vasco de Gama first rounded the coast of Africa from Europe to reach India. Christopher Columbus found the Americas, and Ferdinand Magellan circumnavigated the globe. The compass and first maps for navigation were developed and were used to find and chart new lands.

The greatest invention of the Renaissance (and perhaps the most important invention to modern civilization) was the movable type printing press. For the first time, books, music and maps could be created quickly and inexpensively, making them available to larger segments of the population. As a result, news was easily accessible and ideas were embraced, since more people could read and afford printed materials.

The Protestant Reformation, in which various groups of Christians left the Catholic Church to form their own denominations, brought about a significant change in religion. Bibles and music were translated from the Latin used in the Catholic Church to the languages spoken by the people.

Painters and sculptors created images and figures that were more realistic and lifelike. Among these were Leonardo da Vinci's *Mona Lisa* and Michelangelo's paintings of the ceiling of the Sistine Chapel in Rome. Sculpture developed from a craft to an art form. Michelangelo's *David* was created during this time.

Scientists were aided with refinements in the telescope and microscope. Galileo provided proof that the earth revolved around the sun, and Sir Isaac Newton explained the concept of gravity.

COMPOSERS

Josquin des Prez
(c. 1450–1521)

Giovanni Pierluigi da Palestrina
(c. 1525–1594)

William Byrd
(1543–1623)

Tomás Luis de Victoria
(c.1548–1611)

Giovanni Gabrieli
(1553–1612)

ARTISTS

Sandro Botticelli (1445–1510)

Leonardo da Vinci (1452–1519)

Michelangelo (1475–1564)

Raphael (1483–1520)

El Greco (c.1541–1614)

Michelangelo Merisi da Caravaggio
(1571–1610)

AUTHORS

Nicolo Machiavelli (1460–1527)

Martin Luther (1483–1546)

Miguel de Cervantes (1547–1616)

William Shakespeare (1564–1616)

René Descartes (1569–1650)

VOCABULARY

Renaissance period

polyphony

mass

motet

chorale

madrigal

lute

Music History *Renaissance* **111**

LESSON PLAN
Suggested Teaching Sequence

1. Examine the Renaissance period in a historical perspective.

Direct students to:

- Read and discuss the information found on student page 111.
- Share what they know about the composers, artists and authors listed on this page.
- Turn to the time line on pages 112–113 and read the citations.
- Discuss why these are considered important dates during the Renaissance period.
- Identify specific accomplishments that were made during the Renaissance period and the people associated with those accomplishments.
- Compare each of these events to what occurred after the Renaissance period.

2. Define the musical aspects of Renaissance music.

Direct students to:

- Read and discuss information on Renaissance music found on student page 112.
- Describe the difference between sacred and secular music.
- Define *polyphony, mass, chorale, madrigal, a cappella* and *lute.*

3. Discuss the performance guidelines of Renaissance music.

Direct students to:

- Read the Performance Links found on student page 112.
- Discuss the performance guidelines.

National Standards

6. Listening to, analyzing, and describing music. **(a, b, c, e, f)**

8. Understanding relationships between music, the other arts, and disciplines outside the arts. **(a, b, c, d, e)**

9. Understanding music in relation to history and culture. **(a, c, d, e)**

LISTENING LESSONS

This feature is designed to expand students' appreciation of choral and instrumental music of the Renaissance period.

Choral Selection: "O Magnum Mysterium" by Tomás de Victoria

Direct students to:

- Read the information on student page 113 to learn more about Tomás de Victoria and "O Magnum Mysterium."
- Review the meaning of the musical style of the motet. *(a shorter choral work, set to Latin texts and used in religious services, but not part of the regular mass)*
- After listening to the recorded performance, discuss the interplay of major and minor tonality.
- Use signals such as raising their hands, standing/ sitting, holding up appropriate flash cards to indicate when they hear major and minor tonalities, during a second listening.

Instrumental Selection: "Canzon XV" by Giovanni Gabrieli

Direct students to:

- Read the information on student page 113 to learn more about Giovanni Gabrieli and "Canzon XV."
- After the first listening, discuss the contrast between contrapuntal writing and the sound of big block chords.
- During the second listening, tap a steady beat to find the change in meter and to name the different meters used.

Renaissance Music

During the Renaissance, both sacred and secular music became more complex. The Renaissance period is often referred to as the "golden age of polyphony." **Polyphony**, which literally means, "many-sounding," is *a type of music in which there are two or more different melodic lines being sung or played at the same time.* Each line is independent of each other, and often, each line is of equal importance.

In the Catholic Church, the two prominent forms of music were the **mass**, *a religious service of prayers and ceremonies*, and the **motet**, *a shorter choral work, also set to Latin and used in religious services, but not part of the regular mass.* In the Protestant churches the entire congregation would sing a **chorale**—*a melody that features even rhythms and simple harmonies.* Chorales are sometimes known as hymn tunes, and many hymns still sung in churches today are based on these early chorales.

There were great advances in secular music, as well. For the first time in history, the popularity of secular music rivaled that of sacred music. One of the most common forms of secular music was the **madrigal**, *a musical setting of a poem, generally in three or parts.* Madrigals were generally performed a cappella, and the text was usually based on a romantic or pastoral theme.

During the Renaissance, there was an awakening of interest in instrumental music. Instruments were not only used to accompany voices, but were also featured in solo and ensemble music. The **lute**, *an early form of the guitar*, was as universally used during the Renaissance as the piano is today.

Performance Links

When performing music of the Renaissance period, it is important to apply the following guidelines:

- Sing with clarity and purity of tone.
- Balance the vocal lines with equal importance.
- In polyphonic music, sing the rhythms accurately and with precision.
- When designated by the composer, sing a cappella.

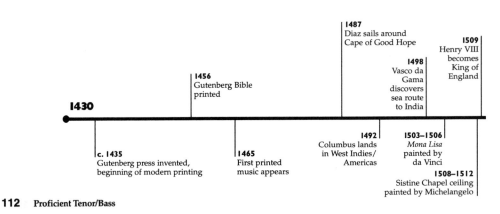

1430

c. 1435
Gutenberg press invented, beginning of modern printing

1456
Gutenberg Bible printed

1465
First printed music appears

1487
Diaz sails around Cape of Good Hope

1492
Columbus lands in West Indies/ Americas

1498
Vasco da Gama discovers sea route to India

1503–1506
Mona Lisa painted by da Vinci

1508–1512
Sistine Chapel ceiling painted by Michelangelo

1509
Henry VIII becomes King of England

112   Proficient Tenor/Bass

MORE ABOUT

Painting

During the Renaissance, there was a renewed focus back to the ancient culture of the Roman Empire and the classical spirit. In visual art, this was represented by a shift from sacred symbolism to realistic art. Leonardo da Vinci, one of the foremost painters and sculptors of the Renaissance, was also an architect, a scientist, an engineer and a musician. Perspective was explored as a result of interest in geometry, and the flat canvas now represented three-dimensional perspective from one point of view outside the plane of the art. The human form was celebrated, and the ideal was a realistic representation. Oil paints, which were first used during the early 1400s, made it possible for painters to revise and refine their ideas as they worked.

Listening Links

CHORAL SELECTION
"O Magnum Mysterium" by Tomás Luis de Victoria (c.1548–1611)

Tomás Luis de Victoria, born in Avila, Spain, was one of the greatest composers of Renaissance polyphony. "O Magnum Mysterium" is a motet that was composed around 1572. The text describes the events surrounding the birth of Christ. The piece features four vocal lines that imitate each other, move together, and weave in and around one another. The texture is quite transparent in the polyphonic sections. Notice how Victoria's use of just a few words during these complex sections make the text easily understood. Of particular interest is the frequent interplay of major and minor chords. Listen to this piece and see if you can hear the contrasting major and minor tonalities.

INSTRUMENTAL SELECTION
"Canzon XV" by Giovanni Gabrieli (c. 1557–1612)

Giovanni Gabrieli spent his most of his life in Venice, Italy, with the exception of the years spent in Munich where he studied with the great composer, Orlando di Lasso (1532–1594). Gabrieli was an organist and resident composer at the Basilica of St. Mark, a huge cathedral right in the center of Venice. "Canzon XV" is written for ten trumpets and trombones. Listen for the contrasts between the contrapuntal writing based on the opening rising theme and the sounds of big block chords. Tap a steady beat to find where a change in meter takes place in the middle of the selection. As you listen to "Canson XV" again, identify and name the different meters that are used.

Check Your Understanding

1. List three major nonmusical changes that took place during the Renaissance period.
2. Describe polyphony as heard in "O Magnum Mysterium."
3. Analyze music from the Renaissance and show how it is different from music of today.

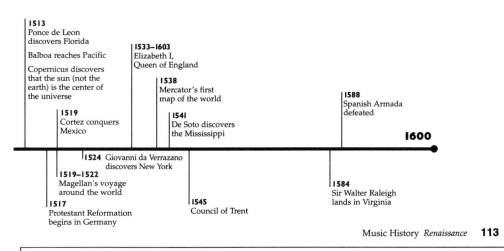

1513
Ponce de Leon
discovers Florida

Balboa reaches Pacific

Copernicus discovers
that the sun (not the
earth) is the center of
the universe

1519
Cortez conquers
Mexico

1519–1522
Magellan's voyage
around the world

1517
Protestant Reformation
begins in Germany

1524 Giovanni da Verrazano
discovers New York

1533–1603
Elizabeth I,
Queen of England

1538
Mercator's first
map of the world

1541
De Soto discovers
the Mississippi

1545
Council of Trent

1588
Spanish Armada
defeated

1600

1584
Sir Walter Raleigh
lands in Virginia

Music History *Renaissance*   **113**

Answers to Check Your Understanding.
1. Answers will vary. For example, the use of the compass made it possible to explore new continents. The invention of the printing press and mass-produced books helped information spread rapidly. The Protestant Reformation led to the formation of many of the world's present-day Protestant denominations.
2. Polyphony is when two or more melodic lines begin at different places and act independently of each other. In "O Magnum Mysterium" polyphony can be heard throughout the piece, in contrast to the sections sung all together.
3. Answers will vary. Today we use many different instruments to provide interesting accompaniments for songs. During the Renaissance most songs were sung a cappella or with simple instruments that echoed the voice lines. One thing the two styles have in common is a frequent use of dissonance.

ASSESSMENT

Informal Assessment

In this lesson, students showed the ability to:
- Share what they know about the Renaissance period.
- Describe musical characteristics, styles and forms found in Renaissance music.
- Describe some characteristics of Renaissance art.

Student Self-Assessment

Direct students to:
- Review the questions in Check Your Understanding on page 113.
- Write a paragraph answering each of the three questions about music and events during the Renaissance period.

ENRICHMENT

Research Project

Direct students to:

Research the development of musical notation from its beginnings in the Middle Ages through the Renaissance period, where its development was spurred by the invention of the printing press. Include how and when the following became used: one line staff, five line staff, *do* clef, treble clef, bass clef, key signatures, rhythmic stem notation, note heads (diamond, triangle, circular), meter signatures, bar lines, dynamics and markings for tempo.

BAROQUE

OVERVIEW

Objectives

After completing this lesson, students will be able to:

- Describe the Baroque period, including important developments.
- Describe characteristics of Baroque music.

VOCABULARY

Have students review vocabulary in student lesson. A complete glossary of terms is found on page 246 of the student book.

Introduce the Baroque period through visual art. Analyze the painting *The Scale of Love* by Jean Antoine Watteau on page 114. Show Fine Art Transparency 3, *The Scale of Love,* (from the Teacher Resource Binder) and direct students to discuss the use of a focal point in this painting. Review the background information about Baroque art as found on teacher page 116.

MUSIC&ART

French painter Jean Antoine Watteau (1684–1721) became the court painter to King Louis XV. He is best known for paintings of characters of scenes from the theater as well as for paintings that show the French aristocracy at play. *The Scale of Love* depicts a guitar player in a brightly colored theatrical costume with a girl seated at his feet as the main focal point. A marble bust of a bearded philosopher appears above the musician, turned to the right where secondary figures, engaged in their own pursuits, pay no attention to the two main actors.

Jean-Antoine Watteau. *The Scale of Love*. c. 1715-18. Oil on canvas. 50.8 x 59.7 cm (19 15/16 x 23 1/2"). National Gallery, London, United Kingdom.

114   Proficient Tenor/Bass

RESOURCES

Teacher Resource Binder

Music and History 5, *Baroque Music*

Music and History 8, *Johann Sebastian Bach*

Fine Art Transparency 2, *The Scale of Love,* Jean-Antoine Watteau

Music and History 9, *Fine Art Teaching Strategy—Baroque*

For additional resources, see Music and History section.

Listening Selections CD

(found in the Teacher Resource Binder)

Track 3: *Te Deum*

Track 4: "Spring" from *The Four Seasons*, First Movement

Focus

- Describe the Baroque Period, including important developments of the time
- Describe characteristics of Baroque music.

The Baroque Period— A Time of Elaboration

The **Baroque period** *(1600–1750)* began in Italy as a result of the Catholic Counter Reformation. This movement was in reaction to the Protestant Reformation of the Renaissance Period. The Church and its wealthy followers sought to impress the world and re-establish the Catholic Church's influence in political and everyday life. The movement soon spread to all of Europe.

The period is characterized by grandeur and opulence, especially among royalty and the upper classes. Elaborate decoration was used in music, art, architecture and fashion. The term *baroque* has its origin's from the French word for "imperfect or irregular pearls." These pearls were often used as decorations on clothing of the period.

Exploration of the world continued and colonies were established in new worlds, thus creating European empires. As goods were brought to Europe from far away lands, a new wealthy merchant class was created.

Support for the arts was high during this time. The nobility sought to have artists, musicians, playwrights and actors in residence, a form of patronage previously seen only in the church and among royalty. However, the public still had little access to the arts, even though the first concerts for which admission was charged occurred during this time. Music and art remained in the church and in the homes of the powerful and wealthy ruling class.

Important scientific discoveries and theories came from this time. Galileo continued his work in astronomy and physics, and Sir Isaac Newton published *Mathematica Principia*, in which he stated the fundamental laws of gravity and motion. Many consider Newton's book to be among the most important scientific book ever written.

COMPOSERS

Johann Pachelbel
(1653–1706)

Henry Purcell
(1659–1695)

Antonio Vivaldi
(1678–1741)

Johann Sebastian Bach
(1685–1750)

George Frideric Handel
(1685–1759)

ARTISTS

Peter Paul Rubens
(1577–1640)

Anthony van Dyck
(1599–1641)

Rembrandt van Rijn
(1606–1669)

Jan Vermeer
(1632–1675)

Jean-Antoine Watteau
(1684–1721)

AUTHORS

John Milton
(1608–1674)

Molière
(1622–1673)

Daniel Defoe
(1550–1731)

Jonathan Swift
(1667–1745)

Samuel Johnson
(1709–1784)

VOCABULARY

Baroque period

homophony

recitatives

figured bass

concerto grosso

opera

oratorio

program music

Music History *Baroque* **115**

National Standards

6. Listening to, analyzing, and describing music. **(a, b, c, e, f)**

8. Understanding relationships between music, the other arts, and disciplines outside the arts. **(a, b, c, d, e)**

9. Understanding music in relation to history and culture. **(a, c, d, e)**

LESSON PLAN

Suggested Teaching Sequence

1. Examine the Baroque period in a historical perspective.

Direct students to:

- Read and discuss the information found on student page 115.

- Share what they know about the composers, artists and authors listed on this page.

- Turn to the time line on pages 116–117 and read the citations.

- Discuss why these are considered important dates during the Baroque period.

- Identify specific accomplishments that were made during the Baroque period and the people associated with those accomplishments.

- Compare each of these events to what occurred before and after the Baroque period.

2. Define the musical aspects of Baroque music.

Direct students to:

- Read and discuss information on Baroque music found on student page 116.

- Discuss developments in music that occurred during this period.

- Define *homophony, recitatives, figured bass, oratorio, opera* and *concerto grosso.*

3. Discuss the performance guidelines of Baroque music.

Direct students to:

- Read the Performance Links found on student page 116.

- Discuss the performance guidelines.

LISTENING LESSONS

This feature is designed to expand students' appreciation of choral and instrumental music of the Baroque period.

Choral Selection:
Te Deum by Henry Purcell
Direct students to:

- Read the information on student page 117 to learn more Henry Purcell and *Te Deum*.
- Listen to the recorded performance and listen for ways in which Purcell dramatized the words through the music.
- While listening again, chart the organization of the piece. Identify sections by instrumentation and voicing; for example—instruments only, chorus and accompaniment, duet, quartet, solo and so forth.

Instrumental Selection:
"Spring" from *The Four Seasons*, First Movement, by Antonio Vivaldi
Direct students to:

- Read the information on student page 117 to learn more about Antonio Vivaldi and "Spring" First Movement from *The Four Seasons*.
- Review the meaning of program music.
- Listen to the recorded performance to identify the elements of spring that Vivaldi chose to portray (birds chirping and singing, streams swiftly moving, sudden and brief thunderstorms, a joyful dance and so forth).

Baroque Music

Music of the Baroque period had a dramatic flair and a strong sense of movement. The quiet a cappella style of the Renaissance gave way to large-scale productions and overall grandeur. Independent instrumental styles evolved, leading to the development of formalized orchestras.

Homophony, *a type of music in which there are two or more parts with similar or identical rhythms being sung or played at the same time,* was very popular during the Baroque period as composers revolted against the polyphony of earlier times.

Other important distinguishing developments in music during the Baroque period were:

- The performance of dramatic **recitatives,** or *vocal solos where the natural inflections of speech are imitated.*
- The singing of solo songs which were homophonic vocal compositions with accompaniment.
- The use of **figured bass,** which is *a set of numbers which are written below the bass line of a piece of music.* These numbers represent different chords and indicate harmonic progressions as a guide for accompanists.

An important form of music in the period was the **concerto grosso,** *a multi-movement composition for a group of solo instruments and orchestra.* Other large works that were developed during this time included the **opera,** *a combination of singing, instrumental music, dancing, and drama that tells a story* and the **oratorio,** *a composition for solo voices, chorus and orchestra, that was an extended dramatic work on a literary or religious theme presented without theatrical action.*

Performance Links

When performing music of the Baroque period, it is important to apply the following guidelines:

- Sing with pitch accuracy, especially in chromatic sections.
- Be conscious of who has the dominant theme, and make sure any accompanying parts do not overshadow the theme.
- Keep a steady, unrelenting pulse in most pieces. Precision of dotted rhythms is especially important.
- When dynamic level changes occur, all vocal lines need to change together.

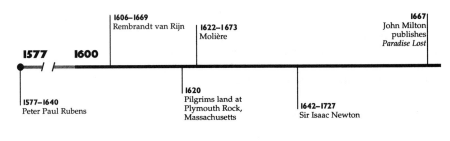

1606–1669
Rembrandt van Rijn

1622–1673
Molière

1667
John Milton publishes *Paradise Lost*

1577   1600

1577–1640
Peter Paul Rubens

1620
Pilgrims land at Plymouth Rock, Massachusetts

1642–1727
Sir Isaac Newton

MORE ABOUT

Art in the Baroque Period

The Baroque period was a time of opulence and ornamentation. Using similar forms as the Renaissance, Baroque artists decorated each element. The distinction between the aristocracy and the common people was highly defined during this period, with the wealthy involved in the arts for their own pleasure and in an effort to represent their status in society. In *The Scale of Love,* the wealthy are represented in their finery.

Listening Links

CHORAL SELECTION

Te Deum (excerpt) by Henry Purcell (1659–1695)

English composer Henry Purcell (1659–1695) came from a family of musicians. As a child, he was a boy chorister at the Chapel Royal. In 1679, he became organist of Westminster Abbey—a position he held for sixteen years. In his later years, Purcell was increasingly prolific, composing some of his greatest church music, including *Te Deum* (1694). In this work, Purcell added an orchestra and a pair of trumpets, never previously used in English church music. The performance was a sensation. Purcell dramatized the words through the music. For example, *heaven* is sung high by the Sopranos, followed by a very low Bass singing the word *earth*. To stress important words, Purcell often used an extended melisma (heard on the words *glorious, goodly* and *praise*). Find other examples of the interplay between the text and music.

INSTRUMENTAL SELECTION

Spring, First Movement from *The Four Seasons* by Antonio Vivaldi (1878–1741)

Antonio Vivaldi was an Italian composer. He is best known as the master of concertos, having written over 500, half of them for solo violin and orchestra. His most well-known work is *The Four Seasons*. It is a set of four solo concertos for violin, string orchestra, and basso continuo. As **program music**, *instrumental music that is composed about a nonmusical subject*, each portrays one of the seasons of the year, corresponding with sonnets that preface each concerto. What elements of spring has Vivaldi chosen to portray in his music?

Check Your Understanding

1. Identify three important developments that took place during the Baroque period.

2. Compare and contrast *oratorio* and *opera*.

3. Analyze characteristics of choral music during the Baroque period as heard in *Te Deum* by Henry Purcell.

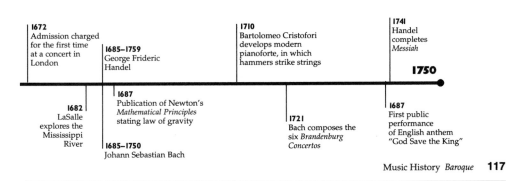

1672 Admission charged for the first time at a concert in London

1685–1759 George Frideric Handel

1710 Bartolomeo Cristofori develops modern pianoforte, in which hammers strike strings

1741 Handel completes *Messiah*

1750

1682 LaSalle explores the Mississippi River

1687 Publication of Newton's *Mathematical Principles* stating law of gravity

1685–1750 Johann Sebastian Bach

1721 Bach composes the six *Brandenburg Concertos*

1687 First public performance of English anthem "God Save the King"

Music History *Baroque*   **117**

Answers to Check Your Understanding.

1. Answers will vary. For example, invention of the telescope, discovery of the law of gravity, exploration and colonization, Pilgrims land at Plymouth Rock.

2. Opera and oratorios are both written for solo voices, chorus and orchestra. They both tell a story. Operas, however, are performed on stage with dancing, costuming and scenery. Oratorios are performed in a church or concert setting.

3. Characteristics of choral music during the Baroque period found in *Te Deum* include dramatic flair, large-scale production and overall grandeur, the words dramatized by the music, the use of melismas, terraced dynamics created by sudden changes in instrumentation or voicings.

ASSESSMENT

Informal Assessment

In this lesson, students showed the ability to:

- Share what they know about the Baroque period.
- Describe musical characteristics, styles and forms found in Baroque music.
- Describe some characteristics of Baroque art.

Student Self-Assessment

Direct students to:

- Review the questions in Check Your Understanding on page 117.
- Write a paragraph answering each of the three questions about the Baroque period.

ENRICHMENT

Research Project

As a small group activity, assign each group one of the following questions to discover what was happening musically in North America during the Baroque period:

- Research music found in North America during the Baroque period (1600–1750). What type of music was being sung or played, and who was creating it?
- What influence did the relationship between Europe and North America have on American music during this period?
- Did the Baroque spirit foster any new musical inventions in North America?
- What types of Native American music were prevalent in North America at this time?
- Present findings to the rest of the class.

CLASSICAL

OVERVIEW

Objectives

After completing this lesson, students will be able to:
- Describe the Classical period, including important developments of the time.
- Describe characteristics of Classical music.

VOCABULARY

Have students review vocabulary in student lesson. A complete glossary of terms is found on page 246 of the student book.

Introduce the Classical period through art. Analyze the photograph of *Grand Piano* created by Joseph Böhm on page 118. Direct students to discuss the piano's history, range and decorations. Review background information of art during the Classical period as found on teacher page 120.

MUSIC & ART The second wife of Napoléon Bonaparte (1769–1821) is believed to have owned this piano. A six-octave range on the piano was customary during the early 1800s. Notice the imperial eagles that crown the legs and nameplate. Joseph Böhm, the builder of this magnificent piano, lived and worked in Vienna, Austria.

Joseph Böhm. *Grand Piano*. c. 1815–20. Wood, various materials. 223.4 cm (87 15/16"). The Metropolitan Museum of Art, New York, New York.

RESOURCES

Teacher Resource Binder

Music and History 10, *Classical Music*

Music and History 11, *Wolfgang Amadeus Mozart*

Fine Art Transparency 3, *Grand Piano, Joseph Böhm*

Music and History 13, *Fine Art Teaching Strategy—Classical*

For additional resources, see Music and History section.

Listening Selections CD

(found in the Teacher Resource Binder)

Track 5: "Gloria" from the *Coronation Mass*

Track 6: *Symphony #100 in G Major*, Second Movement

Focus

- Describe the Classical Period, including important developments of the time.
- Describe characteristics of Classical music.

The Classical Period— The Age of Enlightenment

The **Classical period** *(1750–1820)* was a time when, as a result of archeological findings, society began looking to the ancient Greeks and Romans for examples of order and ways of looking at life. The calm beauty and simplicity of this ancient art inspired artists, architects and musicians to move away from the overly decorated standards of the Baroque period. The elegant symmetry of Greek architecture in particular was recreated in thousands of buildings in Europe and the New World.

This time was also called "The Age of Enlightenment." Writers, philosophers and scientists of the eighteenth century sought to break from the past and replace the darkness and ignorance of outdated thought with the "light" of truth. The spirit of democracy was ignited by the writings of thinkers such as Voltaire and Thomas Jefferson. Their writings suggested that through science and democracy, people could choose their own fate.

These new thoughts and ways of thinking became widespread to many people of the day. The desire for change became so strong that citizens in a number of countries rebelled against leaders who did not grant them basic civil and economic rights. For example, the American Revolution, in which the colonists rebelled against the British government, was based on many of the principles of the "Enlightenment." The French Revolution resulted in the elimination of the monarchy and the establishment of a new government and a new societal structure in that country. Monarchies throughout Europe that were not overthrown became less powerful; many of these countries adopted a democratic form of government.

COMPOSERS

Christoph Willibald Gluck
(1714–1787)

Carl Philipp Emanuel Bach
(1714–1788)

Johann Christian Bach
(1735–1762)

Franz Joseph Haydn
(1732–1809)

Wolfgang Amadeus Mozart
(1756–1791)

ARTISTS

Pietro Longhi
(1702–1788)

Thomas Gainsborough
(1727–1788)

Francisco Göya
(1746–1828)

Jacques-Louis David
(1748–1825)

AUTHORS

Voltaire
(1694–1778)

Jean Jacques Rousseau
(1712–1778)

Johann Wolfgang von Goethe
(1749–1832)

William Wordsworth
(1770–1850)

Jane Austen
(1775–1817)

VOCABULARY

Classical period

symphony

concerto

sonata

string quartet

Music History *Classical* **119**

LESSON PLAN
Suggested Teaching Sequence

1. Examine the Classical period in a historical perspective.

Direct students to:

- Read and discuss the information found on student page 119.
- Share what they know about the composers, artists and authors listed on this page.
- Turn to the time line on pages 120–121 and read the citations.
- Discuss why these are considered important dates during the Classical period.
- Identify specific accomplishments that were made during the Classical period and the people associated with those accomplishments.
- Compare each of these events to what occurred before and after the Classical period.

2. Define the musical aspects of Classical music.

Direct students to:

- Read and discuss information on Classical music found on student page 120.
- Define *symphony, concerto, sonata* and *string quartet.*
- Discuss instruments used in the Classical period.

3. Discuss the performance guidelines of Classical music.

Direct students to:

- Read the Performance Links found on student page 120.
- Discuss the performance guidelines.

National Standards

6. Listening to, analyzing, and describing music. **(a, b, c, e, f)**
8. Understanding relationships between music, the other arts, and disciplines outside the arts. **(a, b, c, d, e)**
9. Understanding music in relation to history and culture. **(a, c, d, e)**

LISTENING LESSONS

This feature is designed to expand students' appreciation of choral and instrumental music of the Classical period.

Choral Selection:
"Gloria" from the *Coronation Mass* by Wolfgang Amadeus Mozart

Direct students to:

- Read the information on student page 121 to learn more about Wolfgang Amadeus Mozart and "Gloria" from the *Coronation Mass*.

- Listen to the recorded performance to identify the sections sung by the full chorus and those sung by the soloists.

- While listening again, identify and list the different ways that the soloists sing together (*a quartet, Soprano and Tenor duet, Soprano and Alto duet, overlapping entries on the word "Amen" in a fugal treatment*).

Instrumental Selection:
***Symphony #100 in G Major,* Second Movement by Franz Joseph Haydn**

Direct students to:

- Read the information on student page 121 to learn more about Franz Joseph Haydn and *Symphony #100 in G Major,* Second Movement.

- Listen to the recorded performance to identify the three large sections and the coda.

- While listening again, write down instruments that are featured in each section.

Music of the Classical Period

Musicians moved away from the heavily ornate styles of the Baroque period and embraced the clean, uncluttered style of the early Greeks and Romans. Instead of many melodies occurring simultaneously, as in the Baroque period, Classical composers wrote clearer music in which one melody sings out while the other parts provide a simple harmonic accompaniment.

The Classical period has been called the "golden age of music." Many forms of music—the **symphony**, *a large scale work for orchestra,* the **concerto**, *a multi-movement for solo instrument and orchestra,* the **sonata**, *a multi-movement piece for solo instrument,* and the **string quartet**, *a form of chamber music which uses two violins, a viola and cello*—were fully developed during this period. The growing popularity of these forms of music led to the establishment of the string, woodwind, brass and percussion sections of today's orchestras. The piano, with its greater sonority than Baroque keyboard instruments, began to become an important instrument in Classical compositions.

Performance Links

When performing music of the Classical period, it is important to apply the following guidelines:

- Listen for the melody line so the accompaniment parts do not overshadow it.
- Sing chords in tune.
- Make dynamic level changes that move smoothly.
- Keep phrases flowing and connected.

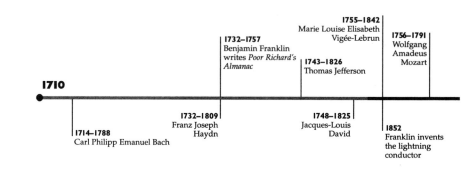

1755–1842
Marie Louise Elisabeth Vigée-Lebrun

1732–1757
Benjamin Franklin writes *Poor Richard's Almanac*

1743–1826
Thomas Jefferson

1756–1791
Wolfgang Amadeus Mozart

1710

1714–1788
Carl Philipp Emanuel Bach

1732–1809
Franz Joseph Haydn

1748–1825
Jacques-Louis David

1852
Franklin invents the lightning conductor

MORE ABOUT...

Art in the Classical Period

The Classical period was highlighted by a return to the ideal of Greek and Roman simplicity and balance. Likewise, social development seemed to swing like a pendulum along a continuum from excess to control. When the Baroque period was at its most opulent, there began to be an upsurge of indignant rebellion from the common people, leading to a return to more sensible, clean, and symmetrical artistic representations. The *Grand Piano* is a beautiful, symmetrical, balanced and uncluttered example of Classical art.

Listening Links

CHORAL SELECTION

"Gloria" from *Coronation Mass* by Wolfgang Amadeus Mozart (1756–1791)

Mozart wrote the *Coronation Mass* for the coronation of Emperor Leopold II of Frankfurt, Germany in 1790. The piece was written for choir, soloists and full orchestra. "Gloria," the second part of the Mass, can be broken into three sections: a beginning, a middle or development, and an ending. Notice that this ending is much like the beginning. The piece ends with a dramatic coda. One melody sings out while the other parts provide a simple accompaniment. As you listen to this piece, pay attention to the innovative interplay between the soloists. List at least three different ways that the soloists sing together.

INSTRUMENTAL SELECTION

Symphony #100 in G Major, Second Movement by Franz Joseph Haydn (1732–1809)

Haydn's *Symphony #100 in G Major* is also known as the "Military Symphony." It is one of two sets of London symphonies written late in Haydn's career in 1794. It calls for a large orchestra for the time, adding instruments from the Turkish military influence—triangle, cymbals, bass drum and bell tree. Listen to this piece of music, paying attention to the contrasting sections.

Check Your Understanding

1. Identify three important developments that took place during the Classical period.

2. What aspects of Mozart's "Gloria" characterize it as being from the Classical period?

3. Describe how music from the Classical period is different from music of the Baroque period.

4. Why do you think this symphony is called the "Military Symphony"?

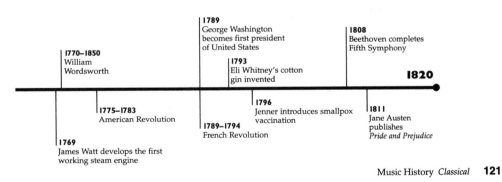

[(A—strings and woodwinds (oboe, bassoon) and French horn; B—triangle, cymbals, woodwinds, strings, trumpet; A'—strings, woodwinds (oboe, flute, bassoon, clarinet), French horn, cymbals, triangle, trumpet; coda—trumpet, tympani, strings, woodwinds, triangle, cymbals)]

ASSESSMENT

Informal Assessment

In this lesson, students showed the ability to:

- Share what they know about the Classical period.
- Describe musical characteristics, styles and forms found in Classical music.
- Describe some characteristics of Classical art.

Student Self-Assessment

Direct students to:

- Review the questions in Check Your Understanding on page 121.
- Write a paragraph answering each of the four questions about the Classical period.

ENRICHMENT

Research Project

As a small group activity, assign each group one of the following leading figures of the Classical period as listed in the sidebar on student page 119. Have each group do research on the contributions of each, and then present findings to the rest of the class.

Music History *Classical* **121**

Answers to Check Your Understanding.

1. Answers will vary. Revolutions in the American colonies and in France that produced new governments and new social structures; oxygen was discovered; the first submarine was produced.

2. Mozart's "Gloria" includes music that is based on balance, clarity, and simplicity, uses of homophonic texture most of the time and uses of interesting dynamic contrast.

3. Answers will vary. The music of the Classical period left the exaggerated embellishments and the use of improvisation behind; it emphasized precision and balance.

4. Instruments from the Turkish military bands such as the triangle and cymbals were added to the orchestra for the first time and featured in this piece. Parts of this piece also sound very march-like.

ROMANTIC

OVERVIEW

Objectives

After completing this lesson, students will be able to:

• Describe the Romantic period, including important developments of the time.

• Describe characteristics of Romantic music.

VOCABULARY

Have students review vocabulary in student lesson. A complete glossary of terms is found on page 246 of the student book.

Introduce the Romantic period through visual art. Analyze the painting by Mary Cassatt on page 122. Direct students to discuss the details in *The Loge*. Why was painter Edgar Degas important to Mary Cassatt? Is there a story in the picture? Review background information on *The Loge* by Cassatt as found on teacher page 124.

MUSIC&ART

American artist Mary Cassatt (1844–1926) is known for her perceptive depictions of women and children. Although born to a prominent Pittsburgh family, Mary Cassatt spent most of her adult life in Paris, France. There her work attracted the attention of French painter Edgar Degas (1834–1917), who invited her to exhibit with his fellow Impressionist painters. In *The Loge*, two women are at the theater. You can see the rings of theater seats and a massive chandelier behind them, which suggests that they are sitting in luxurious boxes.

Mary Cassatt. *The Loge*. 1882. Oil on canvas. 79.8 x 63.8 cm (31 3/8 x 25 1/8"). National Gallery of Art, Washington, D. C. Chester Dale Collection.

122 Proficient Tenor/Bass

RESOURCES

Teacher Resource Binder

Music and History 14, *Romantic Music*

Music and History16, *Camille Saint-Saëns*

Fine Art Transparency 4, *The Loge, Mary Cassatt*

Music and History 18, *Fine Art Teaching Strategy—Romantic*

For additional resources, see Music and History section

Listening Selections CD

(found in the Teacher Resource Binder)

Track 7: "How Lovely Is Thy Dwelling Place" from the *German Requiem*

Track 8: *Symphony #5 in C Minor*, First Movement

Focus

- Describe the Romantic Period, including important developments of the time.
- Describe characteristics of Romantic music.

The Romantic Period— A Time of Drama

The **Romantic Period** *(1820–1900)* was in many ways a reaction against the Classical period, which is often known as the "age of reason." In contrast, the Romantic period could be considered an "age of emotion." A new sense of political and artistic freedom emerged as musicians and artists were no longer employed by the church. The period was characterized by the ideals of liberty and individualism, and of dramatic thought and action.

The Romantic period coincided with the Industrial Revolution. Momentous progress in science and mechanics gave the world the steamboat and rail transportation, and the electric light, telephone and telegraph. Cities grew as nonagricultural jobs developed, and members of the middle classes exerted increasing influence. A new sense of patriotism emerged in Europe as well as in the United States.

The Industrial Revolution produced a wealthy middle class. Their new wealth provided music for the masses to a far greater degree than had existed before. Most musicians' incomes were now provided by the sale of concert tickets and published music rather than by the patronage of the church or royalty. This gave musicians larger audiences and more freedom of expression in their compositions.

The painters of the Romantic period took much of their inspiration from nature. The romantic paintings of William Turner and John Constable express the feelings evoked by nature. Later, Impressionist painters, including Edouard Manet, Claude Monet and Pierre-Auguste Renoir, developed new techniques to bring the sense and feeling of nature alive for the viewer.

COMPOSERS

Ludwig van Beethoven
(1770–1827)

Franz Schubert
(1797–1828)

Frédéric Chopin
(1810–1849)

Robert Schumann
(1810–1856)

Richard Wagner
(1813–1883)

Stephen Foster
(1826–1864)

Johannes Brahms
(1833–1897)

ARTISTS

James Whistler
(1834–1903)

Paul Cezanne
(1839–1906)

Claude Monet
(1840–1926)

Pierre-Auguste Renoir
(1841–1919)

Mary Cassatt
(1845–1926)

Vincent van Gogh
(1853–1890)

AUTHORS

George Sand (1804–1876)

Henry Wadsworth Longfellow
(1807–1882)

Harriet Beecher Stowe (1811–1896)

Charles Dickens (1812–1870)

Leo Tolstoy (1828–1910)

Mark Twain (1835–1910)

VOCABULARY

Romantic period

art song

requiem

motive

Music History *Romantic* **123**

LESSON PLAN
Suggested Teaching Sequence

1. Examine the Romantic period in a historical perspective.

Direct students to:

- Read and discuss the information found on student page 123.
- Share what they know about the composers, artists and authors listed on this page.
- Turn to the time line on pages 124–125 and read the citations.
- Discuss why these are considered important dates during the Romantic period.
- Identify specific accomplishments that were made during the Romantic period and the people associated with those accomplishments.
- Compare each of these events to what occurred before and after the Romantic period.

2. Define the musical aspects of Romantic music.

Direct students to:

- Read and discuss information on Romantic music found on student page 124.
- Name several important Romantic composers and their contributions.
- Define *nationalism* and *art song.*

3. Discuss the performance guidelines of Romantic music.

Direct students to:

- Read the Performance Links found on student page 124.
- Discuss the performance guidelines.

National Standards

6. Listening to, analyzing, and describing music. **(a, b, c, e, f)**
8. Understanding relationships between music, the other arts, and disciplines outside the arts. **(a, b, c, d, e)**
9. Understanding music in relation to history and culture. **(a, c, d, e)**

LISTENING LESSONS

This feature is designed to expand students' appreciation of choral and instrumental music of the Romantic period.

Choral Selection: "How Lovely Is Thy Dwelling Place" from the *German Requiem* by Johannes Brahms

Direct students to:

- Read the information on student page 125 to learn more about Johannes Brahms and "How Lovely Is Thy Dwelling Place" from the *German Requiem*.

- Review the definition of *requiem*.

- Listen to the recorded performance to identify the mood created by this chorus.

- After listening again, describe various ways that Brahms expresses the words of the text through music. *(Answers will vary. An English translation of the words: How lovely is thy dwelling place, O Lord of hosts, for my soul. It longeth, yea fainteth for the courts of the Lord. My soul and body crieth out, yea, for the living God. Blest are they that dwell within Thy house. They praise thy name evermore!)*

Instrumental Selection: *Symphony #5 in C Minor*, First Movement by Ludwig van Beethoven

Direct students to:

- Read the information on student page 125 to learn more about Ludwig van Beethoven and *Symphony #5 in C Minor*.

- Review the definition of motive.

124

Romantic Music

Music of the Romantic period focused on both the heights and depths of human emotion. Complexity, exploration and excitement were characteristics of the new compositions. This was in great contrast to the music of the Classical period, which was based on balance, clarity and simplicity.

Many Romantic compositions reflect the period's spirit of nationalism, or pride in a country's history. Composers used traditional legends, as well as dramas, novels and poems as the basis for both vocal and instrumental works. There was an increased interest in the traditional folk tunes and folk dances of specific nations or regions. For example, German folk songs can be heard in Robert Schumann's (1810–1856) piano pieces and symphonies. In the United States, the songs composed by Stephen Foster (1826–1864) reflected the culture of the South at that time.

Instrumental music became more elaborate and expressive. The symphonies of Beethoven remain among the most popular and critically acclaimed compositions of Western music. Symphony orchestras increased in size, and percussion instruments held a new place of importance.

As the Romantic period progressed, the most important vocal form became the **art song,** *an expressive song about life, love and human relationships for solo voice and piano.* German art songs are known as lieder, and the most famous composer of lieder was Franz Schubert (1797–1828).

Performance Links

When performing music of the Romantic period, it is important to apply the following guidelines:

- Understand the relation of the text to the melody and harmony.
- Concentrate on phrasing and maintaining a clear, beautiful melodic line.
- Perform accurately the wide range of dynamics and tempos.
- Sing confidently in foreign languages to reflect nationalism in music.

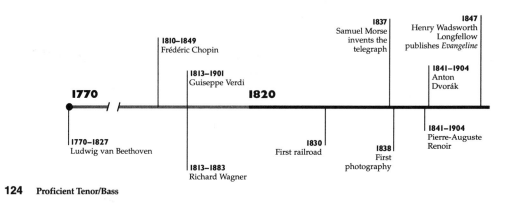

1770

1820

1810–1849 Frédéric Chopin

1813–1901 Guiseppe Verdi

1837 Samuel Morse invents the telegraph

1847 Henry Wadsworth Longfellow publishes *Evangeline*

1841–1904 Anton Dvorák

1770–1827 Ludwig van Beethoven

1830 First railroad

1838 First photography

1841–1904 Pierre-Auguste Renoir

1813–1883 Richard Wagner

124 Proficient Tenor/Bass

MORE ABOUT

Art in the Romantic Period

Visual artists of the Romantic period reflected the era's attitudes with bolder, more colorful works. Point out the details in *The Loge*. An episode in the lives of the middle class is depicted. Ask students to discuss the following question: In which ways does this painter use the elements and principals of art differently than artists of other periods studied?

Listening Links

CHORAL SELECTION

"How Lovely Is Thy Dwelling Place" from *A German Requiem*
by Johannes Brahms (1833–1897)

Johannes Brahms was one of the finest composers of the nineteenth century. A **requiem** *(a mass for the dead)* is a piece containing seven movements combining mixed chorus, solo voices and full orchestra. Brahms intended to portray death as a time of peace and rest. "How Lovely Is Thy Dwelling Place" is a setting of Psalm 84, and is considered to be one of the most beautiful requiem choruses ever written. Toward the end of the piece, the opening melody returns. An unusual use of unison octaves is then heard. Describe the various ways that Brahms expresses the words of the text through his music.

INSTRUMENTAL SELECTION

Symphony #5 in C Minor, First Movement by Ludwig van Beethoven (1770–1827)

Ludwig van Beethoven was one of the greatest composers of all time, particularly noteworthy because he wrote some of his greatest compositions after he had become deaf. His *Symphony #5* has been said to be the musical interpretation of his resolution, "I will grapple with Fate; it shall not overcome me." The first movement has an opening **motive**, *a short rhythmic or melodic idea*, that is immediately recognizable. The development of the motive throughout the piece is a tribute to Beethoven's musical genius. Listen to this piece and identify the motive (short, short, short, long). Describe the differences between the first and second themes in this Movement.

Check Your Understanding

1. Identify three important developments that took place during the Romantic period.

2. Identify characteristics of Romantic music as heard in "How Lovely Is Thy Dwelling Place."

3. Analyze music from the Romantic period and show how it is different from music of the Classical period.

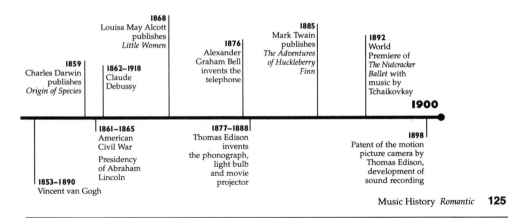

1859
Charles Darwin publishes
Origin of Species

1862–1918
Claude Debussy

1868
Louisa May Alcott publishes
Little Women

1876
Alexander Graham Bell invents the telephone

1885
Mark Twain publishes
The Adventures of Huckleberry Finn

1892
World Premiere of *The Nutcracker Ballet* with music by Tchaikovksy

1900

1861–1865
American Civil War
Presidency of Abraham Lincoln

1877–1888
Thomas Edison invents the phonograph, light bulb and movie projector

1898
Patent of the motion picture camera by Thomas Edison, development of sound recording

1853–1890
Vincent van Gogh

Music History *Romantic* **125**

Answers to Check Your Understanding.

1. Answers will vary. For example, Industrial Revolution, development of railroads, steamboats, the telegraph and telephone, photography and sound recordings are few choices they might use.

2. "How Lovely Is Thy Dwelling Place" reflects several characteristics of Romantic music including complexity; melodies that are long and lyrical; a wide range of dynamics; and so forth.

3. Answers will vary. For example, music of the Classical period was structured, less emotional. It emphasized clarity, repose and balance. Music of the Romantic period was full of emotion and less structured than music of the Classical period. Nationalism was an important element in Romantic music.

- Listen to the recorded performance to identify the opening motive as well as the first and second themes.

- While listening again to the first section, write descriptions of the first and second themes. Discuss the differences between them *(louder/softer; short, disconnected notes/long, flowing phrases; and so forth)*.

ASSESSMENT

Informal Assessment

In this lesson, students showed the ability to:

- Share what they know about the Romantic period.

- Describe musical characteristics, styles and forms found in Romantic music.

- Describe some characteristics of Romantic art.

Student Self-Assessment

Direct students to:

- Review the questions in Check Your Understanding on page 125.

- Write a paragraph answering each of the three questions about the Romantic period.

ENRICHMENT

Research Project

Symphony #5 in C Minor, First Movement, is written in sonata-allegro form. Have students work with a partner to write a story in sonata-allegro form. Share them with the class.

CONTEMPORARY

OVERVIEW

Objectives

After completing this lesson, students will be able to:

- Describe the Contemporary period, including important developments of the time.
- Describe characteristics of Contemporary music.

VOCABULARY

Have students review vocabulary in student lesson. A complete glossary of terms is found on page 246 of the student book.

Introduce the Contemporary period through visual art. Analyze the painting by Marc Chagall on page 126. Direct students to discuss the use of color and form in *Green Violinist*. Review background information on Chagall's Green Violinist as found on page 128.

MUSIC&ART

Marc Chagall (1887–1985) was a Russian-born French painter and designer. Chagall's distinctive use of color and form is derived from the influence of Russian expressionism and French cubism. In *Green Violinist*, Chagall reflects on his Russian homeland by depicting the figure of the violinist dancing in a rustic village.

Marc Chagall. *Green Violinist*. 1923–24. Oil on canvas, 198 x 108.6 cm (78 x 42 3/4").
Solomon Guggenheim Museum, New York, New York. Gift, Solomon R. Guggenheim, 1937.

126 Proficient Tenor/Bass

RESOURCES

Teacher Resource Binder

Music and History 18, *Contemporary Music*

Music and History 20, *Keith Christopher*

Fine Art Transparency 9, *Green Violinist*, Mark Chagall

Music and History 22, *Fine Art Teaching Strategy*

For additional resources, see Music and History section.

Listening Selections CD

(found in the Teacher Resource Binder)

Track 11: "Laudamus Te" from Poulenc's *Gloria*

Track 12: "Street in a Frontier Town" from *Billy the Kid*, Scene I

Focus
- Describe the Contemporary period, including important developments of the time.
- Describe characteristics of Contemporary music.

The Contemporary Period— The End of Isolation

The **Contemporary period** (1900–present) has been a period of rapid change spurred by tremendous technological advances. In less than sixty years, aviation progressed from the first airplane to space exploration and man walking on the moon. Technology brought the emergence of the automobile, television, computer and cellular telephone. The recording of music developed and grew. Recorded sound moved from vinyl LPs and audio cassette tapes to CDs, DVDs and MP3s. Can you imagine a life style without these modern conveniences?

The world has changed from one of many isolated nations to a world where nations come together to attempt to solve worldwide problems such as war, famines, health epidemics and environmental problems such as global warming. People are also less isolated. Rather than staying in one place all their lives as was most common in other periods, many people move from place to place. Some even move to other countries as well. Satellites orbiting the earth allow people to instantly observe what is going on in other parts of the world. One of the most important developments of the Contemporary period is the creation of the World Wide Web that allows individual computers to instantly connect to other computers around the globe. School students in the United States taking classes in French, for example, can communicate directly in real time with students in France during a normal class period.

Some of the Contemporary period leaders in the arts include:

- Composers—Igor Stravinsky (1882–1971), Aaron Copland (1900–1990), Leonard Bernstein (1918–1990), Libby Larson (b. 1950)
- Artists—Romare Bearden (1911–1988), Marc Chagall (1887–1985), Pablo Picasso (1881–1973), Georgia O'Keeffe (1887–1986), Andy Warhol (1930–1987)
- Dancers—Martha Graham (1894–1991) and Bella Zewinsky (b. 1917)

COMPOSERS
Ralph Vaughan Williams (1872–1958)
Béla Bartók (1881–1945)
Igor Stravinsky (1882–1971)
Heitor Villa-Lobos (1887–1959)
William Grant Still (1895–1978)
Francis Poulenc (1899–1963)
Aaron Copland (1900–1990)

ARTISTS
Pablo Picasso (1881–1973)
Diego Rivera (1886–1957)
Marc Chagall (1887–1985)
Georgia O'Keeffe (1887–1986)
Jacob Lawrence (1917–2000)
Andrew Wyeth (b. 1917)

AUTHORS
Robert Frost (1874–1963)
Virginia Woolf (1882–1941)
Ernest Hemingway (1899–1961)
James Baldwin (1924–1997)
Gabriel García Márquez (b. 1928)

VOCABULARY
Contemporary period
dissonance
improvisation
fusion
polyrhythms

Music History *Contemporary* **127**

National Standards
6. Listening to, analyzing, and describing music. **(a, b, c, e, f)**
8. Understanding relationships between music, the other arts, and disciplines outside the arts. **(a, b, c, d, e)**
9. Understanding music in relation to history and culture. **(a, c, d, e)**

LESSON PLAN
Suggested Teaching Sequence

1. Examine the Contemporary period in a historical perspective.
Direct students to:
- Read and discuss the information found on student page 127.
- Share what they know about the composers, artists and authors listed on this page.
- Turn to the time line on pages 128–129 and read the citations.
- Discuss why these are considered important dates during the Contemporary period.
- Identify specific accomplishments that were made during the Contemporary period and the people associated with those accomplishments.

2. Define the musical aspects of Contemporary music.
Direct students to:
- Read and discuss information on Contemporary music found on student page 128.
- Name several important Contemporary composers.
- Discuss three major elements that are often heard in Contemporary music.
- Define *dissonance, minimalism, musical theater, jazz, rock, reggae* and *tejano.*

3. Discuss the performance guidelines of Contemporary music.
Direct students to:
- Read the Performance Links found on student page 128.
- Discuss the performance guidelines.

This feature is designed to expand students' appreciation of choral and instrumental music of the Contemporary period.

**Choral Selection:
"Laudamus Te" from *Gloria*
by Francis Poulenc**

Direct students to:

- Read the information on student page 129 to learn more about Francis Poulenc and "Laudamus Te" from his *Gloria.*

- Listen to the recorded performance to identify sudden changes, accents in the wrong places and beautiful melodies.

- Discuss the different treatments of the repeated phrase "Laudamus Te." (*Usually, the full choir in unison sings this phrase, with accent on "da" and "te." At two places, one part of the choir echoes another on the phrase. It is also sung in big chords with accents on each syllable. The ending adds a new rhythmic emphasis to the phrase.*)

**Instrumental Selection:
"Street in a Frontier Town"
from *Billy the Kid*, Scene I, by
Aaron Copland**

Direct students to:

- Read the information on student page 129 to learn more about Aaron Copland and "Street in a Frontier Town" from *Billy the Kid*, Scene I.

- Define *polyrhythms.*

- Listen to the recorded performance to enjoy the energy and drama of this ballet selection.

Music of the Contemporary Period

By the turn of the twentieth century, musicians of all nationalities were searching for original forms of expression. During the first half of the century, nationalism continued to have a large influence. The study of folk songs in their countries enhanced the music of many composers, such as Ralph Vaughan Williams (England), Aaron Copland (United States), Béla Bartók (Hungary), and Hector Villa-Lobos (Brazil).

Three major elements that are often heard in Contemporary music are (1) harmonies that emphasize **dissonance**, *a combination of tones that sounds harsh and unstable*, (2) melodies with angular contours, and (3) rhythms featuring irregular patterns and shifting meters.

During the mid-twentieth century, there was a shift in classical music. Composer Philip Glass (b. 1937) was searching for a new way of writing. He began to compose music that explored the repetition of simple rhythms and minimal melodies. This new form of writing is call **minimalism**. It is *tonal music that stresses the element of repetition with changes that are dictated by a rule or system.*

Also during this period, many different popular music styles emerged. The list below identifies some of the more important ones.

- Musical Theater—centered on Broadway and Hollywood musicals
- Jazz—strong rhythmic and harmonic structures supporting solo and ensemble improvisation
- Rock—music with strongly accented or emphasized beats
- Reggae—a **fusion** (*a combination of blending of different genres of music*) of rock and Jamaican rhythms, instruments, and language
- Tejano—a fusion of Mexican and country music

Performance Links

When performing music of the Contemporary period, it is important to apply the following guidelines:

- Sing on pitch, even in extreme parts of your range.
- Tune intervals carefully in the skips found in many melodic lines.
- Sing changing meters and unusual rhythm patterns precisely.
- Perform accurately the wide range in dynamics and tempos.

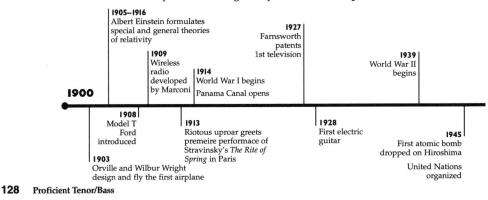

MORE ABOUT...

Art from the Contemporary Period

The word that best describes the art of the Contemporary period is *diversity*. It is indeed a period with a style for everyone, where form, function and art are sometimes inextricably bound together. Old ideas are often used, but are many times abandoned for a new way of looking at the world. Today's artists make use of new materials and techniques to express their ideas, beliefs and feelings. Many of these artists are moving away from traditional styles of art. Art movements of the past have given way to an astonishing array of individual art styles. Some of these styles reflect the influence of earlier artists while others reject entirely any reference to historical models.

Listening Links

CHORAL SELECTION

"Laudamus te" from *Gloria* by Francis Poulenc (1899–1963)

Francis Poulenc was one of France's most colorful twentieth century composers. His style was greatly influenced by Stravinsky, Vivaldi, Palestrina and Victoria. Poulenc's writing is fundamentally tonal, but his music is full of sudden changes in key signatures, dynamics, rhythms and harmonies. He often worked in short musical phrases, repeating them with subtle variations. *Gloria*, written in 1959, is one of his most popular works. He deliberately contrasts text and musical accents. Combinations of different musical styles, accents in all the wrong places, and beautiful melodies make the *Gloria* a Poulenc masterpiece. Discuss how the repeated phrase "Laudamus te" is treated differently on each repetition.

INSTRUMENTAL SELECTION

"Street in a Frontier Town" from *Billy the Kid* by Copland (1900–1990)

Aaron Copland is one of the most famous composers of the twentieth century. Copland was born in Brooklyn, New York, and was famous for adapting American folk themes into his orchestral works. *Billy the Kid* is one such example. Written as a ballet to tell the story of the outlaw Billy the Kid, Copland divides the saga into six parts: "The Open Prairie," "Street in a Frontier Town," "Prairie Night," "Gun Battle," "Celebration," and "Billy's Death." In "Street in a Frontier Town," many American folk songs are used. Copland adapts these folk songs, and uses interesting **polyrhythms**, or *a technique in which several different rhythms are performed at the same time*. Listen to this selection. What folk songs and melodies do you recognize?

Check Your Understanding

1. Identify three important developments that took place during the Contemporary period.

2. Describe musical characteristics of the Contemporary period as heard in *Gloria*: "Laudamus te" by Francis Poulenc.

3. Analyze music from the Contemporary period and show how it is different from music of the Romantic period.

* Listen again to identify the folk songs and familiar melodies used by Copland. (*American folk songs—Great Granddad, The Old Chisholm Trail, Goodbye Old Paint—and a Mexican Jarabe dance tune*).

ASSESSMENT

Informal Assessment

In this lesson, students showed the ability to:

* Share what they know about the Contemporary period.
* Describe musical characteristics, styles and forms found in Contemporary music.
* Describe some characteristics of Contemporary art.

Student Self-Assessment

Direct students to:

* Review the questions in Check Your Understanding on page 129.
* Write a paragraph answering each of the three questions about the Contemporary period.

ENRICHMENT

Creative Project

Abstract art can be represented in sound or dance. Have students choose a piece of abstract art and create a sound composition and dance that reflects the elements of the artwork. Perform the sound composition and dance as the art is exhibited on a large screen behind the performers.

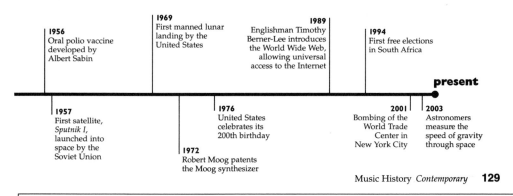

1956 Oral polio vaccine developed by Albert Sabin	**1969** First manned lunar landing by the United States	**1989** Englishman Timothy Berner-Lee introduces the World Wide Web, allowing universal access to the Internet	**1994** First free elections in South Africa
1957 First satellite, *Sputnik I,* launched into space by the Soviet Union	**1976** United States celebrates its 200th birthday	**2001** Bombing of the World Trade Center in New York City	**2003** Astronomers measure the speed of gravity through space
	1972 Robert Moog patents the Moog synthesizer		**present**

Music History *Contemporary* **129**

Answers to Check Your Understanding.

1. Answers will vary. Examples might include the Space Age/Sputnik; developments in travel and communication; WWI and WWII; theory of relativity.

2. Some characteristics of Contemporary music that are heard in "Laudamus Te" from Poulenc's *Gloria* include dissonant chords, shifts in meter, a wide variation in dynamic levels, a combination of several different musical styles, and so forth.

3. Answers will vary. For example, music of the Romantic period focuses on the heights and depths of human emotion. Nationalism is reflected in many musical works. Music of the Contemporary period is marked by change and experimentation—new forms, new instruments, music written with no tonal center, music featuring a fusion of musical styles, and so forth.

CONCERT ETIQUETTE

Objective

- Exhibit informed concert etiquette in a variety of settings.

Suggested Teaching Sequence

Direct students to:

- Read the Spotlight On Concert Etiquette on student page 130 and discuss the importance of concert etiquette in respecting the efforts of others.

- Identify the six elements that constitute proper concert etiquette.

- Compare the elements of concert etiquette to appropriate performance practices. In what ways are they related to one another?

- Apply concert etiquette during live performances in a variety of settings such as school concerts and assemblies, professional symphony and/or opera performances and solo recitals.

- Divide the class into small groups and assign each group one concert venue. Ask each group to make a list of five appropriate and five inappropriate behavior expectations for the assigned venue. Share findings with the class.

Progress Checkpoints

Observe students' progress in:

- ✓ Their ability to identify the elements of concert etiquette.
- ✓ Their ability to understand the importance of concert etiquette.
- ✓ Their ability to apply concert etiquette in a variety of settings.

130

Concert Etiquette

Whether you are attending a rock concert, an athletic event or a musical concert, there are unique criteria for appropriate behavior at each event. The way in which one shows enthusiasm for a school athletic team or a favorite rock band is very different than the way one would express appreciation for a formal musical presentation.

Understanding appropriate expectations specific to individual events is what allows an audience, as well as the performers, to enjoy a presentation. The ultimate goal should be to show consideration and respect to everyone involved in a performance.

The term that describes how one is expected to behave in a formal music concert is *concert etiquette*. Let's examine behavior criteria specific to a formal concert.

- If you arrive late, wait outside the auditorium until a break in the music or until the audience is clapping to enter the hall.

- Wait to exit the hall until a break in the musical selections if a personal emergency occurs.

- Audience members will hear and enjoy the concert if everyone remains quiet and still throughout the performance.

- Take your cue from the performers or conductor and wait for an invitation when it comes to audience participation.

- Affirm your appreciation of the performance by applauding at the end of a selection of music and when the conductor's hands are lowered.

- Cellular telephones and pagers should be set so that no audible sound can be heard. Better yet, turn them off!

Understanding the uniqueness between various events is the first step toward knowing the behavior expectations particular to individual performances. When these guidelines are followed, everyone's enjoyment will be enhanced.

RESOURCES

Teacher Resource Binder

Evaluation Master 5, *Concert Etiquette Quiz*

Reference 16, *Expanding a Musical Vocabulary*

Reference 28, *Writing for the Newspaper*

National Standards

7. Evaluating music and musical performances. **(a, b)**

Choral Library

Away From The Roll Of The Sea

OVERVIEW

Composer: Allister MacGillivray, arranged by Diane Loomer

Text: Allister MacGillivray

Voicing: TTBB

Key: E major

Meter: 3/4

Form: Strophic

Style: Contemporary Canadian Folk Song

Accompaniment: Piano

Programming: Thematic Programming, Festival, Honor Chorus

Vocal Ranges:

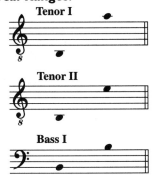

OBJECTIVES

After completing this lesson, students will be able to:

- Demonstrate in ensembles basic performance techniques.
- Read music that incorporates rhythmic patterns in simple meter.

VOCABULARY

Have students review vocabulary in student lesson. Introduce terms found in the music. A complete glossary of terms is found on page 246 of the student book.

Away From The Roll Of The Sea

Composer: Allister MacGillivray, arranged by Diane Loomer
Text: Allister MacGillivray
Voicing: TTBB

VOCABULARY

staggered breathing

legato

lyrics

Focus

- Sing music with legato phrases and staggered breathing.
- Read and perform rhythm patterns with dotted notes and ties.

Getting Started

"Toto, I've a feeling we're not in Kansas any more."
Dorothy, *The Wizard of Oz*

Even in our modern world, some places don't look or feel like any other. These locations often have a singular charm with a distinctive vocabulary. Can you match the following list of descriptive words with the correct location?

Local Vocabulary	Locations
1. mogul, alpine, tarn	a. Sahara Desert, Africa
2. windmill, prairie, peat	b. Cape Breton, Canada
3. cuddy, spar, Acadian	c. Aspen, Colorado, USA
4. oasis, dune, Bedouin	d. Topeka, Kansas, USA

Many of these colorful words have also found their way into the folk songs of each area. These folk songs give us the opportunity to experience places around the world through words and music.

 **SKILL BUILDERS**

To learn more about the key of E major, see Proficient Sight-Singing, *page 155.*

◆ History and Culture

There are active folklorists, songwriters and performers who are committed to keeping this oral tradition alive. Canadian Allister MacGillivray, is such a folk artist. His evocative "Away From The Roll Of The Sea" has brought salty sea air, rolling cliffs and bobbing harbor boats to singers around the world. Listen to the first measure of the accompaniment and you will also be able to hear the gentle slap of the water against the pier. By the time the introduction is over, you will be ready for cuddies (a small cabin or the cook's galley on a ship) and spars (a stout pole—mast, yard, boom, or gaff—for supporting sail rigging) as you sail along the North Atlantic coast.

RESOURCES

Proficient Sight-Singing

Reading Rhythms in 3/4 meter, page 14

Sight-Singing in E major, page 155

Teacher Resource Binder

Teaching Master 21, *Creating in a Folk Style*

Evaluation Master 4, *Checking Out Phrasing*

Evaluation Master 6, *Composing in Triple Meter*

Evaluation Master 8, *Evaluating Musical Expression*

For additional resources, see TRB Table of Contents.

Links to Learning

◆ **Vocal**

You will need to use **staggered breathing** *(the practice of planning breaths so that no two singers take a breath at the same time, thus creating the overall effect of continuous singing)* to sing the long **legato** *(a connected and smooth style of singing)* phrases in "Away From The Roll Of The Sea." Sing the E major scale ascending and descending at a slow tempo. Stagger your breathing so there are no breaks between any scale tones.

◆ **Theory**

It is common in folk music for the rhythm of the melodic line to have variations in each verse to accommodate the **lyrics** *(the words of a song)*. This allows the music to follow the natural speech pattern of the words. The following three rhythm patterns appear in the same place in different verses. Clap or tap each rhythm while you count out loud. Can you locate these patterns in the music?

Evaluation

Demonstrate how well you have learned the skills and concepts featured in the lesson "Away From The Roll Of The Sea" by completing the following:

• With two or three classmates, sing measures 5–26 demonstrating legato style and staggered breathing. Evaluate how well you were able to create the overall effect of continuous singing.

• Compose an eight-measure rhythmic pattern in $\frac{3}{4}$ meter that contains dotted quarter notes and ties. Notate your pattern on staff paper or the computer. Exchange compositions with a classmate and check each other's work for accurate notation. Assess how well you are able to read and write notation in $\frac{3}{4}$ meter.

Choral Library *Away From The Roll Of The Sea* **133**

RESOURCES

Proficient Tenor/Bass Rehearsal/Performance CD

CD 2:1 Voices

CD 2:2 Accompaniment Only

CD 3:13 Vocal Practice Track—Tenor I

CD 4:12 Vocal Practice Track—Tenor II

CD 5:6 Vocal Practice Track—Baritone

CD 6:13 Vocal Practice Track—Bass

National Standards

1. Singing, alone and with others, a varied repertoire of music. **(a, b, c)**

5. Reading and notating music. **(a, b)**

7. Evaluating music and music performances. **(a, c)**

8. Understanding relationships between music, the other arts, and disciplines outside the arts. **(b, c, d)**

9. Understanding music in relation to history and culture. **(d)**

LINKS TO LEARNING

Vocal

The Vocal section is designed to prepare students to develop staggered breathing techniques for ensemble singing.

Have students:

• Practice singing the E major scale ascending and descending on quarter notes.

• Discuss the concept of staggered breathing.

• Sing the scale again as presented on page 133, applying the concept of staggered breathing. Plan the breaths so that there is no audible break in the overall sound when singing the scale.

Theory

The Theory section is designed to prepare students to:

• Accurately read and perform ties and syncopation.

• Identify slight alterations in rhythmic patterns.

• Discover how text and rhythm are related.

Have students:

• Perform the three rhythmic examples.

• Compare and contrast their similarities and differences.

• Locate the patterns in the music. *(example 1: measures 6, 8, 11, 13, 16, 21–22, 27–29, and so forth; example 2: measures 7, 12, 17, 29, 37 and so forth; example 3: measures 75 and 112)*

LESSON PLAN

Suggested Teaching Sequence and Performance Tips

1. Introduce

Direct students to:

- Read and discuss the information found in Getting Started on student page 132. (*Answers: 1=c; 2=d; 3=b; 4=a*) Encourage students to identify and list distinctive characteristics of the area where they live.

- Locate Cape Breton Island on the map. Learn as much about the culture, history and geography of the area as possible.

- Read about staggered breathing and discuss what it means. Sing the example in the Vocal section on page 133, utilizing staggered breathing to create a continuous sound with no audible breaks.

- Practice the three rhythmic patterns in the Theory section on page 133. Ask students to write each pattern on a card or small slips of paper. Use the cards as flash cards. With a partner, drill each other on reading the rhythms correctly.

To Allister with continuing thanks for his songs from the heart. – D.L.

Away From The Roll Of The Sea

For TTBB and Piano

Arranged by DIANE LOOMER

Words and Music by
ALLISTER MAC GILLIVRAY

* The first verse could be sung as solo, in unison by the whole choir, or as suggested in alternating sections.

© 1986 by Cabot Trail Music
5200 Dixie Road – Suite 203
Mississauga, Ontario L4W 1E4

134   Proficient Tenor/Bass

This captivating folk song will be an instant favorite of the students. However, the vocal ranges may be a problem for developing singers. Don't hesitate to rearrange parts, alter notes (substitute another note from the chord, for example) or change octaves to keep each phrase in a comfortable and accessible tessitura for the singers.

no in-di-ca-tion ___ what their ways have been. ___ They ___

rock at their moor-ings ___ all nest-led ___ in dreams ___ a-

- way from the roll of the sea. ___

Progress Checkpoints

Observe students' progress in:
- ✓ Their ability to sing with adequate breath support.
- ✓ Their ability to plan breaths and demonstrate staggered breathing.
- ✓ Their ability to identify and read dotted rhythm patterns.

TEACHING STRATEGY

Concert Etiquette

Have students:

1. Identify appropriate concert etiquette in a variety of settings (formal concerts, informal concerts, large concert halls, small concert halls, and so forth).
2. Attend a variety of live performances.
3. Discuss the appropriate and inappropriate concert behaviors observed.
4. Write a short analysis of appropriate concert etiquette for each setting.

2. Rehearse

Direct students to:

- Use solfège to learn measures 5–26 in unison, paying particular attention to the rhythm patterns outlined in the Theory section on page 133.

- Discuss the technique of ensemble staggered breathing. Work in small groups of four to six singers to perform measures 5–26 on solfège with staggered breathing. Allow groups to perform for each other.

- Follow a similar procedure to learn measures 26–40, or the second verse. Have all sing the Bass melody line. After singers are secure in that, add the Tenor part.

- Work in sectionals and learn the pitches and rhythms for measures 41–47. While each section sings for the choir, have others identify measures that require extra drill or refinement. Perform all of the second verse as written.

CURRICULUM CONNECTIONS

- Listen to recordings of folk music from Cape Breton Island. What characteristics are common to the folk songs? Begin to develop a list of characteristics common to folk music from Cape Breton Island. What can you learn about the culture of Cape Breton Island by listening to its music?

- Find a piece of artwork from a master artist, such as American artists Winslow Homer or George Bingham, or British artist J. M. W. Turner, that would connect to "Away From The Roll Of The Sea." Share your findings with the class.

- Identify the chorus as measures 47–63. Work in sectionals and learn the pitches and rhythms. Rehearse by having two different sections sing together (Tenor I and Bass I, for example). Rotate the combinations until each verse part has sung with the other three at least once.

- Turn to measure 84 and describe how the chorus is different from the way it was originally presented in measure 47. (*Answer: it is a cappella, the harmonies and rhythms are slightly altered*)

- Rehearse both versions of the chorus until learned.

- Look for similarities and differences in the vocal lines between verses 1 and 3. Sing measures 63–84 (verse 3).

- Discover how the third verse is treated differently when repeated in measures 100–121. Sing the Bass I and Bass II part in measures 100–121. After Bass parts are secure, add the Tenor parts.

- Check for tall, uniform vowels sounds while singing.

- Using solfège syllables, sing measures 121–end. Sing a cappella to learn the pitches and rhythms. After secure in part, add text.

TEACHING STRATEGY

Performing from Memory

Have students:

1. Memorize this piece by learning shorter phrases at a time.

2. Perform it from memory on a program or in competition.

3. Further develop memorization skills by memorizing other songs and solos to perform for the class informally or at formal concerts.

Progress Checkpoints

Observe students' progress in:

✓ Singing with a smooth and unforced tone quality.

3. Refine

Direct students to:

• Stand in a circle. Starting at measure 48, go around the circle and sing only one measure while maintaining a steady beat. Sometimes students will have to take over a tied note from another singer. Practice until the tone quality, blend and phrasing are seamless.

• Repeat the circle exercise, singing each vocal line in falsetto! Again, work for a full, supported tone and seamless phrasing.

• Research the local culture of Cape Breton Island, Nova Scotia, Canada. Pay special attention to shipping terms and local expressions. Use the information to create a journal entry from a fisherman moored at the harbor in 1902. The journal entry should echo the "adventures they'd weave" if the fisherman's boat had a "tongue for to speak." Read the entries to the choir and choose several to present during a performance.

138   Proficient Tenor/Bass

Encourage your students to expore **music.glencoe.com**, the Web site for *Experiencing Choral Music.* You may wish to preview the rich content before directing your students online. Options available on the Web site include:

• Web Link Exercises
• Interactive Projects
• Audio Samples

- Illustrate the concept of legato phrasing by having two students tautly hold each end of a 15-foot rope. Let the other students individually pull themselves along the rope from one end (the boat) to the other (the mooring) while singing measures 84-92. The moving singer shouldn't take a breath until he reaches the mooring. Repeat to give all students the experience of constantly moving and pulling along the line. Compare the pull of the rope to the pull of the melodic line. If your singers are adept at nautical knots, you won't need "human" moorings!

Progress Checkpoints

Observe students' progress in:

✓ Their ability to sing with proper vocal placement (head voice).

✓ Their ability to express mood of song through creative writing.

✓ Their understanding of melodic line.

Choral Library *Away From The Roll Of The Sea* **139**

TEACHING STRATEGY

Musical Elements of Style

The combination of musical elements determines the style of a piece.
Have students:

1. Compile a list of musical elements that might affect style.

2. Share the lists to compile one master list.

3. Sing known songs, trying out different styles, and then try to describe the musical elements that are characteristic of that style. (For example, try salsa, opera, Broadway, rock, military, lullaby, and so forth.)

4. Select appropriate literature for a particular style.

ASSESSMENT

Informal Assessment

In this lesson, students showed the ability to:

- Sing with increased breath support.
- Demonstrate legato phrasing.
- Work in small, independent groups.

TEACHING STRATEGY

Shaping with Dynamics

Have students:

- Add another level of sophistication to their performance of "Away From The Roll Of The Sea" by making a small crescendo and diminuendo on every dotted quarter- and eighth-note combination.
- Identify these as falling dynamics within the larger shaping of the whole phrase.

Student Self-Assessment

Have students evaluate their individual performances based on the following:

• Breath Support
• Expressive Singing
• Phrasing
• Accurate Rhythms
• Intonation

Have each student rate his/her performance of this song in the areas above on a scale of 1–5, 5 being the best.

CURRICULUM CONNECTIONS

Technology in Music

Have students:

1. Identify technology used in music (computer, midi, mp3, CD, audio/video recordings, synthesizer, sound equipment, electronic sounds, and so forth).
2. Discuss what effect technology has on music.
3. Create a musical composition using a form of technology.
4. Perform a solo or small ensemble for the class incorporating technology.

Individual and Group Performance Evaluation

To further measure growth of musical skills presented in this lesson, direct students to complete the Evaluation section on page 133.

- In small groups of two or three singers, have students sing measures 5–26. Instruct other members of the class to listen while the small group sings. Ask the class to evaluate how well the group was able to create an overall effect of continuous singing through the use of staggered breathing.

- Direct students to compose an eight-measure rhythmic pattern in 3/4 meter. This pattern may contain dotted quarter notes and ties. After students have written out their patterns, ask them to exchange papers with another student. Check each other's work.

142   Proficient Tenor/Bass

MORE ABOUT...

Composer Allister MacGillivray

Allister MacGillivray was born and raised in the coal mining and fishing town of Glace Bay on Cape Breton Island. As a young boy, he participated in both classical and traditional music opportunities, but by the age of thirteen he was enthralled by British and American folk music. Today he is known as a songwriter, guitarist, record producer, folklorist and author. In addition to "Away From The Roll Of The Sea," MacGillivray is well known for other choral works such as "Song For The Mira" and "Here's To Song."

EXTENSION

Compare and Contrast

- Find the music for a sea chantey in a contrasting style to "Away From The Roll Of The Sea." Have a small group of singers learn it and perform for the class. Compare the characteristics found in both songs.

- Have students create dialogue for a dramatic sketch from the ideas in the fisherman's journals. Conclude the sketch with a performance of "Away From The Roll Of The Sea."

ASSESSMENT

Creating an Assessment Rubric

Have students:

1. Discuss the characteristics of a desirable performance of this piece, using all their knowledge of performance techniques.

2. Identify the criteria by which they think an adjudicator might assess the performance of this piece.

3. For each criterion, decide what characteristics will comprise an adequate, good, very good, and excellent performance.

4. Create a rubric chart.

5. Use the rubric to assess quartets or small ensembles performing all or part of this song.

ENRICHMENT

Large-Ensemble Performance Techniques

Have students listen to a recording of the entire choir singing "Away From the Roll of the Sea." As they listen, have students describe and list the performance techniques they observed. Focus their attention to the techniques of legato singing, staggered breathing, and accurate rhythms. Then, have students perform "Away From the Roll of the Sea" again, demonstrating their understanding of these techniques."

144 Proficient Tenor/Bass

Additional National Standards

The following National Standards are addressed through the Assessment, Extension, Enrichment and bottom-page activities:

1. Singing, alone and with others, a varied repertoire of music. **(a, b, c, f)**

5. Reading and notating music. **(a, b)**

6. Listening to, analyzing, and describing music. **(a, e)**

7. Evaluating music and music performances. **(a, c)**

8. Understanding relationships between music, the other arts, and disciplines outside the arts. **(a, b, c, d, e)**

9. Understanding music in relation to history and culture. **(a, b, d, e)**

SPOTLIGHT

Improvisation

Improvisation is *the art of singing or playing music, making it up as you go.* **Scat singing** is *an improvisational style of singing that uses nonsense syllables instead of words.* Sometimes, these nonsense sounds can imitate the sound of an instrument. Scat singing, especially as a solo, can be the scariest part of singing jazz.

According to Dr. Kirby Shaw, one of the top vocal jazz composers and conductors in the world today, here are some suggestions to help build your confidence in this fun and exciting art form.

- Start your scat solo with a short melodic or rhythmic idea from the tune being performed. There is nothing wrong in having a preconceived idea before starting to sing a scat solo! By gradually developing the idea as you sing, you will have an organized solo that sounds completely improvised.

- Start with scat syllables like "doo" when singing swing tunes. Try "bee," "dee," and "dn" for occasional accented eighth notes on the upbeat of beats (1 *and* 2 *and* 3 *and* 4 *and*). Try "doot" or "dit" for short last notes of a musical phrase.

- Be able to imitate any sound you like from the world around you, such as a soft breeze, a car horn or a musical instrument. There might be a place for that sound in one of your solos.

- Listen to and imitate note-for-note the great jazz singers or instrumentalists. Musicians like Ella Fitzgerald, Jon Hendricks, Louis Armstrong or Charlie Parker can be an inspiration to you.

- Learn to sing the blues. You can listen to artists like B.B. King, Stevie Ray Vaughan, Buddy Guy or Luther Allison. There are many recordings from which to choose.

In short, learn as many different kinds of songs as you can. The best scat singers quote from such diverse sources as nursery rhymes, African chant and even opera. Above all, have fun as you develop your skills!

Composer/arranger Kirby Shaw's music has been sung around the world and has sold millions of copies. As a performer, Dr. Shaw has scatted one-on-one with such notables as Bobby McFerrin, Al Jarreau, Jon Hendricks and Mark Murphy. As a member of the ensemble, he enjoys singing vocal jazz with Just 4 Kicks, a zany four-man a cappella vocal jazz ensemble.

Spotlight *Improvisation* **145**

IMPROVISATION

Objectives

- Create rhythmic and melodic phrases.
- Improvise musical melodies.

Suggested Teaching Sequence
Direct students to:

- Read the Spotlight On Improvisation on student page 145 and define improvisation and scat singing.
- Identify the steps to follow in learning to scat sing.
- Practice scat singing as described on page 145. Teacher may model, students imitate.
- Apply scat singing techniques to a familiar song.
- Make a list of vocal jazz singers they know and identify characteristics of their singing.

Progress Checkpoints

Observe students' progress in:
- ✓ Their ability to define and describe the concept of improvisation.
- ✓ Their ability to demonstrate scat singing.

RESOURCES

Teacher Resource Binder

Evaluation Master 8, *Evaluating Musical Expression*
Skill Builder 14, *Improvising Melodies*
Reference 16, *Expanding a Musical Vocabulary*

National Standards

1. Singing, alone and with others, a varied repertoire of music. **(a, b, c)**
3. Improvising melodies, variations and accompaniments. **(a, b, c)**

Buffalo Gals

OVERVIEW

Composer: Minstrel Song, arranged by Dan Krunnfusz

Text: Folk Song

Voicing: TBB

Key: G major, C major

Meter: 4/4

Form: ABA'B'CAB

Style: American Minstrel Song

Accompaniment: Piano

Programming: Thematic Programming, Festival, Honor Chorus, Americana

Vocal Ranges:

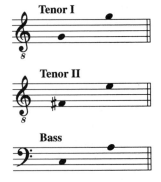

Tenor I

Tenor II

Bass

OBJECTIVES

After completing this lesson, students will be able to:

• Write music that incorporates rhythmic patterns in simple meter.

• Identify uses of music in American culture and history.

• Perform music representing the American heritage.

Have students review vocabulary in student lesson. Introduce terms found in the music. A complete glossary of terms is found on page 246 of the student book.

146

Buffalo Gals

Composer: Minstrel Song, arranged by Dan Krunnfusz

Text: Folk Song

Voicing: TTB

VOCABULARY

minstrel

swing rhythms

Focus

• Create rhythmic phrases using the swing style.

• Define *minstrel* and discuss its role in American music history.

• Perform music representing the American heritage.

🎲 **SKILL BUILDERS**

To learn more about swing rhythms, see Proficient Sight-Singing, *page 171.*

Getting Started

Have you ever heard the phrase "What's old is new again"? What does this mean to you? The song "Buffalo Gals" was written in 1844 and soon it became very popular. People thought it was new, but the roots of this song can be traced back to the old music halls of Germany. Others feel it may have its origins in the English singing game "Pray, Pretty Miss." So the new form of music was a combination of many old ideas in a new package!

◆ History and Culture

During the 1800s, a unique form of musical entertainment emerged in America. The **minstrel** was *a variety show consisting of comic songs, sentimental ballads, soft-shoe dancing and clogging, instrumental playing, comedy skits, sight gags and jokes.* By 1840 minstrel shows had become more numerous and more popular. They were the premier platform for American popular music in the nineteenth century. They also incorporated many of the rich musical traditions that were part of the African American culture at the time.

As the minstrel shows traveled from town to town, "Buffalo Gals" (for Buffalo, New York) became "New York Gals," "Charleston Gals" or "Alabama Gals," depending upon the location of the performance. Some of the well-known minstrel songs that are still sung today are "Oh! Susanna," "Camptown Races," "Turkey In The Straw," and, of course, "Buffalo Gals."

Proficient Sight-Singing

Sight-Singing the C Major Tonic and Dominant Chords, pages 34-35

Sight-Singing in G Major, pages 71–74

Reading Swing Rhythms, page 171

Teacher Resource Binder

Teaching Master 22, *Popular Music Today—My View*

Evaluation Master 8, *Evaluating Musical Expression*

Dalcroze 12, *Moving to the Beat and Beat Subdivisions*

Reference 16, *Expanding a Musical Vocabulary*

For additional resources, see TRB Table of Contents.

Links to Learning

◆ **Vocal**

This song is to be performed using **swing rhythms** (*rhythms in which the second eighth note of each beat is sung like the last third of a triplet, creating an uneven "swing" feel*). Read and perform the following rhythmic patterns to understand and experience the relationship between triplets and swing eighth note patterns.

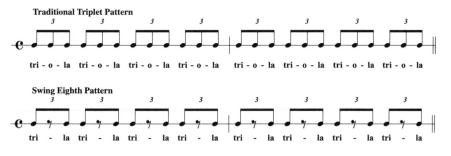

◆ **Artistic Expression**

In a small group, read and perform the following example, while keeping the beat steady and performing in a swing style.

Evaluation

Demonstrate how well you have learned the skills and concepts featured in the lesson "Buffalo Gals" by completing the following:

• Perform measures 29–32 using swing rhythms. Evaluate how well you were able to sing the eighth notes in an uneven, swing style.

• Define *minstrel*. Describe the elements of a minstrel show in nineteenth-century America.

RESOURCES

Proficient Tenor/Bass Rehearsal/Performance CD

CD 2:3 Voices

CD 2:4 Accompaniment Only

CD 3:14 Vocal Practice Track—Tenor I

CD 4:13 Vocal Practice Track—Tenor II

CD 5:7 Vocal Practice Track—Baritone

National Standards

1. Singing, alone and with others, a varied repertoire of music. **(a, c)**

4. Composing and arranging music within specific guidelines. **(a)**

8. Understanding relationships between music, the other arts, and disciplines outside the arts. **(b)**

LINKS TO LEARNING

Theory

The Theory section is designed to prepare students to:

• Develop an understanding of swing rhythms.

• Experience the relationship between triplets and swing eighth-note patterns.

Have students:

• Practice chanting the traditional triplet pattern.

• Chant the swing eighth pattern, feeling the steady pulse of the traditional triplet pattern.

• Divide into two groups. One group claps the traditional triplet pattern while the second group chants the swing eighth pattern. Switch roles.

Artistic Expression

The Artistic Expression section is designed to prepare students to perform standard notation in swing style.

Have students:

• Chant, tap or clap the example as written.

• Do it again, but this time chant, tap or clap in swing style.

• Discuss how swing style feels different from standard notation.

LESSON PLAN

Suggested Teaching Sequence and Performance Tips

1. Introduce

Direct students to:

- Read and discuss the information found in the Getting Started section on student page 146, including what was going on in the United States and elsewhere in the year 1844.

- Share what they know about minstrel shows that became so popular in the United States during the nineteenth century.

- Complete the Links to Learning exercises to gain a better understanding of swing rhythms.

Buffalo Gals

For TTB and Piano

Arranged by
DAN KRUNNFUSZ

Minstrel Song (1844)

Copyright © 2002 Walton Music Corporation
International Copyright Secured   Made in U.S.A. All Rights Reserved
www.waltonmusic.com

148   Proficient Tenor/Bass

TEACHER 2 TEACHER

The syncopated rhythms and light-hearted lyrics will help make this popular American minstrel song one that students will want to sing again and again. It may also be used for sight-singing practice since the rhythms are not too complex, and it is written in the keys of G and C. "Buffalo Gals" is a great song in which to showcase any young men's chorus.

Progress Checkpoints

Observe students' progress in:

✓ Their ability to identify events in American history.

✓ Their ability to understand and perform swing rhythms.

CURRICULUM CONNECTIONS

Technology in Music

Have students:

1. Identify technology used in music (computer, midi, mp3, CD, audio/video recordings, synthesizer, sound equipment, electronic sounds, and so forth).

2. Discuss what effect technology has on music.

3. Create a musical composition using a form of technology.

4. Perform a solo or small ensemble for the class incorporating technology.

2. Rehearse

Direct students to:

- Use solfège syllables to learn the Bass part in measures 1–12. Have all singers learn this part together.
- Ask students to find other occurrences of this passage in the music. *(Answer: measures 21–28 and 55–66)* Sing these passages as well.
- Add the Tenor parts in measures 1–12, 21–28 and 55–66. After all parts are secure on pitch and rhythms, add the words. Sing all patterns swing style.
- In sectional groupings, learn measures 12–20 and 29–36 on solfège syllables. Discover that these two sections are just the same except for the final measure.
- Sight-sing measures 55–end since most of the material is exactly the same as already learned.

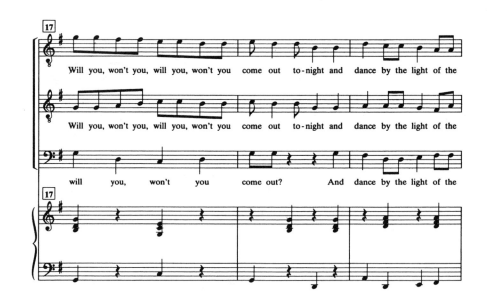

TEACHING STRATEGY

Music as Avocation

One school activity that has some of the characteristics of the early minstrel shows, is the musical variety show, or talent show. If your school periodically produces a variety show, this might be an avocation of interest to some students. Have students compare and contrast this avocational opportunity with others they might have already pursued. (Possible answers: Participation in a community chorus, a church or synagogue choir, or a community theater)

Observe students' progress in:

✓ Sight-singing in the key of G major.

✓ Locating passages in the music that are similar.

✓ Singing rhythms in a swing style.

ENRICHMENT

Improvisation

Some student may be reluctant to try improvisation. As a teacher, it is important to set up guidelines and to create a safe environment. Remind students that any effort is a worthy effort. Praise students often. Follow these steps to lead students to successful improvisation.

1. Play on a keyboard, guitar or some other instrument the I-IV-V-I chord progression. Play it several times until students become familiar with it.

2. Ask for volunteers to improvise a musical melody above the chord progression. Singers may use nonsense or scat syllables.

3. Have students analyze ways in which they can improve their skills in improvisation.

3. Refine

Direct students to:

- Focus on the middle section (measures 37–54) which is written in the key of C major. Sight-sing this section on solfège syllables. After pitches and rhythms are secure, add text.
- Sing the rhythms in measures 37–40 as straight eighth notes, but return to the swing rhythms in measure 41.
- Sing the entire song with the text. Identify sections that need additional practice.
- Perform again with the dynamic and tempo contrasts as indicated in the score.

MORE ABOUT...

Student Evaluation Process

You will find three different evaluation procedures in each lesson. The first is informal, and done by teacher observation at specific checkpoints during the lesson. The second, student self-evaluation, helps students reflect upon what learning has taken place, and self-assess where more work is necessary. Finally, the formal assessment requires each student to make a response or perform in a way that is individually measurable. By mixing techniques, you should be able to construct an objective grading system for students that has many components. Share your assessment plans with students so they will know the benchmarks of success.

Progress Checkpoints

Observe students' progress in:
✓ Their ability to sight-sing in the key of C major.
✓ Their ability to find like and unlike phrases in music.
✓ Distinguishing between straight and swing eighth notes.

Encourage your students to expore **music.glencoe.com**, the Web site for *Experiencing Choral Music*. You may wish to preview the rich content before directing your students online. Options available on the Web site include:

• Web Link Exercises
• Interactive Projects
• Audio Samples

ASSESSMENT

Informal Assessment

In this lesson, students showed the ability to:

- Understand and perform swing rhythms.
- Sight-sing in the key of G major.
- Sight-sing in the key of C major.
- Distinguish between straight and swing eighth notes.

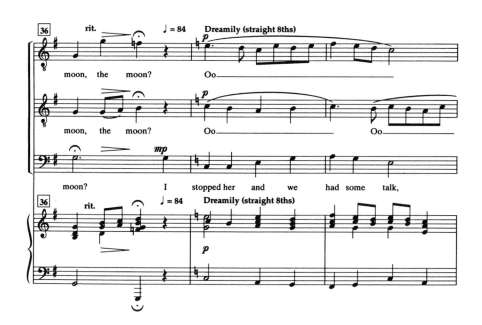

TEACHING STRATEGY

Music Elements of Style

The combination of musical elements determines the styles of a piece. Have students:

- Compile a list of musical elements that might affect style.
- Share the lists to compile one master list.
- Sing known songs, trying out different styles, and then try to describe the musical elements that are characteristic of that style. (Try salsa, operatic, Broadway, rock or lullaby styles for a start.)

Have students evaluate their individual performances based on the following:

- Accurate Rhythms
- Sight-singing Skills
- Swing Style
- Expression
- Intonation

Have each student rate his/her performance of this song in the areas above on a scale of 1–5, 5 being the best.

TEACHING STRATEGY
Composing Music

For students to experience composing, direct student to:

1. Select a meter (simple meter, compound meter, asymmetric meter).
2. Write a four-measure simple or complex rhythmic pattern in that meter.
3. Select a key (major, minor, pentatonic, modal).
4. Using the newly composed rhythmic pattern, write a melody based on the selected key.
5. Exchange compositions with a classmate. Check each other's work for rhythmic and melodic accuracy.
6. Make changes and corrections as necessary, and then read and perform the compositions for the class.

Individual and Group Performance Evaluation

To further measure growth of musical skills presented in this lesson, direct students to complete the Evaluation section on page 147.

- Individually or in small groups, have students sing measures 29–32. Ask the class to evaluate how well they were able to sing the eighth notes in an uneven, swing style.

- Direct students to write a description of a minstrel show in nineteenth-century America. Compare their answers with a classmate.

TEACHING STRATEGY

Sight-Singing

Have students identify strategies they can use to become better sight-singers:

- At first read only the rhythm, then add the pitch, then text.
- Read simple melodies and two parts before trying four.
- Practice a little every day, using new materials.
- Don't worry about making mistakes.
- When a mistake is disastrous, analyze what happened so it can be addressed, practiced, and improved.
- Challenge each other with support and good humor.
- Remember that sight-singing, like any skill, needs to be practiced to improve.

Choral Library *Buffalo Gals* **157**

EXTENSION

Creating a Chordal Accompaniment

Have students:
- Analyze the piano accompaniment for the piece, creating a skeleton of chord tones for each measure.
- Using resonator bells or handbells, play a chordal accompaniment by playing the chord tones once at the beginning of each measure.
- Adjust as necessary, and then add this accompaniment to the piece and piano accompaniment during the whole piece.
- Compose an introduction and coda for bells as well, using a short progression of chords from the piece.

TEACHING STRATEGY

Small-Ensemble Techniques

Divide the class into small groups and invite them to perform "Buffalo Gals" for each other. Ask the class to describe the performance techniques they observed such as singing with good intonation, blend and balance of parts, and energized singing in a swing style.

ENRICHMENT

Writing in the Key of G Major

To help students expand their music literacy, have them:

- In pairs, write the G major scale on a staff.
- Select one partner to point to the pitches randomly, first in stepwise order, then using some skips, creating melodic fragments or phrases. The other partner will sing the pitches, correcting mistakes using a pitched instrument for reference. Switch roles.

TEACHING STRATEGY

Swing Style

If students are not familiar with the swing style, have them:

- Listen to recordings of swing music.
- Move to swing music.
- Watch video footage of swing-style performance.
- Attend a dance-band performance that plays swing-style music.

come out to-night? Won't you come out to-night? Won't you come out to-night?

come out to-night? Won't you come out to-night? Won't you come out to - night?———

come out? Oh, won't you come out? Oh, won't you come out to-night? Oh, please, oh,

- Both listen for melodic phrases that might become part of a melody they could write for others to sight-sing.
- Analyze the thematic sections.
- Contrast the rhythms of the quarter notes against the dotted rhythms in the different parts. Be precise.

Will you, won't you, will you, won't you come out to-night and dance by the light of the

Will you, won't you, will you, won't you come out to-night and dance by the light of the

Will you, won't you come out? And dance by the light of the

Additional National Standards

The following National Standards are addressed through the Assessment, Extension, Enrichment and bottom-page activities:

5. Reading and notating music. **(a, b)**

7. Evaluating music and music performances. **(a, c)**

9. Understanding music in relation to history and culture. **(a)**

Come To The Music

Composer: Joseph Martin
Text: Joseph Martin
Voicing: TTBB

VOCABULARY

mixed meter
interval
perfect fifth
accent

SKILL BUILDERS

To learn more about mixed meter, see Proficient Sight-Singing, pages 107 and 166.

Focus

- Read and perform music that incorporates mixed meters.
- Perform the interval of a perfect fifth.
- Identify and describe the uses of music in society and culture.

Getting Started

"It has a good beat and you can dance to it." The famous Television show *American Bandstand* had a segment called "Rate a Record." Teenagers would listen to a new song and tell what would make the song a hit or a miss. In your opinion, what are the musical elements that make a piece of music interesting to the performer and to the listener? Text, melody, harmony and rhythm are just a few characteristics that make music interesting. Rhythmic intensity and variety are two elements found in "Come To The Music" that make it a hit.

◆ History and Culture

Composers sometimes use irregular rhythmic patterns to give music a driving energy. In "Come To The Music," composer Joseph Martin changes the meter from ⁶⁄₈ to ²⁄₄ to create a medieval dance-like quality. The concept of *using more than one time signature in a song* is called **mixed meter.**

Texas composer and pianist Joseph Martin has performed solo piano recitals and has been the featured artist with symphony orchestras across the United States and Mexico. Recognized throughout the United States for his many choral compositions, both sacred and secular, Mr. Martin has over 450 works in print. Lake Highlands School in Richardson, Texas, commissioned Mr. Martin to write "Come To The Music" for their performance at the Texas Music Educators Association convention in 2000.

RESOURCES

Proficient Sight-Singing

Teacher Resource Binder

Come To The Music

OVERVIEW

Composer: Joseph Martin
Text: Joseph Martin
Voicing: TTBB
Key: E minor/F minor
Meter: 6/8 and 2/4 and 4/4 and 2/8
Form: ABA'
Style: Contemporary American Anthem
Accompaniment: Piano with optional piccolo and percussion
Programming: Concert Opener, Processional, Festival

Vocal Ranges:

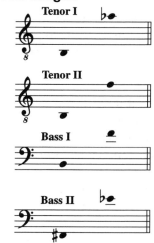

OBJECTIVES

After completing this lesson, students will be able to:

- Demonstrate in ensembles accurate rhythm while performing moderately easy to moderately difficult literature.
- Demonstrate independently, accurate intonation while performing moderately easy to moderately difficult literature.
- Relate music to society and culture.

VOCABULARY

Have students review vocabulary in student lesson. Introduce terms found in the music. A complete glossary of terms is found on page 246 of the student book.

LINKS TO LEARNING

Vocal

The Vocal section is designed to prepare students to sing the interval of the perfect fifth.

Have students:

- Sing the two-part exercise using solfège syllables.
- Sing the exercise using the text.
- Observe the dynamics when performing the exercise.

Theory

The Theory section is designed to prepare students to perform a rhythm pattern in mixed meter.

Have students:

- Chant the exercise counting numbers.
- Chant the exercise on numbers while observing the accents.
- Perform the exercise using the text and accents.

Links to Learning

◆ Vocal

An **interval** is *the distance between two pitches.* The somewhat hollow-sounding intervals of a fourth, fifth and octave of the scale are called "perfect." The interval of a **perfect fifth** *(two pitches that are five notes apart on the staff)* can be difficult to sing in tune. Practice singing and tuning the following example.

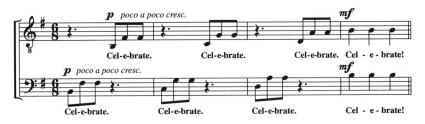

◆ Theory

In "Come To The Music," the time signature sometimes indicates to alternate between one measure of $\frac{6}{8}$ and one measure of $\frac{2}{4}$, creating mixed meter. Although the meter changes, the eighth note pulse remains constant. Read and perform the following rhythmic patterns. Chant the words in rhythm and observe the **accent** *(a note that is sung with extra force or stress)* markings.

Evaluation

Demonstrate how well you have learned the skills and concepts featured in the lesson "Come To The Music" by completing the following:

- Find two examples of mixed meter in "Come To The Music." To show your ability to sing in mixed meter, perform one of the examples for a classmate.
- With a classmate, test your ability to sing a perfect fifth. Sing a pitch. Have a classmate match the pitch and then sing a pitch that is a perfect fifth above. Check that the interval is sung accurately. Switch roles.

RESOURCES

Proficient Tenor/Bass Rehearsal/Performance CD

CD 2:5 Voices

CD 2:6 Accompaniment Only

CD 3:15 Vocal Practice Track—Tenor I

CD 4:14 Vocal Practice Track—Tenor II

CD 5:8 Vocal Practice Track—Bass I

CD 6:14 Vocal Practice Track—Bass II

National Standards

1. Singing, alone and with others, a varied repertoire of music. **(a, c)**

8. Understanding relationships between music, the other arts, and disciplines outside the arts. **(b)**

Commissioned by the Lake Highlands High School Men's Choir,
Michael O'Hern and Terry Berrier, Directors,
for their Texas Music Educators Association 2000 performance

Come To The Music

For TTBB and Piano with Optional Piccolo and Percussion*

Words and Music by
JOSEPH M. MARTIN

*Piccolo and Percussion parts found on pages 176–179.

Copyright © 2002, Malcolm Music
A Division of Shawnee Press, Inc.
International Copyright Secured All Rights Reserved
SOLE SELLING AGENT: SHAWNEE PRESS, INC., DELAWARE WATER GAP, PA 18327

Choral Library *Come To The Music* **163**

LESSON PLAN

Suggested Teaching Sequence and Performance Tips

1. Introduce

Direct students to:

- Read and discuss the information found in the Getting Started section on page 161.
- Practice singing the interval of a perfect fifth as found in the Vocal section on page 162.
- Practice counting the rhythm in mixed meters as found in the Theory section on page 162. Locate where these meters first appear in the score. *(measure 5)*

TEACHER 2 TEACHER

The mixed meters and interesting rhythmic patterns in this piece are the most challenging aspect of "Come To The Music." The rhythm and style give this piece a medieval dance quality. Add the optional instruments for added excitement.

TEACHING STRATEGY

Individual Performance Assessment

To further measure growth of musical skills presented in this lesson, ask students to record the ensemble performance while each student sings his/her own part into a hand-held recorder. Upon playback of the performance, ask students to carefully listen and circle places in the score that need improvement. Have students compile a list of individual problem spots to refine in their own practice.

2. Rehearse

Direct students to:

- Practice with the opening section, which appears in similar form five times in this song (measures 5–12, 13–20, 38–45, 79–86, and 87–94). Work for rhythmic accuracy by chanting the text before adding pitches.
- Practice the contrasting sections (measures 21–37, 57–69, 71–78, 95–108) by chanting the words in rhythm, paying particular attention to the accents.
- Chant again, adding the dynamic contrasts indicated.
- Sing the pitches, adding the accents and dynamics.
- Practice the transitions from one section to the next.

MORE ABOUT...

Composer Joseph Martin

Joseph Martin is recognized internationally for his sacred choral compositions and piano recital skills. He won the Nina Plant Wideman Competition and performed with the Guadalajara Symphony Orchestra; one solo recital in Ex-convento del Carman was broadcast nationally. In addition to his compositional skills, he is Director of Church Music Marketing Development with Shawnee Press, Inc. He continues to perform throughout the country and participate in music conferences, festivals and workshops.

Progress Checkpoints

Observe students' progress in:

✓ Singing with rhythmic accuracy and precision. Remind students to keep the eighth note constant. By keeping a steady eighth-note pulse, the rhythms should become easier to perform.

✓ Singing perfect fifths in tune.

✓ Performing appropriate dynamics and tempos.

166   Proficient Tenor/Bass

TEACHING STRATEGY

6/8 Meter

At this level, 6/8 meter should be quite familiar to students; however, they may need experience improvising in 6/8. Have students echo as you clap improvised rhythmic patterns in 6/8 meter, using the basic rhythms of the meter and shaping phrases with repetition and contrast. (Lead four short patterns that, when clapped in sequence, create a complete phrase. The students echo each pattern, and then clap back all four in sequence from memory.)

3. Refine

Direct students to:

- Practice word stress on the word *celebrate*. Since the middle syllable is generally on a higher pitch, it is easy to emphasize the wrong syllable. The natural instinct is to perform cel-LE-brate. Practice the word as CEL-le-brate.

- Work for tall vowel sounds on "alleluia" which should be sung as All-leh-loo-yah.

- Accents are key when performing this piece. Practice the accents in small and large groups.

- Keep the diction crisp and clear at all times. If the diction is not clear, ask the students to shout the words on a whisper, exaggerating the movement of the mouth.

- Whenever possible, use the piccolo and percussion instruments. They will add to the medieval flavor of the song.

TEACHING STRATEGY

Performance Techniques

Have students:

1. Identify appropriate performance techniques to be used in the performance of this song.

2. Either in small ensembles or with the entire choir (large ensemble), perform the song exhibiting these performance techniques.

3. Describe the performance techniques experienced during the performance.

4. Critique the performance based on the observed performance techniques.

5. Repeat this process often in both informal and formal concert settings.

Progress Checkpoints

Observe students' progress in:

✓ Performing the dynamic contrasts indicated in the music which provides energy and excitement.

✓ Performing the transitions with smooth shifts in rhythm and mood.

✓ Observing all accent marks.

168 Proficient Tenor/Bass

CURRICULUM CONNECTIONS

Technology in Music

Have students:

1. Identify technology used in music (computer, midi, mp3, CD, audio/video recordings, synthesizer, sound equipment, electronic sounds, and so forth).
2. Discuss what effect technology has on music.
3. Create a musical composition using a form of technology.
4. Perform a solo or small ensemble for the class incorporating technology.

Informal Assessment

In this lesson, students showed the ability to:

- Count and perform simple and complex rhythms and meters.
- Use facial expression to communicate the mood and message of the text.
- Apply dynamics and accents as indicated in the score.

TEACHING STRATEGY

Changing Meters

Have students:

- Walk about the room with the eighth-note pulse rhythm in their feet, with no accents.
- Add accents with claps and leaning for 3/4 meter, emphasizing the first, third, and fifth steps of each six-step pattern.
- Change to accents for 6/8 meter, emphasizing the first and fourth steps.
- Now change to accents for 2/4 meter, emphasizing the first and third steps of each four-step pattern.
- Create combination of meters to walk.

Have students evaluate their individual performances based on the following:

- Diction
- Tall Vowels
- Expressive Singing
- Intonation
- Accurate Rhythms

Have each student rate his/her performance of this song in the areas above on a scale of 1–5, 5 being the best.

170   Proficient Tenor/Bass

MUSIC LITERACY

To help students expand their music literacy, have them:

- Conduct the changing meters, feeling the eighth-note unit of measure.
- Recognize that when the meter is challenging, it is necessary to work to get the rhythm accurate. At the same time, the piece only works musically if the musical phrases are shaped.
- Identify the musical phrases, using the text to help when there are differences of opinion.
- Review strategies for shaping phrases.
- Sing the piece, focusing on shaping phrases.

Individual and Group Performance Evaluation

To further measure growth of musical skills presented in this lesson, direct students to complete the Evaluation section on page 162.

- After finding two examples of mixed meter in "Come To The Music," sing those measures for a classmate. Find two other examples and switch roles.

- After singing a perfect fifth above a pitch sung by a classmate, evaluate the performance by asking, "Was the higher pitch in tune? If not, how could it be improved?" Check the results with a piano and then switch roles.

CONNECTING THE ARTS

Processes in the Arts

Have students:

1. Find examples of artwork or art forms from the Contemporary period, describing how they exhibit the characteristics of the period. (Choose from visual art, architecture, dance, drama, poetry or literature.)

2. Discuss how the processes used in the other areas are the same and different from music, taking into consideration the roles of artists, performers and audience.

3. Find other examples from the same art category, but from a different style, period or culture.

4. Discuss similarities and differences between the examples.

EXTENSION

Conducting

Demonstrate the conducting patterns of 6/8, 2/4, 4/4 and 2/8. Practice these patterns together as a group. Next, ask the students to conduct the first section of "Come to the Music." Then have students conduct the contrasting sections. Ask for volunteers to conduct various sections of the music. As an added challenge, suggest that a student conduct the entire piece as the choir performs it.

172   Proficient Tenor/Bass

ASSESSMENT

Creating an Assessment Rubric

Have students:

1. Discuss the characteristics of a desirable performance of this piece, using all their knowledge of performance techniques.
2. Identify the criteria by which they think an adjudicator might assess the performance of this piece.
3. For each criterion, decide what characteristics will comprise an adequate, good, very good and excellent performance.
4. Create a rubric chart.
5. Use the rubric to assess quartets or small ensembles performing all or part of this song.

ENRICHMENT

Composing Music

When composing music, a writer must take into consideration both melody and rhythm. Sometimes a composer will start with a rhythmic idea, while at other times he or she will start with a melody. Direct students to:

1. Select a meter:
   - simple meter (2/4, 2/4, 4/4)
   - compound meter (6/9, 9/8, 3/8)
   - asymmetric meter (5/8, 7/8)
2. Write a four-measure simple or complex rhythmic pattern in that meter.
3. Select a key (major, minor, pentatonic, modal).
4. Using the newly composed rhythmic pattern, write a melody based on the selected key.
5. Exchange compositions with a classmate. Check each other's work for rhythmic and melodic accuracy.
6. Make changes and corrections as necessary.
7. Perform their compositions for the class.

MORE ABOUT...

Compare and Contrast

Listen to recordings of other compositions by Joseph Martin (e.g., "The Awakening" and "Toccata of Praise") and compare similarities and differences to "Come To The Music."

Additional National Standards

The following National Standards are addressed through the Assessment, Extension, Enrichment and bottom-page activities:

5. Reading and notating music. **(b)**

6. Listening to, analyzing, and describing music. **(a)**

7. Evaluating music and music performances. **(b)**

Encourage your students to expore **music.glencoe.com**, the Web site for *Experiencing Choral Music.* You may wish to preview the rich content before directing your students online. Options available on the Web site include:

- Web Link Exercises
- Interactive Projects
- Audio Samples

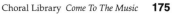

TEACHING STRATEGY

Performing to a Common Beat and Watching the Conductor

Have students:

- Each feel his or her pulse and pat it.
- Listen to all the pulses in the room, and slowly come to a common pulse, which they all pat very softly.
- Stop patting and sing "Come To The Music" without a conductor, staying exactly together.
- Sing the same piece with you conducting, with them following exactly.
- Discuss the role of the conductor in keeping a group together, and the importance of watching the conductor.

Commissioned by the Lake Highlands High School Men's Choir,
Michael O'Hern and Terry Berrier, Directors,
for their Texas Music Educators Association 2000 performance

Come To The Music

PICCOLO

Words and Music by
JOSEPH M. MARTIN

Copyright © 2002, Malcolm Music
A Division of Shawnee Press, Inc.
International Copyright Secured   All Rights Reserved
SOLE SELLING AGENT: SHAWNEE PRESS, INC., DELAWARE WATER GAP, PA 18327

176   Proficient Tenor/Bass

TEACHING STRATEGY

Creating an Assessment Rubric for "Come To The Music"

Have students:

- Discuss the characteristics of a desirable performance of this piece, using all their knowledge of performance.
- Identify the criteria by which they think an adjudicator might assess the performance of the piece.
- For each criterion, decide what characteristics will comprise an adequate, good, very good, and excellent performance.
- Create a rubric chart and reproduce it for each student.
- Use the rubric to assess quartets or double quartets performing all or part of "Come To The Music."

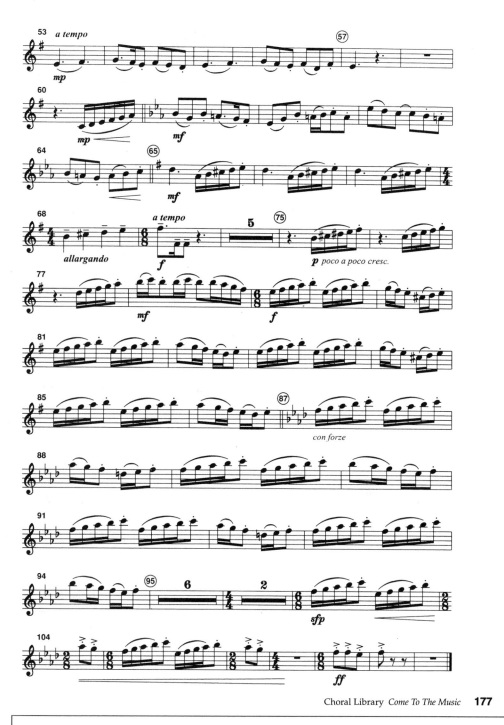

REHEARSAL STRATEGY

Teaching in a "Whole-Parts-Whole" Sequence

To help students gain a better understanding of each piece, direct them to:

- Sing through the entire piece at the beginning of each rehearsal segment. Take note of which sections need the most work.

- Rehearse the individual parts of the song based on your evaluation of the read-through performance.

- Perform the entire piece again to end the rehearsal segment. Don't stop. Remember that it is possible to rehearse and improve the choir even while they are singing.

Commissioned by the Lake Highlands High School Men's Choir,
Michael O'Hern and Terry Berrier, Directors,
for their Texas Music Educators Association 2000 performance

Come To The Music

PERCUSSION

Words and Music by
JOSEPH M. MARTIN

Copyright © 2002, Malcolm Music
A Division of Shawnee Press, Inc.
International Copyright Secured   All Rights Reserved
SOLE SELLING AGENT: SHAWNEE PRESS, INC., DELAWARE WATER GAP, PA 18327

178   Proficient Tenor/Bass

CONNECTING THE ARTS

Phrasing in the Arts

Have students:

- Discuss how the phrase is represented in arts other than music—dance, drama, visual art or poetry.
- Watch, look at, listen to, or read in language or visual arts to experience how the phrase is managed.
- Discuss with artists how they do or do not use the concept of phrasing.
- Discuss with performers whether and how they consider phrasing in their work.
- Share the information collected and construct a presentation based on their finding entitled "Phrasing in the Arts," or a title of their own choosing.

MORE ABOUT...

Breathing

Both deep breaths and the control of the breath allow students to interpret music appropriately. There are several images that may work for students to achieve a deep breath. Have students:

- Take a "cool sip" of air through an imaginary straw, feeling the lungs fill deeply.
- Hold hands around the waist gently, fingertips pointed toward the backbone, and then push them out as the breath is taken. Expand back, sides and front to achieve the maximum breath support.
- Imagine a "belt of noses" around the waist, and breathe in through the noses to achieve a deep breath.

Do You Hear The People Sing?

OVERVIEW

Composer: Claude-Michel Schönberg, arranged by Ed Lojeski

Text: Herbert Kretzmer, additional text by Alain Boublil and Jean-Marc Natel

Voicing: TTBB

Key: E♭ major, B♭ major

Meter: 4/4

Form: ABA'B'A'A'Coda

Style: Broadway

Accompaniment: Piano

Programming: Concert, Festival, Concert Closer

Vocal Ranges:

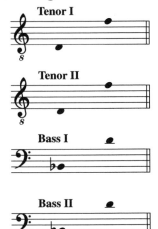

OBJECTIVES

After completing this lesson, students will be able to:

• Demonstrate in ensembles accurate rhythm while performing.

• Relate music to history and culture.

VOCABULARY

Have students review vocabulary in student lesson. Introduce terms found in the music. A complete glossary of terms is found on page 246 of the student book.

Do You Hear The People Sing?

Composer: Claude-Michel Schönberg, arranged by Ed Lojeski
Text: Herbert Kretzmer, additional text by Alain Boublil and Jean-Marc Natel
Voicing: TTBB

VOCABULARY

musical

triplet

Focus

• Notate and perform triplets.

• Relate music to history and culture.

• Perform music representing the American musical theater.

Getting Started

Will you join in our crusade?

Who will be strong and fight with me?

Somewhere beyond the barricade

Is there a world you long to see?

All this for a loaf of bread? In the **musical** *(a play or film in which the story is expressed through speaking, acting, singing and dancing)* Les Misérables, a stolen loaf of bread sets in motion a series of events surrounding the French Revolution. The young revolutionaries believe that if they band together and fight injustice, they will have the power to change the world. Do you know of other historical personalities who have fought for social justice?

◆ **History and Culture**

The popular musical *Les Misérables* is based on the epic novel of the same name by French author Victor Hugo (1802–1885). The novel was published in 1862, and people lined up at bookstores in Paris to buy one of the 48,000 copies available for sale on the first day of publication. In the story, the main character, Jean Valjean, is released on parole after 19 years in prison. Spanning two decades, *Les Misérables* is a story of love and courage set during the post-revolutionary chaos of nineteenth-century France. The musical debuted in Paris in 1980 and opened in New York in 1987. In the musical, "Do You Hear The People Sing?" is sung by the young revolutionaries.

SPOTLIGHT

To learn more about musical theater, see page 209.

RESOURCES

Proficient Sight-Singing

Teacher Resource Binder

Links to Learning

◆ **Theory**

Perform the following example that includes **triplet** (*three notes that are played in the space of two notes of equal value*) rhythms. Make a clear distinction between the dotted eighth and sixteenth note patterns and the triplets.

◆ **Artistic Expression**

Working in a group of four or more singers, discuss the theme of this song. What could have led these students to the point of revolt? How would you feel if you were in their position? What characteristics in the music convey these feelings? Share your ideas with another group. How might this information strengthen your performance of "Do You Hear The People Sing?"

Evaluation

Demonstrate how well you have learned the skills and concepts featured in the lesson "Do You Hear the People Sing?" by completing the following:

- Compose a four-measure rhythmic pattern that includes dotted eighth and sixteenth note patterns and triplets. Notate your pattern on staff paper or computer. Check your work for accurate rhythms and notation.

- Write a short essay describing the relationship between the song "Do You Hear The People Sing?" and the historical events of the story. Share your ideas with others.

- Perform expressively a varied repertoire of music representing styles from diverse cultures.

LINKS TO LEARNING

Theory

The Theory section is designed to prepare students to perform a rhythm pattern that includes triplets.

Have students:

- Chant the rhythm using a counting system.
- Perform the exercise by clapping the rhythms.

Artistic Expression

The Artistic Expression section is designed to prepare students to convey the message of the lyrics.

Have students:

- Discuss the lyrics with a group of four or more students.
- Relate the song to their personal convictions.
- Share their thoughts with another group.

RESOURCES

Proficient Tenor/Bass Rehearsal/Performance CD

CD 2:7 Voices

CD 2:8 Accompaniment Only

CD 3:16 Vocal Practice Track—Tenor I

CD 4:15 Vocal Practice Track—Tenor II

CD 5:9 Vocal Practice Track—Baritone

CD 6:15 Vocal Practice Track—Bass

National Standards

1. Singing, alone and with others, a varied repertoire of music. **(a, c)**
8. Understanding relationships between music, the other arts, and disciplines outside the arts. **(b)**

LESSON PLAN

Suggested Teaching Sequence and Performance Tips

1. Introduce

Direct students to:

- Read and discuss the information found in the Getting Started section on page 180.

- Practice the rhythm exercise found in the Theory section on page 181. Find similar rhythms in the score.

- Review and discuss the lyrics as described in the Artistic Expression section on page 181.

Do You Hear The People Sing?

From LES MISÉRABLES

For TTBB and Piano

Arranged by
ED LOJESKI

Music by CLAUDE-MICHEL SCHÖNBERG
Lyrics by HERBERT KRETZMER
Original Text by ALAIN BOUBLIL
and JEAN-MARC NATEL

Music and Lyrics Copyright © 1980 by Editions Musicales Alain Boublil
English Lyrics Copyright © 1986 by Alain Boublil Music Ltd. (ASCAP)
This edition Copyright © 1998 by Alain Boublil Music Ltd. (ASCAP)
Mechanical and Publication Rights for the U.S.A. Administered by Alain Boublil Music Ltd. (ASCAP)
c/o Stephen Tenebaum & Co., Inc., 1775 Broadway, Suite 708, New York, NY 10019, Tel. (212) 246-7204, Fax (212) 246-7217
International Copyright Secured   All Rights Reserved   This music is copyright   Photocopying is illegal
All Performance Rights Restricted

*This arrangement is for concert use only. The use of costumes, choreography or other elements
that evoke the story or characters of this musical work is prohibited.*

182   Proficient Tenor/Bass

TEACHER2TEACHER

This dramatic piece offers much opportunity for the choir to perform a song about an important event in history. It begins with three inspiring solos and builds from there. The students should be engaged both musically and personally when singing "Do You Hear The People Sing?"

mu - sic of a peo - ple___ who will not be slaves a - gain! When the

beat - ing of your heart___ ech - oes the beat-ing___ of the drums, there is a

Tenor Solo

life a - bout to start when to - mor - row comes. Will you

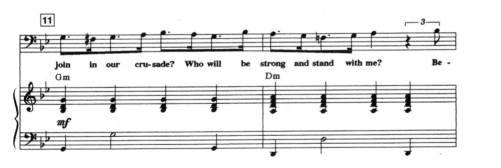

11

join in our cru-sade? Who will be strong and stand with me? Be -

Gm   Dm

Choral Library Do You Hear The People Sing? **183**

Progress Checkpoints

Observe students' progress in:

✓ Their ability to perform a rhythm including dotted eighths and sixteenth notes and triplets.

✓ Their ability to relate to a song about a revolution.

ASSESSMENT

Evaluating the Quality of a Performance

Have students:

1. Watch a video or listen to an audio recording of this piece as performed by the choir.

2. Compare this performance to exemplary models such as other recordings or other live performances of the piece.

3. Develop constructive suggestions for improvement based on the comparison.

2. Rehearse

Direct students to:

- Rehearse measures 2–10 with all Basses, paying attention to accurate intonation. When pitches are secure, ask for volunteers to sing this section as a solo.

- Rehearse measures 10–14 with all Tenors. When pitches are secure, ask for volunteers to sing this section as a solo.

- Rehearse measures 14–16 with all Baritones. When pitches are secure, ask for volunteers to sing this section as a solo. Sing measures 2–16 with soloists.

- Rehearse measures 16–46 in vocal sections and then combine once pitches and rhythms are secure. Notice the similarity in the music (measures 16–24 with 31–38 and 38–44; 24–30 with 10–16).

- Focus on any problem spots and drill until secure.

- Sing the entire piece, once all parts and secure.

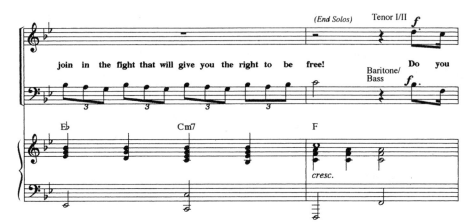

Online

Encourage your students to expore **music.glencoe.com**, the Web site for *Experiencing Choral Music*. You may wish to preview the rich content before directing your students online. Options available on the Web site include:

- Web Link Exercises
- Interactive Projects
- Audio Samples

Progress Checkpoints

Observe students' progress in:

✓ Their ability to read all rhythms correctly.

✓ Their ability to sing all pitches accurately and in tune.

✓ Their use of clear diction.

3. Refine

Direct students to:

- Go to the beginning and sing the song again, focusing on all dynamic, expressive and tempo markings.

- Show a contrast between tempo established at the beginning and the slower, even more dramatic tempo beginning at measure 39.

MORE ABOUT...

Arranger Ed Lojeski

Ed Lojeski is acknowledged as one of the finest choral arrangers/directors in the business today. Mr. Lojeski has served as an accompanist and musical consultant for movie productions such as *Where The Boys Are, The Unsinkable Molly Brown, Hello Dolly* and *Shaft* and on TV films for *Mannix, Medical Center, Gunsmoke* and *Mystery Movie of the Week.* Mr. Lojeski has also written shows for Robert Goulet, Trini Lopez, The Nicholas Brothers and George Shearing. He has served a pianist-conductor and/or vocal coach for Elvis Presley, Johnny Mathis, Kathryn Grayson, The Lettermen, Tony Martin, Cyd Charisse, Charles Nelson Reilly and Karen Morrow. Choral groups under his direction have appeared on television and in the Hollywood Bowl.

join in our cru-sade? Who will be strong and stand with me? Some-where be-

B♭ **B♭/D** **E♭** **B♭** **B♭/A**

f

yond the bar-ri-cade is there a world you long to see? Do you

Gm **C** **Fsus** **F** **F/A**

hear the peo-ple sing, say do you hear the dis-tant drums? It is the

B♭ **B♭/D** **E♭** **B♭** **F/A**

Observe students' progress in:

✓ Their correct use of dynamics and expression.

✓ Performing with an audible contrast between tempos.

CURRICULUM CONNECTIONS

Dramatic Reading

Have students:

• Choose a dramatic poem from English class or a famous speech from history.

• Discuss and identify how the work with vowels in this lesson might relate to these pieces of literature.

• Practice and recite their piece, focusing on good vowel production and clear diction.

ASSESSMENT

Informal Assessment

In this lesson, students showed the ability to:

- Perform rhythms accurately including triplets.
- Identify and describe a piece about revolution.
- Describe and perform music from a Broadway musical.

Student Self-Assessment

Have students evaluate their individual performances based on the following:

- Diction
- Expressive Singing
- Phrasing
- Accurate Rhythms
- Intonation

Have each student rate his/her performance of this song in the areas above on a scale of 1–5, 5 being the best.

188   Proficient Tenor/Bass

CAREERS IN MUSIC
Music as Avocation

One school activity that helps develop students' stage presence is participation in musical theater. If your school periodically stages plays or musicals (or if there is a community theater that accepts volunteers), this might be an avocation of interest to some students. Explain that a role in the musical theatre or a play can be varied. It can be as simple as being a member of the background chorus or "crowd scene" to playing the lead role and learning numerous lines and solo numbers. Have students compare and contrast this avocational opportunity with others they might have already pursued.

Additional National Standards

The following National Standards are addressed through the Assessment, Extension, Enrichment and bottom-page activities:

4. Composing and arranging music within specified guidelines. **(a)**

6. Listening to, analyzing and describing music. **(b)**

7. Evaluate music and music performances. **(b)**

Individual and Group Performance Evaluation

To further measure growth of musical skills presented in this lesson, direct students to complete the Evaluation section on page 181.

- After notating a four-measure rhythmic pattern on staff paper or the computer, have the rhythm performed by a classmate. Switch roles and then perform the rhythms one after the other.

- After writing a short essay on the historical events that relate to "Do You Hear The People Sing?" share it with other students. Read several essays for the choir possibly selecting a few to be read before a performance of the song at your next concert.

EXTENSION

Solos

Students should be given many opportunities to perform solos. This can be done as part of the rehearsal process or ultimately for a performance. If there are solo and ensemble festivals nearby, plan a trip to one. Initially it can be as observers. Ultimately it should afford as many students as are interested the chance to perform a solo for evaluation and critique.

Honey-Little 'Lize Medley

OVERVIEW

Composer: Harry Freeman, arranged by Floyd Connett
Text: Harry Freeman and Traditional
Voicing: TTBB
Key: B♭ major
Meter: 4/4
Form: Medley
Style: Barbershop
Accompaniment: A cappella
Programming: Concert

Vocal Ranges:

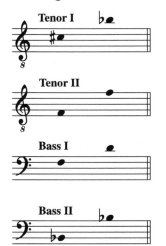

OBJECTIVES

After completing this lesson, students will be able to:

- Demonstrate accurate intonation while performing.
- Perform music in the key of B♭ major.
- Perform music representing the American heritage.

VOCABULARY

Have students review vocabulary in student lesson. Introduce terms found in the music. A complete glossary of terms is found on page 246 of the student book.

Honey-Little 'Lize Medley

Composer: Harry Freeman and Traditional, Arranged by Floyd Connett
Text: Harry Freeman and Traditional
Voicing: TTBB

VOCABULARY

barbershop singing
avocation
tag

Focus

- Sing with accurate intonation.
- Read and perform music notation in the key of B♭ major.
- Perform music representing our American heritage.

Getting Started

What do the Broadway musicals *The Unsinkable Molly Brown, The Music Man,* and *Annie Get Your Gun* have in common? Each of these famous productions features a barbershop quartet. **Barbershop singing** (*an original American style of a cappella singing in four-part harmony, usually four singers of the same gender*) is one of the oldest traditions of American singing. Many men and women sing in barbershop choruses as an **avocation** (*not related to a job or career*). When a barbershop quartet or chorus locks into a chord, both singers and listeners are treated to a great sensation.

⬛ SPOTLIGHT

To learn more about careers in music, see page 193.

◆ History and Culture

Barbershop music is a uniquely American folk art. Barbershop singing flourished in the early twentieth century in the United States and was actually sung in barbershops, on street corners, at social functions and in parlors. It was sometimes called "curbstone" harmony.

Barbershop singing evolved in much the same way as other forms of vocal music. These were songs characterized by sentimental lyrics and uncomplicated melodies that could be harmonized with a variety of four-part chords. The voice parts in barbershop music are still called by their traditional names— Tenor, Lead, Baritone, Bass—whether referring to men or women's vocal groups. One of the distinctive qualities of barbershop harmony is that the melody, sung by the Lead voice, is voiced below the Tenor harmony. The barbershop harmony of today is a highly stylized art form requiring a high degree of singing skill.

RESOURCES

Proficient Sight-Singing
Sight-Singing in B♭ Major, pages 90–93

Teacher Resource Binder
Teaching Master 26, *Barbershop Characters!*

Evaluation Master 2, *Analyzing Intonation*

Evaluation Master 16, *Performance Evaluation: Part-Singing*

Reference 10, *Career: Comparing Performance Opportunities*

For additional resources, see TRB Table of Contents.

Links to Learning

◆ **Theory**

This song is written in B♭ major and is based on the B♭ major scale. To locate B♭ on the keyboard, find a set of three black keys. B♭ is the black key on the right. The B♭ scale consists of the notes B♭, C, D, E♭, F, G, A, B♭. Play the B♭ major scale.

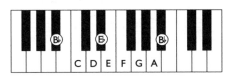

Sing the B♭ major scale.

◆ **Artistic Expression**

Every barbershop song contains a **tag** (*the ending of a barbershop song, usually the last four to eight bars, and often considered the best chords in the song*). Find the tag in the music (measures 17–18). Sing the tag and hold each chord until it is completely in tune.

Evaluation

Demonstrate how well you have learned the skills and concepts featured in the lesson "Honey-Little 'Lize Medley" by completing the following:

- In a quartet with one singer on a part, sing the tag ending (measures 17–18). Evaluate each group's ability to sing the tag in tune.

- Using solfège syllables, sing your part in measures 1–4 to demonstrate how well you can read music notation in the key of B♭ major. Evaluate how well you did.

Theory

The Theory section is designed to prepare students to sing and play the B♭ major scale.

Have students use the keyboard as a guide and play and sing the scale.

Artistic Expression

The Artistic Expression section is designed to prepare students to sing the tag in the medley.

Have students sing the tag, making sure each chord is perfectly in tune.

RESOURCES

Proficient Tenor/Bass Rehearsal/Performance CD

CD 2:9 Voices

CD 2:10 Accompaniment Only

CD 3:17 Vocal Practice Track—Tenor I

CD 4:16 Vocal Practice Track—Tenor II

CD 5:10 Vocal Practice Track—Baritone

CD 6:16 Vocal Practice Track—Bass

National Standards

1. Singing, alone and with others, a varied repertoire of music. **(a, b, c)**

5. Reading and notating music. **(a)**

7. Evaluating music and music performances. **(a, b)**

9. Understanding music in relation to history and culture. **(b)**

Honey-Little 'Lize Medley

For TTBB, a cappella

Arranged by
FLOYD CONNETT

Words and Music to "Honey" by
HARRY FREEMAN
"Little 'Lize" Traditional

LESSON PLAN

Suggested Teaching Sequence and Performance Tips

Direct students to:

- Read and discuss the information found in the Getting Started section on student page 190.
- Practice the example in the Vocal section.
- Sing the song using your preferred method of sight-singing.
- Locate each cadence and practice singing these in tune and with good balance.
- Bring out the melody at all times. Make sure they know which part has the melody at all times.
- Listen for the overtones produced when chords are totally locked in, encouraging the choir to work toward that goal of producing the overtones.

Progress Checkpoints

Observe students' progress in:

- ✓ Their ability to sight-sing with accurate pitch.
- ✓ Their ability to sing each cadence in tune.
- ✓ Their awareness of where the melody is being sung
- ✓ Their ability to produce overtones.

ASSESSMENT

Develop a scale for student self-assessment and complete the evaluation section on page 191 for further assessment.

© 1959 SPEBSQSA, Inc.
6315 3rd Avenue, Kenosha, WI 53143

192 Proficient Tenor/Bass

TEACHER 2 TEACHER

Barbershop music is a great style of music for teaching intonation and blend. Take the time to explain the history and tradition of barbershop music. This song is sure to be a favorite of your singers and your audience.

SPOTLIGHT

Careers In Music

Music Industry

The music industry provides career opportunities that encompass the area of business as well as music. This article will focus on music publishing, retail sales and instrumental sales.

Music publishing involves the process of finding music to publish, preparing the music for print (editing and proofreading), marketing and distributing the music for sales, and supporting the composers for their contribution. The skills required for this type of job may vary greatly. On the business side of the company, training in business, accounting, marketing, advertising and sales would be necessary. The ability to communicate, both in writing and orally, is vital in business. On the editorial side, there are job opportunities as an editors, proofreaders, graphic designers and music engravers. Some of these jobs require a music background, as well as writing skills and specific computer skills. Quite often, there will be on-the-job training to learn the mechanical techniques and specialized software systems used at the company.

Music retail sales requires music experience or training specific to the area of sales. Music stores may feature different instruments, pianos, vocal music, textbooks or accessories. Anyone considering a career in instrumental sales should have a working knowledge of the instruments and be able to demonstrate on the instrument for the customer. The same is true for the other area of sales—one must have a working knowledge of the item being sold. Another job opportunity in music retail sales is the store manager, who oversees the entire operation of the store. This would require skills in business, management and inventory control. It would also require the hiring and training of new employees. Anyone interested in this field should have a background in business and a working knowledge of music.

An instrument sales representative is someone who represents an instrument manufacturing company. While the position requires skills in sales, it is also important to have an in-depth knowledge of the instrument, skill in playing the instrument and a passion for the instrument or music in general. The salesperson will most likely be required to work in the field. This involves hard work and possibly time away from home. In addition to music training, a sales representative must also have skills in sales, accounting and bookkeeping.

Spotlight *Careers in Music* **193**

RESOURCES

Teacher Resource Binder

Reference 9, *Career: Music Education*
Reference 10, *Career: Comparing Performance Opportunities*

National Standards

8. Understanding relationship between music, the other arts, and disciplines outside the arts. **(b)**

9. Understanding music in relation to history and culture. **(c)**

CAREERS IN MUSIC

Objective

- Identify and describe music-related career opportunities.
- Define the relationship of the processes of other subjects and those of music.

Suggested Teaching Sequence

Direct students to:

- Read the Spotlight On Careers in Music on page 193 and identify the career opportunities in the music industry.
- Divide into small groups and make a list of as many different career opportunities available in the music business or industry. Share the list with the rest of the class.
- Discuss the training requirements needed to enter a career in music business.
- Compare and contrast a career in music business versus a career in nonmusical business. Include training, job market, salary, specialized skills, and so forth.
- Search the Internet or research the library to find other job opportunities in the field of music.

Progress Checkpoints

Observe students' progress in:

✓ Their ability to identify what is meant by the music industry.

✓ Their ability to describe the training and job opportunities available in the music industry.

Kalinka

OVERVIEW

Composer: Russian Folk Song, arranged by Stan Engebretson
Text: Russian
Voicing: TTBB
Key: G minor
Meter: 2/4 and 3/4
Form: AABB¹AAABB¹AAA¹
Style: Russian Folk Song
Accompaniment: Piano
Programming: International Folk, Festival, Contest

Vocal Ranges:

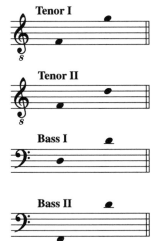

OBJECTIVES

After completing this lesson, students will be able to:

• Define concepts of musical performances using standard terminology.

• Perform expressively from notation a varied repertoire of music representing styles from diverse cultures.

VOCABULARY

Have students review vocabulary in student lesson. Introduce terms found in the music. A complete glossary of terms is found on page 246 of the student book.

194

Kalinka

Composer: Russian Folk Song, arranged by Stan Engebretson
Text: Russian
Voicing: TTBB

VOCABULARY

folk song
accelerando
crescendo
piu mosso
meno mosso

Focus

• Define *accelerando* and *crescendo*.

• Perform music representing the Russian culture.

 SPOTLIGHT

To learn more about diction, see page 201.

Getting Started

What do these things have in common?

• hand-painted Easter eggs

• matryoshka nesting dolls

• Cossack dances

• *Peter and the Wolf*

They are all a part of Russian heritage. Russia is a country with a rich folk tradition in the arts. This tradition also includes a great amount of expressive folk music that is filled with drama and emotion. The folk song "Kalinka" is a wonderful example of this proud heritage. Part of the charm of singing "Kalinka" is the use of the Russian language. This **folk song** *(a song that has been passed down by word of mouth from generation to generation)* depicts a winter scene where a young man is singing of his love for his sweetheart, asking the "snowball" trees (trees laden with snow) to bring her back.

◆ History and Culture

One distinctive feature of the folk song "Kalinka" is the dramatic changes of tempo. The opening section includes an **accelerando** *(a musical term that indicates a gradual increase in tempo)* paired with a **crescendo** *(a dynamic marking that indicates to gradually sing louder)*. Subsequent sections are marked as **piu mosso** *(a tempo marking that indicates a little more motion, or faster)* and **meno mosso** *(a tempo marking that indicates a little less motion, or slower)*. Find these tempo markings in the music.

194 Proficient Tenor/Bass

RESOURCES

Proficient Sight-Singing

Sight-Singing in G Minor, pages 97–99

Reading Rhythms in 2/4 Meter, pages 66–67

Reading Rhythms in 3/4 Meter, page 14

Reading Eighth Notes and Eighth Rests, pages 23–24

Teacher Resource Binder

Teaching Master 27, *Pronunciation Guide for "Kalinka"*

Evaluation Master 6, *Diction Checkup*

Reference 16, *Expanding a Musical Vocabulary*

Reference 26, *IPA Vowels*

For additional resources, see TRB Table of Contents.

Links to Learning

◆ **Vocal**

Russian vowels should be pronounced as Italian vowels. The "li" combination should be pronounced "lyee." For example, "kalinka" should be pronounced "ka-lyeen-ka."

◆ **Artistic Expression**

Perform the following example on the syllables "lin-ka." Gradually increase the tempo of each note to practice singing an *accelerando.*

Perform the following example on the syllables "lin-ka." Gradually increase the volume of each note to practice singing a crescendo.

Perform the following example on the syllables "lin-ka." Gradually increase the tempo and the volume of each note to practice singing an accelerando paired with a crescendo.

Evaluation

Demonstrate how well you have learned the skills and concepts featured in the lesson "Kalinka" by completing the following:

• Record yourself singing measures 1–9 with the Russian text. Listen to the recording and evaluate your performance for correct Russian pronunciation.

• Define the musical terms *accelerando* and *crescendo.* Demonstrate an understanding of these terms by singing a familiar song. While performing the familiar song, add an *accelerando* and a *crescendo.* Evaluate how well you were able to demonstrate both.

LINKS TO LEARNING

Vocal

The Vocal section is designed to prepare students to pronounce Russian vowels.

Have students repeat the word "kalinka" with the suggested pronunciation.

Artistic Expression

The Artistic Expression section is designed to prepare students to perform an example using accelerando and crescendo.

Have students:

• Sing the example while gradually getting faster.

• Sing the example while gradually getting louder.

• Sing the example while gradually getting faster and louder.

RESOURCES

Proficient Tenor/Bass Rehearsal/Performance CD

CD 2:11 Voices

CD 2:12 Accompaniment Only

CD 3:18 Vocal Practice Track—Tenor I

CD 4:17 Vocal Practice Track—Tenor II

CD 5:11 Vocal Practice Track—Bass I

CD 6:17 Vocal Practice Track—Bass II

National Standards

1. Singing, alone and with others, a varied repertoire of music. **(a)**

6. Listening to, analyzing, and describing music. **(b)**

Kalinka

For TTBB and Piano

Arranged by
STAN ENGEBRETSON

Russian Folk Song

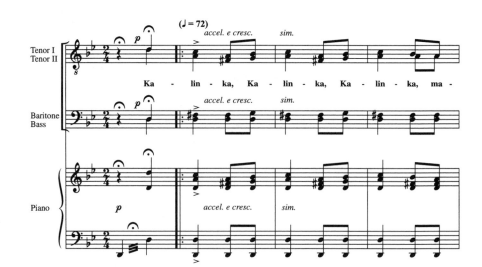

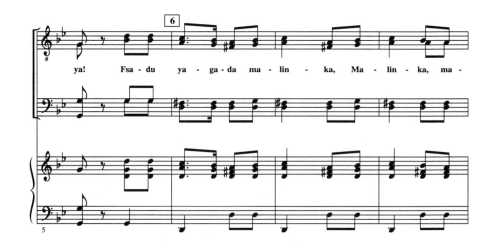

Copyright © 1993 Plymouth Music Co., Inc. 170 N.E. 33rd Street, Ft. Lauderdale, FL 33334
International Copyright Secured   Made in U.S.A.   All Rights Reserved

LESSON PLAN

Suggested Teaching Sequence and Performance Tips

1. Introduce

Direct students to:

- Read and discuss the information found in Getting Started section on page 194.
- Practice pronouncing the word "kalinka" as described in the Vocal section on page 195. Locate the word in the score (first used in measures 1–2).
- Practice singing the ascending melody in the Artistic Expression section on page 195. Gradually get faster the first time, gradually get louder the second time and combine the faster tempo and louder dynamic the third time.

Progress Checkpoints

Observe students' progress in:

✓ Pronouncing the Russian text.
✓ Singing key phrases in the song.

196

Begin with the image of a steam-engine locomotive picking up speed from rest. Through this work the student will begin to make the relationship between the printed accelerando and crescendo to the performance of these musical elements. The key to achieving this is through the eighth-note subdivision.

2. Rehearse

Direct students to:

- Practice singing measures 1–9 using solfège syllables while gradually getting faster and louder.
- Sing measures 1–9 using a neutral syllable such as "dee."
- Sing measures 20–27 using a neutral syllable such as "dee."
- Sing measures 37–44 using a neutral syllable such as "dee."
- Practice Russian pronunciation by chanting the words in rhythm.
- Sing above measures using Russian language.

Progress Checkpoints

Observe students' progress in:

- ✓ Their ability to sing gradual accelerandos and crescendos while maintaining a relatively even subdivision.
- ✓ Their rhythmic and pitch accuracy.
- ✓ Singing with accurate diction, unified vowel sounds and stress.
- ✓ Singing with proper vowel sounds and unique consonants.

MORE ABOUT...

Folk Music

Folk music is music that has been passed on from generation to generation, often in the oral tradition. Typically, folk song composers are unknown, and a song may change slightly when one person learns it then shares it with someone else. Folk songs exist in "tune families," which include all songs that originated from a specific one. Any related song in a tune family can be shorter or longer than the original, or the rhythm, melody, scale or form can be altered.

3. Refine

Direct students to:

- Drill and practice rhythms using Russian language.
- Sight-sing the solo part in measures 10–36.
- Combine the solo part as sung by individuals with choral sections.
- Sing the entire song using Russian language.

Progress Checkpoints

Observe students' progress in:

✓ Their accuracy of rhythms and pitch.

✓ Using the correct Russian pronunciation of the text.

✓ Performing a natural accelerando and crescendo with accuracy of rhythms and proper volumes.

✓ Singing solos with confidence on correct pitches and rhythms.

ASSESSMENT

Evaluating the Quality of a Performance

Have students:

1. Listen to a video or audio recording of this piece as performed by the choir.

2. Compare this performance to exemplary models such as other recordings or other live performances of the piece.

3. Develop constructive suggestions for improvement based on the comparison.

ASSESSMENT

Informal Assessment

In this lesson, the students showed the ability to:

- Perform a gradual accelerando over eight measures.
- Perform a gradual crescendo over eight measures.
- Sing a gradual accelerando with a gradual crescendo.
- Perform the previous alterations while singing a Russian text.

Student Self-Assessment

Have students evaluate their individual performances based on the following:

- Foreign Language
- Expressive Singing
- Intonation
- Accurate Pitches
- Accurate Rhythms

Have each student rate his/her performance of this song in the areas above on a scale of 1–5, 5 being the best.

TEACHING STRATEGY

Identifying a Key as Minor

Have students discuss and identify strategies for determining whether a piece is in major or minor, and, if minor, what type of minor key it might be. Some possible strategies include:

- Look at the key signature, and determine the possible major key.
- Look at the notation, especially the beginning chord, and the chords at the ends of phrases, identifying the tonal center.
- Determine if the tonal center matches the major key, or is a third below, indicating the relative minor.

Individual and Group Performance Evaluation

To further demonstrate musical growth, direct students to complete the Evaluation section on page 195.

- After recording measures 1–9 evaluate the performance by asking, "How accurate was the pronunciation of the Russian text? Which word(s) could use improvement?"
- After defining accelerando and crescendo, sing a familiar song incorporating those changes in the performance. Sing the song for a classmate and see if he/she can hear the song getting gradually faster and louder. Switch roles.

EXTENSION

Compare and Contrast

Ask students to find another example of a work that uses a gradual accelerando with a crescendo (e.g., Dukas' *The Sorcerer's Apprentice,* Grieg's *In the Hall of the Mountain King*). Also locate examples of music that maintain the same tempo and dynamics. Use pieces that are being currently performed by the choir as a possible source for comparison purposes.

200   Proficient Tenor/Bass

Additional National Standards

The following National Standards are addressed through the Assessment, Extension, Enrichment and bottom-page activities:

1. Singing, alone and with others, a varied repertoire of music. **(c)**
5. Reading and notating music. **(b)**
6. Listening to, analyzing, and describing music. **(a)**
7. Evaluating music and music performances. **(a)**

SPOTLIGHT

Diction

Singing is a form of communication. To communicate well while singing, you must not only form your vowels correctly, but also say your consonants as clearly and cleanly as possible.

There are two kinds of consonants: voiced and unvoiced. Consonants that require the use of the voice along with the **articulators** (*lips, teeth, tongue, and other parts of the mouth and throat*) are called voiced consonants. If you place your hand on your throat, you can actually feel your voice box vibrate while producing them. Unvoiced consonant sounds are made with the articulators only.

In each pair below, the first word contains a voiced consonant while the second word contains an unvoiced consonant. Speak the following word pairs, then sing them on any pitch. When singing, make sure the voiced consonant is on the same pitch as the vowel.

Voiced:	Unvoiced Consonants:	More Voiced Consonants:
[b] bay	[p] pay	[l] lip
[d] den	[t] ten	[m] mice
[g] goat	[k] coat	[n] nice
[dʒ] jeer	[tʃ] cheer	[j] yell
[z] zero	[s] scenic	[r] red
[ʒ] fusion	[ʃ] shun	
[ð] there	[θ] therapy	More Unvoiced Consonants:
[v] vine	[f] fine	[h] have
[w] wince	[hw] whim	

The American "r" requires special treatment in classical choral singing. To sing an American "r" at the end of a syllable following a vowel, sing the vowel with your teeth apart and jaw open. In some formal sacred music and English texts, you may need to flip or roll the "r." For most other instances, sing the "r" on pitch, then open to the following vowel quickly.

Spotlight *Diction* **201**

RESOURCES

National Standards

1. Singing, alone and with others, a varied repertoire of music. **(b)**
8. Understanding relationships between music, the other arts, and disciplines outside the arts **(b)**

DICTION

Objectives

- Demonstrate basic performance techniques using proper diction.

Suggested Teaching Sequence

Direct students to:

- Read the Spotlight On Diction on student page 201 and identify the importance of diction in singing.
- Define articulators.
- Describe the difference between voiced and unvoiced consonants.
- Speak the voiced and unvoiced consonants out loud and find examples in music.
- Compare the concept of proper diction to effective performance practices.
- Discuss on the proper use of the "r" consonant when singing.

Progress Checkpoints

Observe students' progress in:

- ✓ Their ability to speak voiced and unvoiced consonants properly.
- ✓ Their ability to name the parts of the body that are the articulators.
- ✓ Their ability to recognize voiced and unvoiced consonants in other music they are studying.
- ✓ Their ability to relate the importance of proper diction in other areas such as drama, speech and public speaking.

Linden Lea

OVERVIEW

Composer: Ralph Vaughan Williams (1872–1958), arranged by Julius Harrison

Text: William Barnes

Voicing: TTBB

Key: B♭ major

Meter: 3/4

Form: Strophic

Style: Contemporary English Art Song

Accompaniment: A cappella

Programming: Contest, Festival

Vocal Ranges:

OBJECTIVES

After completing this lesson, students will be able to:

• Identify melodic parts.

• Demonstrate in ensembles basic performance techniques while performing moderately easy to moderately difficult literature.

VOCABULARY

Have students review vocabulary in student lesson. Introduce terms found in the music. A complete glossary of terms is found on page 246 of the student book.

Linden Lea

Composer: Ralph Vaughan Williams (1872–1958), arranged by Julius Harrison
Text: William Barnes (1801–1886)
Voicing: TTBB

VOCABULARY

melodic contour

close harmony

Focus

• Identify and demonstrate melodic contour.

• Sing independently in small ensembles.

• Perform music representing the British culture.

Getting Started

Have you ever found yourself at a loss for words to express a feeling or situation? Poets often capture an idea and put ideas into words we cannot find. The poet William Barnes (1801–1886) was a schoolmaster from North Dorset, England. Barnes had a deep love for the English countryside where he lived. In his poetry, Barnes expressed and explained his feelings for an area of Dorset known as Linden Lea. Ralph Vaughan Williams set this poem to music in 1901.

🎲 SKILL BUILDERS

To learn more about the key of B♭ major, see Proficient Sight-Singing, *page 90.*

◆ History and Culture

Ralph Vaughan Williams (1872–1958) has been described as one of the leading British composers of the Contemporary period. His music is expressive, powerful and noble. In the early 1900s, Vaughan Williams traveled to the English countryside and collected folk songs, notating them for future generations. Folksongs were not his only interest, however. Vaughan Williams was a productive composer and wrote for many different mediums. He is credited with writing nine symphonies, five operas, film music and many choral works. He believed that a composer should "make his art an expression of the whole life of the community." A quiet, unassuming gentleman, Vaughan Williams shied away from all honors except the Order of Merit (the highest honor for the advancement of the Arts in England). He is buried in Westminster Abbey, London, England, near fellow composer Henry Purcell (1659–1695).

RESOURCES

Proficient Sight-Singing

Sight-Singing in B♭ Major, pages 90–94

Reading Rhythms in 3/4 Meter, page 14

Reading Eighth Notes and Eighth Rests, pages 23–24

Reading Dotted Half and Dotted Quarter Notes, page 51

Teacher Resource Binder

Teaching Master 29, *Connecting With the Audience*

Evaluation Master 4, *Checking Out Phrasing*

Skill Builder 30, *Solfège Hand Signs*

Vocal Development 16, *Warm-up: Part Singing*

For additional resources, see TRB Table of Contents.

Links to Learning

◆ Vocal

Melodic contour is *the overall shape of the melody.* Read and perform the following example with a supported tone and dynamic contrast to create the rise and fall of the phrase.

sol do re mi sol la sol fa mi re do la do do re do

◆ Theory

Close harmony is *harmony in which notes of the chord are kept as close together as possible, often within an octave.* Perform the following example to practice singing in close harmony.

loo loo loo loo_____ loo loo loo loo loo_ loo loo loo loo loo

loo loo loo loo loo loo loo loo loo loo loo loo loo_ loo

Evaluation

Demonstrate how well you have learned the skills and concepts featured in the lesson "Linden Lea" by completing the following:

- Expressively sing the example in the Vocal section, showing the melodic contour of the phrase. Were you able to begin and end the phrase softly? Did you sing louder to the peak of the phrase? Was the outline of the phrase clearly heard?

- In a duet with one singer on a part, sing the example in the Theory section above. Demonstrate your vocal independence while singing in close harmony. Evaluate how well you were able to stay on your own part (sing independently) and sing in tune.

Choral Library *Linden Lea* **203**

RESOURCES

Proficient Tenor/Bass Rehearsal/Performance CD

CD 2:13 Voices

CD 2:14 Accompaniment Only

CD 3:19 Vocal Practice Track—Tenor I

CD 4:18 Vocal Practice Track—Tenor II

CD 5:12 Vocal Practice Track—Bass I

CD 6:18 Vocal Practice Track—Bass II

National Standards

1. Singing, alone and with others, a varied repertoire of music. **(a, c)**

6. Listening to, analyzing, and describing music. **(b)**

- Perform expressively from notation a varied repertoire of music representing styles from diverse cultures.

LINKS TO LEARNING

Vocal

The Vocal section is designed to prepare students to create rise and fall of a phrase by using a supported tone and dynamic contrast.

Have students:

- Sing the melodic contour using solfège syllables.
- Sing the melody on the neutral syllable "loo."
- Sing the melody on a neutral syllable and observe the dynamic markings.

Theory

The Theory section is designed to prepare students to sing close harmony in tune.

Have students:

- Learn the top melody using solfège syllables.
- Learn the bottom melody using solfège syllables.
- Divide into two sections and sing both melodies at the same time on the neutral syllable "loo."

LESSON PLAN

Suggested Teaching Sequence and Performance Tips

1. Introduce

Direct students to:

- Read and discus the information found in the Getting Started section on page 202.

- Practice singing a portion of the melody used in the song as shown in the Vocal section on page 203. Sing the example with a rise and fall to the phrase.

- Locate and practice singing the melody as found throughout the piece (Tenor I verses 1 and 2; Bass I verse 3). Note that the style of this piece is chordal, with the lower three parts accompanying the melody in the Tenor I part. In verse 3, Bass I has the melody in measures 18–26. The melody should always be the dominant voice part.

- Practice each voice part separately using solfège syllables for measures 1– 9. Discuss and demonstrate stressing the first of the two slurred eighth notes in the lower three voice parts. Pay particular attention to the rise and fall of each phrase.

- Once parts are independent, combine them. All parts should listen for the melody and move together for expressive phrasing.

Linden Lea
(A Dorset Song)

For TTBB, a cappella

Arranged by
JULIUS HARRISON

Words by WILLIAM BARNES
Music by RALPH VAUGHAN WILLIAMS
(1872–1958)

Copyright arrangement 1950 in U.S.A. by Boosey & Co. Ltd.
Copyright for all countries
U.S. Edition 1954

TEACHER 2 TEACHER

The intertwining harmonies found in "Linden Lea" will challenge the members of your chorus to sing close harmonies while rewarding them with a charming and haunting melody.

Progress Checkpoints

Observe students' progress in:

✓ Their ability to sing phrases expressively.

✓ Their ability to locate and sing the melody throughout the piece.

✓ Their ability to sing slurred eighth notes in correct style.

✓ Their ability to sing the first phrase in four-part harmony.

CURRICULUM CONNECTIONS

Geographically Speaking

Locate Dorset County on a map of England. You will find it in southern England, fronting the English Channel. The coastline of Dorset extends from Lyme Regis in the west to Christchurch in the east. Dorset is often described as "The Best of Both Worlds." Some of the finest sandy beaches in the British Isles are located along the coastline. Behind the coastline there are rural villages and lovely countryside. The history of Dorset dates back prior to Roman times. Use the Internet to locate pictures of Dorset. Research life in Dorset today.

2. Rehearse

Direct students to:

- Divide the remaining music into four-bar sections. Practice each voice part separately using solfege syllables. When secure, combine two, then three, then four parts.

- Notice that while the melodic material often repeats, the harmony in the underlying three parts changes each time.

- Pay particular attention to the accidentals throughout. Isolate chords containing accidentals and check for accuracy. Note that several of the accidentals marked are actually courtesy accidentals used to clarify, and since they are found in the key signature they do not alter the sound of the chord.

Progress Checkpoints

Observe students' progress in:

✓ Singing all voice parts securely.

✓ Singing accidentals correctly.

MORE ABOUT...

Poet William Barnes

Born in 1801 at Bagber, near Sturminister Newton in North Dorset, William Barnes worked as a solicitor's clerk until 1823, when he became a school teacher. He married Julia Miles in 1827. He was deeply affected by her death in 1852, and many of his poems describe his love for her. In 1848 he was ordained and appointed curate at Whitcombe near Dorchester. He died in 1886. In his obituary in the *Saturday Review* Barnes was described as "the best pastoral poet we possess, the most sincere, the most genuine, the most theocritan. The dialect is but a very thin veil hiding from us some of the most delicate and finished verse written in our time."

3. Refine

Direct students to:

- Sing while observing the dynamic and editorial markings in the score. *Andante con moto* is a walking tempo with forward motion. *Animato* means to sing in an animated style. *Risoluto* means to sing in a marked, determined style.

- Isolate and sing sections on a neutral syllable, listening for balance and blending of parts.

- Read the text. Read the information about William Barnes in the Getting Started section on page 202. Discuss the ideas found in the poem and determine the expressive elements that will help convey these ideas to the listener. *(i.e., good diction, forward motion, word stress at the peaks of phrases, dynamic contrasts)*

- Strive for outstanding diction. Remember to place an "oo" in front of the words beginning with "w," for ease in beginning the tone.

- A lea is a grassy meadow. The poet is describing a beautiful scene in the English countryside where he lived. Investigate the meaning of any other words that are unfamiliar.

Progress Checkpoints

Observe students' progress in:

✓ Singing expressively, as directed by the dynamic and editorial markings.

✓ Performing with parts that are balanced and blended.

✓ Effectively communicating the text by using clean, concise diction.

MORE ABOUT...

Composer Ralph Vaughn Williams

Born at Down Ampney in 1872, Ralph Vaughn Williams was an English composer. He studied composition with important teachers as well as the composer Maurice Ravel. He started collecting folk songs in 1903, which greatly affected his writing. He was also an editor of the *English Hymnal* in 1906, which influenced his larger works. Many of his pieces have a quiet, serene sound to them, which is even identified in the title of his *Pastoral Symphony*. He also wrote music for films including *Scott of Antarctic* which came about because of his ability to convey bleakness in the music of his later period.

ASSESSMENT

Informal Assessment

In this lesson, students showed the ability to:

- Sing expressively with appropriate phrasing.
- Sing in four-part harmony.
- Balance parts with the melody.
- Comprehend the text and convey its meaning.
- Sing using the dynamics and editorial markings found in the score.

Student Self-Assessment

Have students evaluate their individual performances based on the following:

- Phrasing
- Diction
- Expressive Singing
- Intonation
- Correct Part-Singing

Have each student rate his/her performance of this song in the areas above on a scale of 1–5, 5 being the best.

Individual and Group Performance Evaluation

To further measure growth of musical skills presented in this lesson, direct students to complete the Evaluation section on page 203.

- Pair up with a student from the same section and sing the melodic contour from the Vocal section. Review each performance.
- After singing the example from the Theory section in a duet with one singer on a part, evaluate the performance.

Additional National Standards

The following National Standards are addressed through the Assessment, Extension, Enrichment and bottom-page activities:

5. Reading and notating music. **(a)**

7. Evaluating music and music performances. **(a)**

SPOTLIGHT

Musical Theater

Tim McDonald, the current creative director of Music Theatre International in New York, was asked to share his ideas on musical theater in today's schools. This is what he has to say:

"Musical theater (sometimes spelled 'theatre') is a uniquely American art form like jazz and rock-and-roll that has become popular all over the world. Recently, musicals have been in the spotlight with major motion picture releases and television specials. Also, performers like Tom Cruise, Britney Spears and Tom Hanks as well as directors Baz Luhrmann and Tim Burton have credited their success to participating in their high school's musical.

An annual student musical has become a regular part of the school calendar. In fact, it is estimated that 50,000 productions are presented in school auditoriums and over 2.5 million young people participate in their school musical each year. Most everyone can participate in a student musical on some level. Each person's contribution adds to the success of the production. For those who enjoy singing, dancing or acting, there's probably a role for you, or a place in the ensemble. For those who like to be behind the scenes, there's directing, stage managing, choreography and the technical crew. If your interests lean more towards visual art, there are sets to be designed and painted, props to be imagined, and costumes to be crafted.

The best part of participating in a musical is that it's a lot of fun! So the next time you see an audition notice, take a chance and audition, or talk to the director about working behind the scenes. Who knows, one day you may credit your school musical with the success of your career."

In 1952, Frank Loesser transformed a fledgling business into what is now known throughout the world as "MTI." Music Theatre International is a theatrical licensing company specializing in Broadway musicals. It has been instrumental in extending the production life of the great American musicals such as Guys and Dolls, West Side Story, Fiddler On The Roof, Les Misérables, Annie, Of Thee I Sing, Ain't Misbehavin', Damn Yankees, The Music Man, Godspell, Little Shop Of Horrors *as well as the musical theater collaboration of composer/lyricist Stephen Sondheim, among others.*

Spotlight *Musical Theater* **209**

RESOURCES

Teacher Resource Binder

Reference 10, *Career: Comparing Vocal Performance Opportunities*

National Standards

7. Evaluating music and music performances. **(b)**

8. Understanding relationships between music, the other arts, and disciplines outside the arts. **(a)**

9. Understanding music in relation to history and culture. **(b)**

MUSICAL THEATER

Objectives

- Relate music to history.
- Identify the relationships between the content of the other fine arts and those of music.
- Describe music-related career options including performance.

Suggested Teaching Sequence

Direct students to:

- Read the Spotlight On Musical Theater on student page 209 and define musical theater.
- Discuss the history of American musical theater.
- Identify important musical theater composers and popular shows.
- Make a list of musical theater shows that they have seen live, on a video or DVD.
- Discuss the advantages of participating in a school musical. In small groups, brainstorm about the different types of performers and behind-the-scenes people it takes to put on a school production.

Progress Checkpoints

Observe students' progress in:

- ✓ Understanding musical theater and its background.
- ✓ Identifying the different types of people it takes to put on a musical theater production.
- ✓ Their ability to actively participate in a school musical.

Loch Lomond

OVERVIEW

Composer: Traditional Scottish Folk Song, arranged by Dede Duson
Text: Lady John Scott (1810–1900) (Alicia Anne Spottiswoode)
Voicing: TTBB
Key: A major
Meter: 4/4
Form: ABA'B'
Style: Scottish Folk Song
Accompaniment: A cappella
Programming: Concert, Contest

Vocal Ranges:

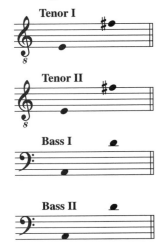

OBJECTIVES

After completing this lesson, students will be able to:

- Demonstrate in ensembles accurate intonation while performing.
- Perform expressively from notation a varied repertoire of music representing styles from diverse cultures.

VOCABULARY

Have students review vocabulary in student lesson. Introduce terms found in the music. A complete glossary of terms is found on page 246 of the student book.

210

Loch Lomond

Composer: Traditional Scottish Folk Song, arranged by Dede Duson
Text: Lady John Scott (Alicia Anne Spottiswoode) (1810–1900)
Voicing: TTBB

VOCABULARY

glee
legato
dot

Focus

- Sing with accurate intonation and balance.
- Sing with expressive phrasing.
- Perform music representing the Scottish culture.

Getting Started

Another term for a men's choir or chorus is *glee club.* Many men's choruses around the country still claim that name today. A **glee** is *an unaccompanied and homophonic piece of vocal music in three or four parts.* "Loch Lomond" is a wonderful glee club song. The rich four-part harmonies capture the attention of both the singer and the audience. The romantic text allows for expressive singing as only a men's choir can do. Dede Duson, whose music always winds and spins around a constant energy of eighth note patterns, has beautifully set this traditional Scottish song for men.

◆ **History and Culture**

It has been called one of the most beautiful spots on Earth— Loch Lomond—the single biggest expanse of inland water in the British Isles. The lake brings together two very different Scotlands—the low shallows in the South with the steep mountains of the West. You might want to search the Internet to find pictures of this lovely place.

"Loch Lomond" is an old Jacobite Air. (A song from the Jacobites—those who followed King James VII after his disposition from the throne of Scotland and England in 1689.) The words are attributed to Lady John Scott, born Alicia Anne Spottiswoode (1810–1900) in Berwickshire, Scotland. The version we are familiar with today is said to have first appeared in print in *Poets and Poetry of Scotland* (1876). It is interesting to note that Lady John Scott also wrote the song "Annie Laurie" found on page 12 of this book.

⬡ SPOTLIGHT

To learn more about vocal health, see page 244.

RESOURCES

Proficient Sight-Singing

Sight-Singing in A Major, pages 138–139

Reading Rhythms in 4/4 Meter, pages 2, 6

Reading Dotted Eighth and Sixteenth Note Combinations, pages 76–77

Teacher Resource Binder

Evaluation Master 2, *Analyzing Intonation*

Evaluation Master 8, *Evaluating Musical Expression*

Skill Builder 24, *Rhythm and Kodály*

Reference 6, *Note Values*

For additional resources, see TRB Table of Contents.

Links to Learning

◆ **Vocal**

Read and perform the following example to practice singing a **legato** *(a connected and sustained style of singing)* line. Use adequate breath support to carry the tone from one note to the next. After you have sung the example on "loo," sight-sing it using solfège syllables. Hint: The first note is *sol*.

◆ **Theory**

A **dot** is *a symbol that increases the length of a given note by half its value. It is placed to the right of the note.* Read and perform the following example to practice rhythm patterns similar to those found in the music.

Evaluation

Demonstrate how well you have learned the skills and concepts featured in the lesson "Loch Lomond" by completing the following:

• In a quartet with one singer on a part, perform measures 10–13. Were you able to sing a legato line? Were you able to sing in tune as a group?

• Can you sustain the four-measure phrases with adequate breath support while keeping the pitch in tune? Sing measures 18–21 to demonstrate how well you can sing a four–bar phrase expressively.

RESOURCES

Proficient Tenor/Bass Rehearsal/Performance CD

CD 2:15 Voices

CD 2:16 Accompaniment Only

CD 3:20 Vocal Practice Track—Tenor I

CD 4:19 Vocal Practice Track—Tenor II

CD 5:13 Vocal Practice Track—Baritone

CD 6:19 Vocal Practice Track—Bass

National Standards

1. Singing, alone and with others, a varied repertoire of music. **(a, c)**

9. Understanding music in relation to history and culture. **(a)**

LINKS TO LEARNING

Vocal

The Vocal section is designed to prepare students to sing a melody using legato articulation.

Have students:

• Sing the melody on the neutral syllable "loo."

• Sing the melody using solfège syllables.

Theory

The Theory section is designed to prepare students to perform a rhythmic pattern that includes dotted eighth notes and sixteenth notes.

Have students:

• Perform the rhythm pattern by chanting the counting syllables.

• Clap or tap the rhythm of rhythm pattern.

LESSON PLAN

Suggested Teaching Sequence and Performance Tips

Direct students to:

- Sight-sing the song using solfège syllables.

- Practice measures 8–9, 17–18, 24–25 carefully. Be sure the altered notes are sung correctly.

- Rehearse the piece on a connected sound—either "loo" or a "hum," establishing where you will breathe and create the phrase shape.

- Keep an active eighth-note pulse. Students should tap the pulse as the eighth-note feeling must stay alive and move each phrase forward as it is sung. It will also establish the pulse with which to breathe or place consonants.

- Tune each chord as it sounds. Freeze every chord as you rehearse—adjusting the intonation until it rings absolutely in tune.

- Push each weak beat to the strong beat—especially beat 4 to beat 1. The "push notes" will propel the musical thought forward and make the phrases more interesting.

Progress Checkpoints

Observe students' progress in:

✓ Singing the accidentals correctly.

✓ Performing with a sustained legato articulation in four-measure phrases.

✓ Students actively keeping the eighth note alive as they tap or pat that note. Long notes move forward

To the men of Lee and Mesquite, for "A Concert VI"

Loch Lomond

For TTBB, a cappella

Scottish Folk Song
Arranged by DEDE DUSON

Any reproduction, adaption or arrangement of this work in whole or in part without
consent of the copyright owner constitutes an infringement of copyright
© 1982 Neil A. Kjos Music Co., San Diego, California
International Copyright Secured   All Rights Reserved   Printed in U.S.A.

212   Proficient Tenor/Bass

TEACHER 2 TEACHER

"Loch Lomond" is a wonderful harmonization of a great Scottish folk song. It creates a glee club sound that students love to sing and audiences love to hear. Students need to understand the romantic emotion in the story, i.e., the love for one's country and the love for one's true love. There are some Gaelic words used that might be unfamiliar to the students. Be sure they learn the meaning of all text.

bon-nie, bon-nie banks— o' Loch Lo-mond. 'Twas— there that we part-ed in

there that we part-ed— in

yon shad-y glen on the steep, steep— side— o' Ben Lo - mond,— where

yon— shad-y glen—

in— pur-ple hue— the heath-er hills we view and the

moon com-in' out— in the gloam - in'. Oh,—

Oh,

nev-er meet a-gain, on the bon-nie, bon-nie bon-nie, bon-nie banks— o' Loch Lo - mond.

Additional National Standards

The following National Standards are addressed through the Assessment, Extension, Enrichment and bottom-page activities:

5. Reading and notating music. **(b)**

6. Listening to, analyzing, and describing music. **(a)**

7. Evaluating music and music performances. **(a)**

---

as the inner pulse is felt.

✓ Finely tuning every beat and every chord of the song.

✓ Expressive, musical phrasing.

ASSESSMENT

Informal Assessment

In this lesson, students showed the ability to:

- Sight-sing their voice part as other parts were sung.
- Understand the D.S. al Coda and coda by observing the correct form.
- Sustain four-measure phrases without taking a breath.

Student Self-Assessment

Have students evaluate their individual performances based on the following:

- Breath Management
- Phrasing
- Expressive Singing
- Intonation
- Accurate Rhythms

Have each student rate his/her performance of this song in the areas above on a scale of 1–5, 5 being the best.

Individual and Group Performance Evaluation

To further measure growth of musical skills presented in this lesson, direct students to complete the Evaluation section on page 211.

- After singing measures 10–13 in quartets with one person on a part, review each performance.
- After singing measures 18–21 as a solo with another

The Star-Spangled Banner

OVERVIEW

Composer: John Stafford Smith (1759–1836), arranged by Barry Talley
Text: Francis Scott Key
Voicing: TTBB
Key: C major
Meter: 4/4 and 3/4
Form: Medley
Style: Patriotic
Accompaniment: A cappella
Programming: Concert Opener, Festival, Patriotic Concert

Vocal Ranges:

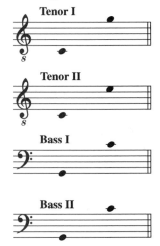

OBJECTIVES

After completing this lesson, students will be able to:

- Define concepts of music notation, including accidentals.
- Demonstrate in ensembles accurate rhythm, including dotted rhythms.
- Relate music to history, society and culture.

VOCABULARY

Have students review vocabulary in student lesson. Introduce terms found in the music. A complete glossary of terms is found on page 246 of the student book.

214

The Star-Spangled Banner

Composer: John Stafford Smith (1759–1836), arranged by Barry Talley
Text: Francis Scott Key
Voicing: TTBB

VOCABULARY

national anthem
accidental

SPOTLIGHT

To learn more about concert etiquette, see page 130.

Focus

- Describe and sign an accidental accurately.
- Read and perform rhythmic patterns that contain dotted rhythms.
- Relate the music to history, to society and to culture.

Getting Started

The flag and the **national anthem** *(a patriotic song adopted by a nation through tradition or decree)* are symbols of national pride and patriotism. What does the phrase "O'er the land of the free and the home of the brave" mean to you? What images do you visualize when you sing the "The Star-Spangled Banner"? Write down your thoughts and share them with the class.

◆ **History and Culture**

You may know who wrote the words to "The Star-Spangled Banner," but do you know who wrote the original music? His name is John Stafford Smith (1750–1836). Smith was an English composer and organist who composed "To Anachreon in Heaven" in 1770 for the London Anacreonic Society, an aristocratic group dedicated to the promotion of the arts. Later, the words, written by Francis Scott Key, were set to this tune.

During the War of 1812, the British fleet attacked Fort McHenry, which is located outside Baltimore, Maryland. During the attack, Francis Scott Key was aboard a British warship trying to gain the release of an American prisoner. The next morning, the flag, though battered and torn, was still there. Inspired by this sight, Key wrote the words to "The Star-Spangled Banner" on the back of a letter he had in his pocket. It was printed on flyers the next day and distributed throughout Baltimore. In 1931, the United States Congress officially recognized "The Star-Spangled Banner" as our national anthem. It is proper protocol and concert etiquette to stand whenever "The Star-Spangled Banner" is performed.

214   Proficient Tenor/Bass

RESOURCES

Proficient Sight-Singing

Sight-Singing in C Major, pages 7, 9, 13, 26–27, 34–35

Reading Rhythms in 4/4 Meter, page 2

Reading Rhythms in 3/4 Meter, page 14

Reading Dotted Eighth/Sixteenth Note Rhythms, page 76

Teacher Resource Binder

Teaching Master 30, *Reflections on "The Star-Spangled Banner"*

Evaluation Master 5, *Concert Etiquette Quiz*

Skill Builder 30, *Solfège Hand Signs*

Reference 16, *Expanding a Musical Vocabulary*

For additional resources, see TRB Table of Contents.

Links to Learning

◆ **Vocal**

Although this arrangement is written in the key of C major, it uses **accidentals** *(a sharp, flat or natural that is not included in the key signature of a piece of music)* to change the pitch of some notes. The pitch *fa* is sometimes raise to *fi*, and the pitch *sol* is sometimes raised to *si*. Perform the following C major scale with accidentals.

do re mi fa fi sol si la ti do ti la si sol fi fa mi re do

For more practice singing accidentals, perform the following example.

do re mi fa sol la ti do do   do ti la sol fa mi re do do

do re mi fi sol si la ti do   do ti la si sol fi fa mi re do do

◆ **Theory**

Read and perform the following rhythmic patterns that contain dotted rhythms.

ti ti ti ti ti ti   tim ka ta   tim ka ta   tim ka ta   ta–a–a

ti ti ti ti tim ka ta   ti ti tim ka ta   tim ka ti ti   ta–a–a

Evaluation

Demonstrate how well you have learned the skills and concepts featured in the lesson "The Star-Spangled Banner" by completing the following:

• Sing the Vocal examples above to show your ability to sing altered pitches in tune. You may do this with a partner taking turns singing for each other. Critique each other's performance.

• Chant or clap the rhythms in measures 5–13 that contain dotted notes. Evaluate how well you were able to perform the dotted rhythms accurately. Rate your performance as (1) all rhythms were correct, (2) most rhythms were correct, or (3) only a few of the rhythms were correct.

Choral Library *The Star-Spangled Banner* **215**

LINKS TO LEARNING

Vocal

The Vocal section is designed to prepare students to:

• Understand the use of accidentals.

• Accurately sing accidentals.

Have students:

• Sing the Vocal exercises using solfège syllables.

• Vary the tempo by first singing slowly, then faster.

Theory

The Theory section is designed to prepare students to:

• Perform dotted rhythm patterns that appear in the score.

• Perform various rhythms in 3/4 meter.

Have students:

• Divide into two groups. One group taps a steady sixteenth-note pulse and the other group claps the rhythm. Switch parts.

• All speak the rhythm using rhythm syllables.

RESOURCES

Proficient Tenor/Bass Rehearsal/Performance CD

CD 2:17 Voices

CD 2:18 Accompaniment Only

CD 3:21 Vocal Practice Track—Tenor I

CD 4:20 Vocal Practice Track—Tenor II

CD 5:14 Vocal Practice Track—Bass I

CD 6:20 Vocal Practice Track—Bass II

National Standards

1. Singing, alone and with others, a varied repertoire of music. **(a, b)**

9. Understanding music in relation to history and culture. **(a)**

Suggested Teaching Sequence and Performance Tips

Direct students to:

- Read and discuss the information found in the Getting Started section on page 214.
- Sight-sing the C major scale with accidentals in the Vocal section on page 215.
- Clap and speak the dotted rhythm patterns in the Theory section on page 215.
- Locate and circle the accidentals in the music. Sight-sing measures 1–4 with accurate pitches.
- Locate all dotted rhythms in the music. Sight-sing measures 1–4 again, this time focusing on pitch as well as rhythm.
- Sing through entire piece.
- Sing expressively by singing all dynamic levels as indicated in the score.
- Bring out the melody when it shifts from part to part.

Progress Checkpoints

Observe students' progress in:

- ✓ Singing accidentals with accuracy.
- ✓ Their ability to accurately perform dotted rhythms.
- ✓ Their ability to successfully transfer altered pitches from the Vocal section to the music itself.
- ✓ Singing with accurate pitch and rhythm.
- ✓ Singing with dynamic contrast throughout the piece.
- ✓ Balancing the melody within the ensemble.

The Star-Spangled Banner

For TTBB, a cappella

Arranged by
BARRY TALLEY

Words by FRANCIS SCOTT KEY
Music by JOHN STAFFORD SMITH

Copyright © 2000 by HAL LEONARD CORPORATION
International Copyright Secured   All Rights Reserved

216   Proficient Tenor/Bass

The feeling of our nation's pride and patriotism has never been stronger. This arrangement of our national anthem brings together the familiar and resounding final chorus of one of America's favorite choral works, "The Battle Hymn of the Republic," to set the stage for "The Star-Spangled Banner." Discuss whether "The Star-Spangled Banner" has taken on a more personal meaning since the events of September 11, 2001. Write down or share the images that come to mind when performing this piece.

ASSESSMENT

Informal Assessment

In this lesson, the students showed the ability to:

- Identify and successfully sing chromatic lines found in the music.
- Sing with appropriate dynamics and balance.

Student Self-Assessment

Have students evaluate their individual performances based on the following:

- Posture
- Expressive Singing
- Intonation
- Accurate Pitch
- Accurate Rhythms

Have each student rate his/her performance of this song in the areas above on a scale of 1–5, 5 being the best.

Individual and Group Performance Evaluation

To further measure growth of musical skills presented in this lesson, direct students to complete the Evaluation section on page 215.

- After singing the Vocal examples with a partner, evaluate the performance by asking, "Were the altered pitches in tune?"
- After chanting or clapping the rhythms in measures 5–13 that contain dotted notes, rate the performance using the following scale: (1) all rhythms were correct, (2) most rhythms were correct, (3) only a few rhythms were correct

Additional National Standards

The following National Standards are addressed through the Assessment, Extension, Enrichment and bottom-page activities:

5. Reading and notating music. **(b)**

6. Listening to, analyzing, and describing music. **(b)**

7. Evaluating music and music performances. **(a)**

Tears In Heaven

OVERVIEW

Composer: Eric Clapton and Will Jennings, arranged by Michael Jothen

Text: Eric Clapton and Will Jennings

Voicing: TB

Key: F major

Meter: 4/4

Form: IntroABAB'CBAB'Coda

Style: American Pop

Accompaniment: Keyboard, Guitar

Programming: General Concert

Vocal Ranges:

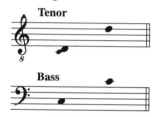

OBJECTIVES

After completing this lesson, students will be able to:

- Relate music to culture.
- Perform expressively from notation a varied repertoire of music representing styles from diverse cultures.
- Demonstrate independently, fundamental skills while performing moderately easy to moderately difficult literature.

VOCABULARY

Have students review vocabulary in student lesson. Introduce terms found in the music. A complete glossary of terms is found on page 246 of the student book.

Tears In Heaven

Composer: Eric Clapton and Will Jennings, arranged by Michael Jothen

Text: Eric Clapton and Will Jennings

Voicing: TB

VOCABULARY

head voice

chest voice

refrain

phrase

SPOTLIGHT

To learn more about the physiology of singing, see page 227.

Focus

- Identify and describe uses of music in society and culture.
- Perform and interpret expressively a varied repertoire of music.
- Extend the vocal range with a smooth transition between registers.

Getting Started

Throughout human existence, music has served as a way for people to share their feelings. As we move through life, we encounter both sorrows and joys. We may for a moment experience happiness and elation, and then suddenly have sadness and confusion prevail. It is always changing. Music provides a means by which we can share our emotions with others as they share theirs with us. It allows us to gain confidence in observing what others have experienced in their lives and knowing that we may be experiencing the same in our own.

◆ History and Culture

Eric Clapton (b. 1945) is considered one of the greatest rock guitarists of today. He started playing the guitar at age fourteen by imitating the blues guitarists he heard on the radio or through recordings. He has remained at the forefront of rock performances for over forty years.

In 1991, Clapton's four-year-old son was tragically killed in a falling accident. For a long time, Clapton avoided public performances and focused on the events surrounding his son's death. When he returned to the stage, he was a different person. A real-life event had influenced his music. Gone was the hard edge of his earlier musical style. The 1992 Grammy awards earned Clapton six Grammy awards, including Record of the Year, Song of the Year, and Best Male Pop Vocal Performance for his song "Tears In Heaven."

RESOURCES

Proficient Sight-Singing

Sight-Singing in F Major, pages 45–46, 54

Reading Rhythms in 4/4 Meter, pages 2, 6

Reading Tied Notes, page 42

Reading Dotted Half and Dotted Quarter Notes, page 51

Teacher Resource Binder

Teaching Master 31, *Culture and Music: A Connection*

Teaching Master 32, *Stage Presence Helps Connect*

Vocal Development 11, *Flexibility and Range*

Dalcroze 15, *Phrase Building*

For additional resources, see TRB Table of Contents.

Links to Learning

◆ **Vocal**

Establishing and maintaining consistent and beautiful vocal tone when moving from the **head voice** *(higher range of a singer)* to the **chest voice** *(the lower range of a singer)* is important for expressive performance of the melody. Perform the following example on the neutral syllable "loo."

◆ **Artistic Expression**

The **refrain**, *a repeated section at the end of each phrase or verse in a song*, of this song is particularly expressive and meaningful. Sing the refrain of "Tears In Heaven" with **phrases** *(musical ideas that have a beginning and an end)* that are softer at the beginning and end and loudest at its peak. Work for expressive facial expression and movements that help convey the depth of the text.

Evaluation

Demonstrate how well you have learned the skills and concepts featured in the lesson "Tears In Heaven" by completing the following:

- Compare how the cultural context for "Tears In Heaven" is similar and/or different from other choral compositions you are currently studying.

- Identify performance practices that would improve your performance of "Tears In Heaven." Apply these performance practices to individual and group performances of the song.

RESOURCES

Proficient Tenor/Bass Rehearsal/Performance CD

CD 2:19 Voices

CD 2:20 Accompaniment Only

CD 3:22 Vocal Practice Track—Tenor

CD 6:21 Vocal Practice Track—Bass

National Standards

1. Singing, alone and with others, a varied repertoire of music. **(a)**

8. Understanding relationships between music, the other arts, and disciplines outside the arts. **(b)**

LINKS TO LEARNING

Vocal

The Vocal section is designed to prepare students to meld singing in the upper and lower registers of the voice.

Have students sing the pitches in the exercise on the neutral syllable "loo" working on beautiful tone in all registers.

Artistic Expression

The Artistic Expression section is designed to prepare students to enhance presentations of the composition through actively engaging the body in performance.

Have students sing the refrain of the song in phrases where the beginning and end of each phrase is softer than the peak.

LESSON PLAN

Suggested Teaching Sequence and Performance Tips

1. Introduce

Direct students to:

- Read and discuss the information found in the Getting Started section on page 218.
- Practice singing the descending pitches in the Vocal section on page 219. Work on a smooth transition from the upper register to the lower register.
- Practice singing the refrain as described in the Artistic Expression section on page 219. Involve facial expressions to convey the emotion of the text.

Progress Checkpoints

Observe students' progress in:

✓ Singing descending pitches in various vocal registers.

✓ Singing with appropriate facial expressions.

Tears In Heaven

For TB and Piano

Arranged by
MICHAEL JOTHEN

Words and Music by
ERIC CLAPTON and WILL JENNINGS

Copyright © 1992 by E.C. Music Ltd. and Blue Sky Rider Songs
This arrangement Copyright © 2005 by E.C. Music Ltd. and Blue Sky Rider Songs
All Rights for E.C. Music Ltd. Administed by Unichappell Music, Inc.
All Rights for Blue Sky Rider Songs Adminstered by Irving Music, Inc.
International Copyright Secured   All Rights Reserved

220   Proficient Tenor/Bass

TEACHER 2 TEACHER

Helping students express the text of a vocal composition is a key to enhancing vocal performances. The suggestions under the Artistic Expression section are presented to assist students in grasping the depth of feeling underlying the text. Consider starting the learning process with this strategy.

MORE ABOUT...

Performance Space

Musical performances are changed by the physical space, the architectural characteristics of the space, in which a performance is given. Perform "Tears In Heaven" on stage, in the gymnasium or cafeteria, outside, a small or large room and so on. Compare and contrast the differences between performances.

2. Rehearse

Direct students to:

- Sight-sing the melody for the solo in measures 5–19. Sing it on a neutral syllable and once pitches are secure, add the text.

- Sight-sing the parts in measures 23–37 using solfège syllables. Add text once pitches are sung correctly.

- Sight-sing the parts in measures 41–49.

- Sight-sing the parts in measures 53–59. Compare this section with measures 13–19. Notice the melody is primarily the same but is split between the two voice parts.

- Discuss the road map of the music when observing the D.S. al Coda (perform the music through measure 62, go back to measure 23 and sing the third verse, after measure 36 go to the coda, perform measure 63 to the end).

- Sight-sing the coda. Note the similar pitches but slightly different rhythms.

Progress Checkpoints

Observe students' progress in:

- ✓ Singing the correct pitches and rhythms.

- ✓ Singing the melody and harmony parts.

- ✓ Following the structure of an arrangement that includes a D.S. al Coda.

3. Refine

Direct students to:

- Sing the entire song using the text and correct rhythms.
- Sing measures 5–19 as solos. Allow for individual interpretations once pitches and rhythms are learned.
- Articulate the text clearly from measure 23 to the end. Encourage active facial expressions.
- Work for a balance between parts. The melody should always be prominent. Perform the voice parts and only sing when your part has the melody.
- Perform the song from measure 23 to the end with the piano. Only sing when your part has the harmony.
- Perform all parts with the melody being sung slightly louder than the harmony.
- Observe the dynamic and tempo markings suggested by the arranger and adjust the volume and speed of the beat accordingly.

Progress Checkpoints

Observe students' progress in:

- ✓ Balancing the parts so that the melody is prominent.
- ✓ Using clean diction with appropriate facial expressions.
- ✓ Singing solos that convey the message of the text.
- ✓ Performing the dynamics and tempos as notated in the score.

222   Proficient Tenor/Bass

COMMUNITY CONNECTION

Twenty-first-Century Composers

Have students:

- Contact local arts agencies to learn the names of any composers in the community.
- Invite a local composer to visit the classroom. (You will need to screen choices for appropriateness.)
- Plan questions to ask about the art of composing music.
- Listen to some compositions by this composer.
- Plan a performance or video using the composer's piece.

ASSESSMENT

Informal Assessment

In this lesson, students showed the ability to:

- Sight-sing in the key of F major.
- Create a smooth transition from one vocal register to the next.
- Have balanced dynamics between the melody and harmony.
- Observe suggested dynamic and tempo markings.

TEACHING STRATEGY

Solo and Small Ensemble Performances

Have students:

1. Prepare solos and small ensembles for performance or competition.

2. Interpret music symbols and terms referring to dynamics, tempo and articulation during the performance.

3. Critique and analyze the quality of the performance using standard terminology.

Student Self-Assessment

Have students evaluate their individual performances based on the following:

- Phrasing
- Diction
- Expressive Singing
- Intonation
- Correct Part-Singing

Have each student rate his/her performance of this song in the areas above on a scale of 1–5, 5 being the best.

MORE ABOUT...

Arranger Michael Jothen

Michael Jothen is Professor of Music, Program Director of Graduate Music Education and Division Chairperson of Music Education at Towson University, Baltimore, Maryland. An active choral and general music educator, he is composer, guest conductor and clinician, coauthor of the Basal textbook series *Music and You* and *Share the Music.* He is also author of articles in *The Choral Journal, Music Educators Journal, Letters,* and *NASSP Bulletin.* Dr. Jothen is a graduate of St. Olaf College, Case-Western Reserve University, and Ohio State University.

Individual and Group Performance Evaluation

To further measure growth of musical skills presented in the lesson, direct students to complete the Evaluation section on page 219.

- After looking through the music being studied, write a one-page report on the piece that is most similar to "Tears In Heaven" and the one that is least similar. Why were these two pieces cited?

- After viewing a videotape of the choir's performance of "Tears In Heaven," evaluate the performance by asking, "How could the text be sung with more meaning? Which section conveyed the song's message the best? Which section could improve with their visual affect? Who in the choir has the appropriate facial expression when singing the song?"

Encourage your students to expore **music.glencoe.com**, the Web site for *Experiencing Choral Music*. You may wish to preview the rich content before directing your students online. Options available on the Web site include:

- Web Link Exercises
- Interactive Projects
- Audio Samples

MUSIC LITERACY

Expressive Elements and Phrasing

To help students expand their music literacy, have them:

- Read the text of "Tears In Heaven," identifying where the natural phrase breaks are and therefore, where they should breathe.
- Look through the notation, finding all dynamic and tempo markings.
- Sing through the phrases, following the dynamic and tempo markings.
- Analyze the thematic sections of the song.
- Contrast the quarter-note rhythms against the tied-note rhythms in the different parts. Be precise.

EXTENSION

Researching Eric Clapton

Eric Clapton is not only a great composer and guitarist, he was also the member of some very important bands. By using the Internet, the library or the CD and record collections of friends and family, have students research Eric Clapton's past and prepare a written or oral report on his life and musical importance. Share findings with a friend or the choir. Are there any other songs written or performed by Eric Clapton that would be good for a choral performance? Why or why not?

Small-Ensemble Performance Techniques

Have students divide into quartets with at least one singer on a part. Have the quartets perform "Tears in Heaven" for the class. Ask the class to describe three positive characteristics of the choral sound they heard.

Then ask each quartet to self-evaluate the performance by answering these questions:

- Did your group sing in tune?
- Was there a balance of voices or did one singer dominate over the others?

Ask the class to evaluate the performance of each quartet by answering the following:

- Could you understand the words?
- Did they sing with correct dynamics?
- Did you hear musical phrasing tasking place?

226 Proficient Tenor/Bass

Additional National Standards

The following National Standards are addressed through the Assessment, Extension, Enrichment and bottom-page activities:

5. Reading and notating music. **(b)**

7. Evaluating music and music performances. **(b)**

9. Understanding music in relation to history and culture. **(c)**

SPOTLIGHT

Physiology Of Singing

Physiology is a branch of biology that deals with living organisms and their parts. It is interesting to see how the parts of the human body affect our singing. Familiarize yourself with "Physiology of the Voice" on page 21 before studying this page.

Vocal Pitch, Range and Timbre

- Pitch is related to the length of the vocal folds. The longer and more stretched the folds are, the higher the pitch; the shorter and more relaxed, the lower the pitch.

- Range is related to the length and thickness of the vocal folds. Longer, thinner folds vibrate more easily at higher pitches; shorter, thicker folds vibrate more easily on lower pitches.

- Timbre or "tone color" of the voice is related to the size of the larynx, the relative thickness of the vocal folds, and resonance factors (see below). A large larynx with thicker vocal folds produces a deeper, richer sound; a small larynx with thinner vocal folds produces a lighter, simpler sound.

Resonance

- Resonance is related to the size, shape and texture of the surface of the resonators and how we utilize them.

- Some resonators are fixed in size, shape and texture; for example, the sinus and nasal cavities (except when you have a cold!).

- Others such as the oral, pharyngeal and laryngeal cavities change depending on how we utilize the articulators in shaping the vowels and defining the consonants.

Projection

- Projection is related to many factors. Some of these factors include (1) the amount of air pressure used at the onset of the tone and throughout the phrase, (2) utilization of the resonators, (3) the amount of tension in the body, (4) the health of the vocal mechanism, (5) the physical and emotional energy level of the singer, and (6) the acoustics of the room.

Spotlight *Physiology Of Singing* **227**

RESOURCES

Teacher Resource Binder

Vocal Development 11, *Flexibility and Range*
Vocal Development 14, *Resonance*
Reference 16, *Expanding a Musical Vocabulary*

National Standards

1. Singing, alone and with others. **(b)**
8. Understanding the relationships between music, the other arts, and disciplines outside the arts. **(b)**

PHYSIOLOGY OF SINGING

Objectives

- Sing individually.
- Define the relationship between the content of other subjects and those of music.

Suggested Teaching Sequence

Direct students to:

- Read the Spotlight article on page 227 and discuss.
- Discuss the difference between fixed resonators and changeable resonators. Identify parts of the body for each.
- Identify five factors that have an effect on projection of the voice.
- Sing or speak into a microphone to record their voices. Play the recording and identify the person speaking or singing based on the timbre of the voice.
- Relate the information about physiology of the parts of the voice to what they have studied in science class.

Progress Checkpoints

Observe students' progress in:

- ✓ Their ability to identify the parts of the body used for speech and for singing.
- ✓ Their ability to identify the elements of the human body that affect pitch, range and timbre in the voice.
- ✓ Their ability to understand the importance of knowing how the voice works in becoming a better singer.

Two Excerpts from *Liebeslieder Walzer*

OVERVIEW

Composer: Johannes Brahms (1833–1875), edited by Stacey Nordmeyer

Text: from *Polydora,* English text by J. Mark Baker

Voicing: TB

Keys: B♭ major and E♭ major

Meter: 3/4

Form: AABB and AABB

Style: German Romantic Art Song

Accompaniment: Piano

Programming: Contest, Festival

Vocal Ranges:

OBJECTIVES

After completing this lesson, students will be able to:

• Sing in groups a varied repertoire of music.

• Demonstrate fundamental skills while performing.

• Demonstrate accurate rhythm while performing.

VOCABULARY

Have students review vocabulary in student lesson. Introduce terms found in the music. A complete glossary of terms is found on page 246 of the student book.

Two Excerpts from *Liebeslieder Walzer*

Composer: Johannes Brahms (1833–1875), edited by Stacey Nordmeyer
Text: from *Polydora,* English text by J. Mark Baker
Voicing: TB

VOCABULARY

Romantic period

head voice

¾ meter

Ländler

MUSIC HISTORY

To learn more about the Romantic period, see page 122.

Focus

• Perform and describe music from the Romantic period.

• Extend the vocal range and demonstrate proper use of head voice.

• Read and perform rhythmic notation in ¾ meter.

Getting Started

Imagine walking down the hallway of your school and not being allowed to speak to any of the girls. Courtship between men and women in the nineteenth century was guided by highly restrictive customs and practices. Men and women were not allowed to speak to one another without a prior introduction. Likewise, a couple's meeting could occur only in the presence of adult supervision. The *Liebeslieder Waltzes* by Johannes Brahms celebrate love and courtship within the confines of these social norms.

◆ History and Culture

The German composer Johannes Brahms (1833–1897) is regarded as one of the greatest composers of the **Romantic period** *(1820–1900).* He endeavored to show a range of extreme emotions within his music. Joy, pain, love and unrequited love are just a few of the themes found throughout his music.

German poet Georg Friedrich Daumer (1800–1875) made a name for himself by collecting and translating poems of other cultures. Brahms selected the entirety of Opus 52, including "O die Frauen" and "Sieh', wie ist die Welle klar," from Daumer's collection of international poetry called *Polydora.* The English translation of the German text is as follows:

No. 3 "O die Frauen"

Oh, women, women,
How they melt one with bliss!
I'd have become a monk long ago
Except for women!

No. 14 "Sieh', wie ist die Welle klar"

See how clear the waters are
When the moon shines down!
You who are my love,
Love me in return.

RESOURCES

Proficient Sight-Singing

Sight-Singing in B♭ Major, pages 90–93

Sight-Singing in E♭ Major, pages 115–116, 119

Reading Rhythms in 3/4 Meter, page 14

Reading Dotted Half Notes, page 51

Teacher Resource Binder

Teaching Master 33, *Pronunciation Guide for "Two Excerpts from 'Liebeslieder Walzer'"*

Evaluation Master 15, *Diction Check-up*

Skill Builder 28, *Rhythm Challenge in Triple Meter*

Vocal Development 11, *Flexibility and Range*

For additional resources, see TRB Table of Contents.

Links to Learning

◆ Vocal

The extended ranges found in these songs will require you to sing in your **head voice,** *the highest part of your vocal range.* Perform the following example on "loo" to practice singing in your upper range.

◆ Theory

In $\frac{3}{4}$ **meter,** *a time signature in which there are three beats per measure and the quarter note receives the beat,* each beat has a distinctive name and purpose. Beat 1 is the strongest beat (crusis), beat 2 receives less stress (metacrusis), and beat 3 receives even less stress (anacrusis). The anacrusis also serves as the upbeat to the next measure.

◆ Artistic Expression

A **Ländler** is *a slow Austrian dance similar to a waltz that is performed in* $\frac{3}{4}$ *meter.* Speak or sing the words to "O die Frauen" while stepping to the pulse. Step beat 1 the strongest, but lighten up on beats 2 and 3. When comfortable with text and movement, repeat the process while clapping a dotted half note in a large circular motion for each measure. Discuss how movement can enhance the performance of a piece of music.

Evaluation

Demonstrate how well you have learned the skills and concepts featured in the lesson in "Two Excerpts from *Liebeslieder Walzer*" by completing the following:

- Discuss the musical characteristics of the Romantic period.
- Form a large circle with room enough to walk. Perform "O die Frauen" while walking in a waltz step or a $\frac{3}{4}$ pattern. Evaluate how well you were able to sing and move to the beat in $\frac{3}{4}$ meter.

Choral Library Two Excerpts from Liebeslieder Walzer **229**

RESOURCES

Proficient Tenor/Bass Rehearsal/Performance CD

CD 2:21 Voices
CD 2:22 Accompaniment Only
CD 3:23 Vocal Practice Track—Tenor
CD 6:22 Vocal Practice Track—Bass

National Standards

1. Singing, alone and with others, a varied repertoire of music. **(a, c)**

LINKS TO LEARNING

Vocal

The Vocal section is designed to prepare students sing using their head voice.

Have students:

- Sing the exercise using solfège syllables.
- Sing the exercise on the neutral syllable *loo.*

Theory

The Theory section is designed to prepare students to perform music in 3/4 meter.

Have students locate the time signatures in the songs and relate them to 3/4 meter.

Artistic Expression

The Artistic Expression section is designed to prepare students to experience and understand the expressive effect of waltz-like rhythms through movement.

Have students:

- Speak the lyrics to "O die Frauen" while stepping to the pulse.
- Place more emphasis on beat one than beats two and three while stepping to the beat.
- Clap using large circular motions to the half note while stepping to the beat and placing an emphasis on beat one of each measure.

No. 3 O die Frauen

For TB and Piano

Edited by STACEY NORDMEYER
English text by J. MARK BAKER

Text from *Polydora*
JOHANNES BRAHMS (1833–1897)

LESSON PLAN

Suggested Teaching Sequence and Performance Tips

1. Introduce

Direct students to:

- Read and discuss the information found in the Getting Started section on page 228.
- After listening to a recording of the music ask students to discuss how the elegance of the music coincides with the social and political milieu of late nineteenth-century Europe.
- Practice singing the two-part exercise in the Vocal section on page 229. Relate using the head voice to the high pitches in the songs.
- Discuss 3/4 meter as described in the Theory section on page 229. Relate that meter to the one used in the songs (*they are the same*).
- Practice the movements suggested in the Artistic Expression section on page 229. Once students can speak the text while doing this movement, have them sing the pitches and move.

Progress Checkpoints

Observe students' progress in:

✓ An understanding of the social and cultural atmosphere from which this music arises.

✓ Singing upper pitches with the head voice.

✓ Rhythmic precision regarding the reading and clapping of each measure. The movement should be at the very least "errhythmic" (regular and mechanically correct).

Copyright © 2005 by HAL LEONARD CORPORATION
International Copyright Secured   All Rights Reserved

230   Proficient Tenor/Bass

TEACHER 2 TEACHER

These two masterpieces by Brahms are choral writing at its best. The music is simple, supple and quite elegant. It is entirely diatonic yet possesses some interesting modulations. The *Liebeslieder Waltzes* afford a wonderful opportunity for your students to vocally project the grace and elegance of the late nineteenth century German waltz.

2. Rehearse

Direct students to:

- Analyze the musical score, identifying the meter and beats within the measures.

- Rehearse by clapping and/or stepping each of the measures as described in the Links to Learning section. Because of the waltz-like feel of this music, it is vital that the rhythm become "eurhythmic" (i.e., flowing and expressive in movement).

- First have your students clap each measure circularly. That is, beat one (crusis) will be at the six o'clock position, beat two (metacrusis; this is the follow-through beat) will be at two o'clock and beat three (anacrusis; the preparatory beat) will be at 10 o'clock. This relationship will create a flowing template into which any quarter/half combination can easily pour. Now step the rhythm. As indicated in the Links to Learning section, have the students step the rhythm in a flowing dancelike manner. In "O die Frauen" they should begin by initiating the movement with an inhalation on the rest. Have them take a back step at the cadences, which occur at the end of measures 2, 4 and 8. This will give the phrase a settled feeling.

- Do the movement described previously while singing.

MORE ABOUT...
Johannes Brahms

In 1833 Brahms was born into a very poor musical family. He studied with Remenyi, a violinist, and toured Europe with him as his accompanist. He met famous composers on the tour: Joachim, Liszt, and Schumann. He became acquainted with gypsies, their culture, and their music. After his tour he concentrated on learning the classics composed by Beethoven and Bach.

His music reflected these earlier influences. He wrote every kind of music except opera: symphonies, concerti, overtures, variation, piano compositions, sonatas, intermezzi, rhapsodies, caprices, ballads, waltzes and lieder. Brahms was a conservative in the Romantic era, writing pure or absolute music, not program, story or tone painting.

Observe students' progress in:

✓ Their joyful response to moving.

✓ Accurate and expressive clapping and stepping. In order for the elegance of the waltz to be fully felt it is essential that the students move in a free, uninhibited—yet controlled—fashion. Help them loose any inhibitions by making this activity challenging and fun.

3. Refine

Direct students to:

- Sing entire song one part at a time while moving rhythmically in a flowing manner. Try singing both pieces while: (1) Stepping the underlying quarter-note pulse. (2) Stepping the dotted half. Make sure that the space used is approximately three times that used for the quarter note. (3) Stepping the rhythm as outlined above.

- Divide into sections. Have the Tenors step and sing their rhythms while the Basses do the same. If possible, have them link arms with a member of the other section (if this is too uncomfortable they could also move in close proximity to each other). When the rhythm is parallel it will be relatively easy. However, in measure 6 of "O die Frauen" the Tenors have a half note while the Basses have two quarter notes. At this point they will need to adjust to each other's spatial demand. The adjustment should enhance the music making.

232

CONNECTING THE ARTS
Processes in the Arts

Have students:

1. Find examples of artwork or art forms from the Romantic period, describing how they exhibit the characteristics of the period. (Choose from visual art, architecture, dance, drama, poetry or literature.)

2. Discuss how the processes used in the other areas are the same and different from music, taking into consideration the roles of artists, performers and audience.

3. Find other examples from the same art category, but from a different style, period or culture.

4. Discuss similarities and differences between the examples.

Two Excerpts from Liebeslieder Walzer, *Opus 52*

No. 14 Sieh', wie ist die Welle klar

For TB and Piano

Edited by STACEY NORDMEYER
English text by J. MARK BAKER

Text from Polydora
JOHANNES BRAHMS (1833–1897)

Copyright © 2005 by HAL LEONARD CORPORATION
International Copyright Secured   All Rights Reserved

Choral Library *Two Excerpts from* Liebeslieder Walzer   **233**

- Divide the chorus in half and have one half step the quarter note while the other half steps and sings the rhythm. So both groups can kinesthetically and musically benefit from the other, have the "pulse" steppers circle move outside the "rhythm" steppers.

Progress Checkpoints

Observe students' progress in:
- ✓ Precise eurhythmic and spatial precision.
- ✓ Their ability to maintain perfect focus and concentration in the midst of the other parts.
- ✓ Their ability to experience the waltz-like mood of the occasion while stepping either the pulse or the rhythm.
- ✓ Perfect spatial relations— i.e., the half-note step should twice as big as the quarter note.

ASSESSMENT

Informal Assessment

In this lesson, the students showed the ability to:
- Maintain a steady beat.
- Move to each part in the midst of other movements.
- Internalize and communicate the kinesthetic-eurhythmic power of the German waltz vocally.

TEACHING STRATEGY

Compare and Contrast Form

The form or style used in Two Excerpts from *Leiberslieder Walzer* is a waltz. Have students:

- Identify the form of "O die Frauen" and "Sieh', wie ist die Welle klar" as a waltz. What characteristics are found in a waltz?
- Analyze the form and discuss how each song is treated differently.
- Compare and contrast the waltzes used in both songs. How are they similar? How are they different? Compare and contrast the elements of texture, harmony, placement of melody, dynamics, tempo, text and so forth.

Student Self-Assessment

Have students evaluate their individual performances based on the following:

- Phrasing
- Foreign Language
- Intonation
- Accurate Rhythms
- Correct Part-Singing

Have each student rate his/her performance of this song in the areas above on a scale of 1–5, 5 being the best.

Individual and Group Performance Evaluation

To further measure growth of musical skills presented in this lesson, direct students to complete the Evaluation section on page 229.

- After learning the two pieces by Brahms, write a one-page report on musical characteristics of the Romantic period that are evident in the two songs. Compare the results with other students.
- After videotaping the choir walking in a waltz step while singing "O die Frauen," evaluate the performance.

EXTENSION

Composition

Compose a rhythmic phrase of four to six measures in length using values that have been learned. Have students notate then clap and step their compositions. Combine phrases by performing them one after the other as well as at the same time. Determine if any of the motions could be performed with the two songs by Brahms.

Additional National Standards

The following National Standards are addressed through the Assessment, Extension, Enrichment and bottom-page activities:

4. Composing and arranging music within specific guidelines. **(a)**

5. Reading and notating music. **(b)**

7. Evaluating music and music performances. **(a)**

8. Understanding relationships between music, the other arts, and disciplines outside the arts. **(a)**

SPOTLIGHT

Gospel Music

Gospel music is *religious music that originated in the African American churches of the South.* Characteristics of gospel music include improvisation, syncopation and repetition. Following the Civil War, African American churches began to form. The spirituals previously sung by the slaves served as their main source of sacred music. By the early 1900s, some sectors of the church moved to more spirited songs accompanied by tambourines, drums and piano. This new music was the beginning of the gospel style.

African American gospel music gained national recognition during the 1940s and the 1950s with the recordings and live concerts by the singing great Mahalia Jackson (1912–1972). Also of influence was composer and bandleader Thomas Andrew Dorsey (1899–1993). He published over 400 gospel songs and is known as the father of gospel music. His featured music used lively rhythms and syncopated piano accompaniments. "Precious Lord, Take My Hand" is probably his most famous song.

When asked about the correct way to sing gospel music, the contemporary composer Rollo Dilworth said that singers often debate about the appropriate use of chest and head voice registers when performing gospel style. While some believe that excessive use of the chest voice might cause vocal damage, others believe that singing in the African American idiom is not "authentic" if performed in head voice. Dilworth suggests that successful singing in most any genre requires a balanced, healthy singing tone in both head and chest registers. Vocal techniques used in gospel singing include (1) percussive singing (a style that lies between legato and staccato styles); (2) swell (an exaggerated crescendo that adds weight and breadth to an accented syllable); and (3) pitch bending (the scooping up to a pitch, often coupled with a swell or a falling off of a pitch). The rhythm is felt in an accurate yet relaxed style. Basic movements may include stepping, clapping and rocking. Improvisation of the melody is frequently heard in gospel music.

Listen to recordings of gospel music. Identify and analyze the characteristics of gospel style that you hear.

Spotlight *Gospel Music* **235**

RESOURCES

Teacher Resource Binder

Reference 2, *Listening Guide*

Reference 16, *Expanding a Musical Vocabulary*

Reference 37, *Quiz Master: Rubric Construction Form*

National Standards

1. Singing, alone and with others, a varied repertoire of music. **(a, b, c)**

7. Evaluating music and music performances. **(a, b)**

GOSPEL MUSIC

Objective

• Classify aurally presented music representing diverse styles.

Suggested Teaching Sequence

Direct students to:

• Read the Spotlight On Gospel Music on student page 235 and list the characteristics.

• Make a list of familiar gospel songs or artists/composers. If possible, play an example of Thomas Dorsey's "Precious Lord, Take My Hand."

• List and demonstrate the vocal techniques used in gospel singing.

• Demonstrate movements often seen in performances of gospel music.

• Share with the class any experience they may have had with gospel music, such as performing, attending a concert, and so forth.

• Listen to exemplary recordings of gospel groups and determine what makes them exemplary examples.

Progress Checkpoints

Observe students' progress in:

✓ Their ability to define and gospel music.

✓ Their ability to list the characteristics of gospel music.

✓ Their ability to list and demonstrate the vocal techniques used in gospel singing.

Witness

OVERVIEW

Composer: Traditional Spiritual, arranged by Moses Hogan (1957–2003)

Text: Traditional

Voicing: TTBB

Key: C major

Meter: 2/4

Form: Strophic

Style: Spiritual

Accompaniment: A cappella

Programming: Concert, Festival, Multicultural

Vocal Ranges:

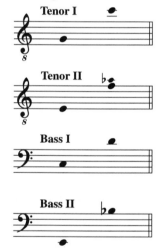

OBJECTIVES

After completing this lesson, students will be able to:

- Identify melodic parts when listening to music.
- Compare elements of music through literature selected for performance.
- Perform expressively from notation a varied repertoire of music representing diverse cultures.

VOCABULARY

Have students review vocabulary in student lesson. Introduce terms found in the music. A complete glossary of terms is found on page 246 of the student book.

Witness

Composer: Traditional Spiritual, arranged by Moses Hogan (1957–2003)

Text: Traditional

Voicing: TTBB

VOCABULARY

call and response

syncopation

portamento

Focus

- Identify call and response aurally and in notation.
- Describe characteristics of the spiritual.
- Perform music representing the African American spiritual.

🔺 **SPOTLIGHT**

To learn more about gospel music, see page 235.

Getting Started

Picture in your mind a courtroom scene. A witness has been asked to take the stand. Once the witness is sworn in, he is asked to testify. As the witness tells the story and tries to make a point, certain words are emphasized. During the telling of a dramatic tale, the jury and the spectators occasionally respond with sighs of disbelief and gasps of amazement! As the witness finishes, he stands to his feet and says to the court in a loud and emphatic tone, "And that is the whole truth, and nothing but the truth." Moses Hogan's setting of the spiritual "Witness" presents a story that will challenge you as the singer to put yourself in the shoes of the man in the courtroom who confidently testified before a crowd of spectators.

◆ History and Culture

"Witness" is an African American spiritual. Characteristic of most spirituals, this setting features **call and response** *(in music when a leader or group sings a phrase, or call, followed by a response of the same phrase by another group).* The response may use some of the same words as the call, or it may use different words altogether. In some cases, a response phrase actually completes the thought of the call phrase. Other features found in this arrangement include syncopated rhythms, sliding vocals, changes in tempo, sudden dynamic shifts, and a stirring descant that is sure to bring an audience to its feet!

RESOURCES

Proficient Sight-Singing

Sight-Singing in C Major, pages 7, 9, 13

Reading Rhythms in 2/4 Meter, pages 66–67

Reading Eighth Notes and Eighth Rests, pages 23–24

Reading Tied Notes, pages 42, 50

Teacher Resource Binder

Teaching Master 34, *Analyzing for Musical Characteristics*

Evaluation Master 3, *Assessing Performing Syncopation*

Skill Builder 1, *Building Harmony*

Skill Builder 24, *Rhythm and Kodály*

Reference 30, *Writing Program Notes*

For additional resources, see TRB Table of Contents.

Links to Learning

◆ Vocal

To practice singing the harmonies found in this arrangement, perform the following example. Sing on the neutral syllable "dah."

◆ Theory

Syncopation is *the placement of accents on a weak beat or a weak portion of the beat.* Read and perform the following example. Find these patterns in the music.

◆ Artistic Expression

Perform the following example to gain experience in singing vocal slides, a style that is sometimes referred to as **portamento** *(a smooth glide from one note to another).*

Evaluation

Demonstrate how well you have learned the skills and concepts featured in the lesson "Witness" by completing the following:

- Select two people to serve as listeners. As the choir sings "Witness," the listeners are to identify the passages of call and response that they heard. They are also to listen critically for correct tuning and harmonies. Repeat the process with new listeners.

- List characteristics of spirituals found in this arrangement of "Witness."

Choral Library *Witness* **237**

RESOURCES

Proficient Tenor/Bass Rehearsal/Performance CD

CD 2:23 Voices

CD 2:24 Accompaniment Only

CD 3:24 Vocal Practice Track—Tenor I

CD 4:21 Vocal Practice Track—Tenor II

CD 5:15 Vocal Practice Track—Baritone

CD 6:23 Vocal Practice Track—Bass

National Standards

1. Singing, alone and with others, a varied repertoire of music. **(a)**

6. Listening to, analyzing, and describing music. **(a, b)**

LINKS TO LEARNING

Vocal

The Vocal section is designed to prepare students to sing harmonic progressions that will be found in the piece.

Have students:

- Sing the four parts using solfège syllables.
- Sing the exercise using the neutral syllable "dah."

Theory

The Theory section is designed to prepare students to read and perform various syncopated patterns.

Have students:

- Chant the rhythmic pattern using the counting syllables written below the staff.
- Clap the exercise while tapping a quarter-note pulse.

Artistic Expression

The Artistic Expression section is designed to prepare students to sing harmonic progressions and vocal slides that will be found in the piece.

Have students:

- Sing the three-part exercise using solfège syllables.
- Sing the exercise using the neutral syllable hum.
- Sing the exercise using hum and add the portamento articulation.

LESSON PLAN

Suggested Teaching Sequence and Performance Tips

1. Introduce

Direct students to:

- Read and discuss the information found in the Getting Started section on page 236.
- Practice singing the harmonic progression as shown in the Vocal section on page 237. Relate it to the harmony in measures 9–17.
- Practice performing the syncopated rhythmic patterns as shown in the Theory section on page 237. Relate it to measures 1–8.
- Practice singing the three-part exercise in the Artistic Expression section on page 237. Locate a similar example in the upper three parts in measures 50–59.

Progress Checkpoints

Observe students' progress in:

- ✓ Their ability to sing four-part harmony with accuracy.
- ✓ Their ability to perform syncopated rhythms with precision.
- ✓ Their ability to sing a three-part exercise that includes portamento.

Commissioned by the Ithaca College Men's Chorus
Sean Conor Anderson, Conductor

Witness

For TTBB, a cappella

Arranged by
MOSES HOGAN

Traditional Spiritual

Copyright © 2002 by HAL LEONARD CORPORATION
International Copyright Secured   All Rights Reserved

TEACHER2TEACHER

Moses Hogan's arrangement of "Witness" is a good piece for exploring syncopation and expression markings. In addition to the chromatic harmonies found in this arrangement, students will get an opportunity to examine the compositional concepts that make the African American spiritual tradition a unique one.

for my Lord,__ my soul is a wit-ness for my Lord.__

__ will be a wit-ness

be a, be a wit-ness for my Lord?__ My soul is a wit - ness

a for my Lord?__

for my Lord.__ Yes! I'm a wit - ness for my Lord,__ my

Who__ will be a wit - ness

soul is a wit - ness for my Lord.__ be a, be a wit-ness

a

for my Lord?__ Hum__ Hum__

Marcato p

for my Lord?__ Oh, I have-n't been to heav-en but-a I been told__ that the

2. Rehearse

Direct students to:

- Review the syncopated patterns found in the Theory section of the lesson.
- Chant the first 17 measures of the piece in rhythm using Kodály syllables as suggested in the Theory section of the lesson. When all rhythms are secure, practice the Tenor parts together. When pitches are secure, add text. Practice the Bass parts, and then add text. Combine parts and rehearse.
- While maintaining a steady quarter-note pulse, chant the rhythms beginning with the pickup to measure 18. Continue through the first beat of measure 33. When rhythms are secure, the Tenors sight-sing their parts on a neutral syllable. When pitches are secure, add text. Repeat the procedure for Bass parts. If necessary, separate parts to insure clarity, especially with inter-vals of a second. When pitches are secure, combine Tenor and Bass parts. Check for accuracy of pitches.
- Sight-sing the section from beat two of measure 33 through the first beat of measure 49. Notice that this section is identical to the previous one (measures 17–33).

TEACHING STRATEGY

Compare and Contrast

Hall Johnson (1888-1970) was one of the most respected and prolific arrangers of spirituals. His arrangement of "Witness" has been recorded by many outstanding vocalists, including Jessye Norman and Kathleen Battle. Locate and listen to a recording of this solo arrangement and compare it to Mr. Hogan's arrangement. In terms of melody, text, and form, how are they similar and how are they different? What are the characteristics of each arrangement that make it unique?

- On the neutral syllable "doo," sight-sing the Bass II part pitches from measures 49–65. When pitches are secure, add text. Using the piano for support, practice the "hums" in the Baritone and Tenor parts, isolating each part and practicing the vocal slides. Also, practice the pitches for these parts at measures 64–65. When pitches for the upper parts are secure, add the Bass melody and sing all parts together.

- Beginning with the pickup to measure 82, sight-sing all parts in the section through measure 113 (with piano), as it is similar to the previous section. If necessary, review any parts to obtain accuracy.

- Sight-sing measures 114 through the downbeat of measure 129, as it contains the same chorus material as before.

- Beginning with the word *Well* in measure 129, chant the rhythms of all voice parts through the end of the piece. When rhythms are secure, chant the text. The Tenor parts practice together, noticing the divisi that occurs beginning in measure 145. When pitches are secure, add text. The Bass parts practice beginning in measure 131. Notice the divisi that occurs in measure 155. When pitches are secure, slowly combine parts. Practice the descant (measures 145–153) with a small group of Tenor Is. Review measure 129 to the end.

240   Proficient Tenor/Bass

MORE ABOUT...

Arranger Moses Hogan

Moses George Hogan (1957-2003) was an internationally renowned pianist, conductor, and arranger who helped renew interest in the African American spiritual as a choral art form. He received a Bachelor of Music degree in performance from Oberlin Conservatory and pursued further studies at the Julliard School and Louisiana State University. Hogan taught at Dillard University and at Loyola University in his hometown of New Orleans, Louisiana. He was the founder and artistic director of the New World Ensemble, the Moses Hogan Chorale, and the Moses Hogan Singers. Hogan was a prolific arranger of spirituals, and he composed other choral works that reflected African American musical styles.

Observe students' progress in:

✓ Their ability to sing all rhythms, especially syncopation, with accuracy.

✓ Singing the correct pitches.

✓ Singing harmonies in divisi sections.

3. Refine

Direct students to:

• Go back to the beginning of the piece. Review all dynamic and articulation markings. Demonstrate an understanding of articulation markings such as accent marks and portamento.

• In the verse sections of the piece (measures 49–65; measures 81–113) and the coda (measures 129–end), call-and-response patterns are found.

• Perform the piece, keeping in mind the expression markings and the structure of the call-and-response patterns.

Progress Checkpoints

Observe students' progress in:

✓ Their ability to observe all the dynamic and expression markings in the score.

✓ Their ability to perform the types of call-and-response patterns employed by the arranger.

CULTURAL CONNECTIONS

Spirituals

The enslaved Africans brought music with the following elements to the New World: syncopation, polyrhythm, pentatonic and gap scales, and the idea of music combined with body movements.

From the suffering of the ocean crossing and a life of subjugation, they create a new genre, the "spiritual," or religious folk song of the slave. It revealed their unhappiness and suffering, taught facts, sent messages, provided a common language, and shared religious rituals and beliefs. In the spiritual, the singer must express a personal connection with God. The spiritual reflects a true historical picture of the lives of slaves as told by slaves themselves.

ASSESSMENT

Informal Assessment

In this lesson, students showed the ability to:

- Sing syncopated rhythm patterns with accuracy.
- Recognize the elements of call and response that appear in the score.

Student Self-Assessment

Have students evaluate their individual performances based on the following:

- Phrasing
- Expressive Singing
- Intonation
- Accurate Rhythms
- Correct Part-Singing

Have each student rate his/her performance of this song in the areas above on a scale of 1–5, 5 being the best.

Individual and Group Performance Evaluation

To further measure growth of musical skills presented in this lesson, direct students to complete the Evaluation section on page 237.

- After the choir has performed "Witness" for the two listeners, evaluate the performance by asking, "How in tune were the parts? Which section(s) need more work on singing the correct pitches?" Switch roles with two other listeners.
- After listing the characteristics of spirituals found in "Witness," compare the results with another student.

242   Proficient Tenor/Bass

TEACHING STRATEGY

Performing from Memory

Have students:

1. Memorize this piece by learning shorter phrases at a time.
2. Perform it from memory on a program or in competition.
3. Further develop memorization skills by memorizing other songs and solos to perform for the class informally or at formal concerts.

Additional National Standards

The following National Standards are addressed through the Assessment, Extension, Enrichment and bottom-page activities:

1. Singing, alone and with others, a varied repertoire of music. **(c)**
5. Reading and notating music. **(a, b)**
6. Listening to, analyzing, and describing music. **(a)**
7. Evaluating music and music performances. **(a)**
9. Understanding music in relation to history and culture. **(a)**

EXTENSION

Call and Response

Two types of call and response are employed in this arrangement. "Testifying" call and response, as the term implies, means that the singer presents his personal convictions. "Narrative" call and response, the other type found in this arrangement, is a device that attempts to tell or recall a story about some person or event, usually from scripture. In addition to syncopated rhythms and sliding vocals, Mr. Hogan adds tempo changes, sudden dynamic shifts and an upper register descant that is sure to bring an audience to its feet!

Which patterns are of the narrative type and which patterns are of the testifying type? [*Answers: measures 50–65 (testifying); measures 81–113 (narrative); measures 129–end (narrative).*]

ENRICHMENT

Improvising Musical Melodies

Encourage students to improvise musical melodies while performing. Select an eight-bar phrase from "Witness." Ask volunteers to improvise a melodic descant above the melody as the choir sings the written notation. Have students take turns improvising.

VOCAL HEALTH

Objectives

- To introduce and experience healthy vocal production as related to musical vocal performance.

Suggested Teaching Sequence

Direct students to:

- Read Spotlight On Vocal Health on student page 244.
- Identify and write down (for their own viewing) any of the directives on the student page that might impact them on a regular or sometimes basis.
- Incorporate as many of the directives as possible for the next six weeks.
- Keep a record of any noticeable improvements in their vocal health.
- Share their results with the choir if they are willing.

Progress Checkpoints

Observe students' progress in:

- ✓ Demonstrating body awareness.
- ✓ Using proper posture and breath management.
- ✓ Shaping vowels correctly with clear diction.
- ✓ Seemingly effortless singing.
- ✓ Vocal projection
- ✓ Vocal health awareness

 SPOTLIGHT

Vocal Health

Since our voices are a result of physical processes in our bodies, we need to learn a few things we can do to ensure that our voices will be healthy and function well for years to come.

To experience, explore and establish good habits for vocal health, try the following:

- Limit shouting and trying to talk over loud noise.
- Do not smoke. Avoid smoky environments.
- Avoid beverages with caffeine and fried foods (acid reflux).
- Limit talking on the telephone. Use a supported voice when you do.
- Avoid whispering if you lose your voice.
- Rest your voice if it is tired or if it takes more muscular effort to sing.
- Keep your voice hydrated. Drink lots of water every day and use nonmentholated, sugar-free lozenges if your throat is dry.
- Gargle with warm salt water if your throat is sore.
- Use a humidifier in your bedroom when the air conditioning or furnace is on.
- Try not to clear your throat. Swallow or clear with a puff of air instead.
- Avoid coughing, if at all possible.
- Cover your nose and mouth with a scarf in cold weather.
- Get plenty of sleep, especially the night before a performance.

As you can see, maintaining good vocal health is a matter of common sense in taking care of your body. By taking good care of yourself, you can continue to enjoy a strong, healthy singing voice. Take care and sing long!

244 Proficient Tenor/Bass

RESOURCES

Teacher Resource Binder

Vocal Development 1–6, *Developing the Voice*

National Standards

1. Singing, alone and with others. **(b)**

Glossary

2/2 meter A time signature in which there are two beats per measure and the half note receives the beat.

2/4 meter A time signature in which there are two beats per measure and the quarter note receives the beat.

3/2 meter A time signature in which there are three beats per measure and the half note receives the beat.

3/4 meter A time signature in which there are three beats per measure and the quarter note receives the beat.

3/8 meter A time signature in which there is one group of three eighth notes per measure and the dotted quarter note receives the beat. When the tempo is very slow, this meter can be counted as having three beats per measure, with the eighth note receiving the beat.

4/4 meter A time signature in which there are four beats per measure and the quarter note receives the beat.

5/8 meter A time signature in which there are five beats per measure and the eighth note receives the beat.

6/4 meter A time signature in which there are two groups of three quarter notes per measure and the dotted half note receives the beat. When the tempo is very slow, this meter can be counted as having six beats per measure, with the quarter note receiving the beat.

6/8 meter A time signature in which there are two groups of three eighth notes per measure and the dotted quarter note receives the beat. When the tempo is very slow, this meter can be counted as having six beats per measure, with the eighth note receiving the beat.

9/8 meter A time signature in which there are three groups of three eighth notes per measure and the dotted quarter note receives the beat. When the tempo is very slow, this meter can be counted as having nine beats per measure, with the eighth note receiving the beat.

12/8 meter A time signature in which there are four groups of three eighth notes per measure and the dotted quarter note receives the beat.

A

a cappella *(ah-kah-PEH-lah)* [It.] A style of singing without instrumental accompaniment.

a tempo *(ah TEM-poh)* [It.] A tempo marking that indicates to return to the original tempo of a piece or section of music.

ABA form A form in which an opening section (A) is followed by a contrasting section (B), which leads to the repetition of the opening section (A).

accelerando *(accel.) (ah-chel-leh-RAHN-doh)* [It.] A tempo marking that indicates to gradually get faster.

accent A symbol placed above or below a given note to indicate that the note should receive extra emphasis or stress. (>)

accidental Any sharp, flat or natural that is not included in the key signature of a piece of music.

adagio *(ah-DAH-jee-oh)* [It.] Slow tempo, but not as slow as *largo*.

ad libitum *(ad. lib.)* [Lt.] An indication that the performer may vary the tempo or add or delete a vocal or instrumental part.

Aeolian scale *(ay-OH-lee-an)* [Gk.] A modal scale that starts and ends on *la*. It is made up of the same arrangement of whole and half steps as a natural minor scale.

al fine *(ahl FEE-neh)* [It.] To the end.

aleatory music *(AY-lee-uh-toh-ree)* A type of music in which certain aspects are performed randomly. Also known as *chance music*.

alla breve Indicates cut time; a duple meter in which there are two beats per measure, and half note receives the beat. *See* cut time.

allargando (*allarg.*) (*ahl-ahr-GAHN-doh*) [It.] To broaden, become slower.

allegro (*ah-LEH-groh*) [It.] Brisk tempo; faster than *moderato*, slower than *vivace*.

allegro non troppo (*ah-LEH-groh nohn TROH-poh*) [It.] A tempo marking that indicates not too fast. Not as fast as *allegro*.

altered pitch Another name for an accidental.

alto (*AL-toh*) The lowest-sounding female voice.

andante (*ahn-DAHN- teh*) [It.] Moderately slow; a walking tempo.

andante con moto (*ahn-DAHN- teh kohn MOH-toh*) [It.] A slightly faster tempo, "with motion."

andantino (*ahn-dahn-TEE-noh*) [It.] A tempo marking that means "little walking," a little faster than *andante*.

animato Quickly, lively; "animated."

anthem A choral composition in English using a sacred text.

answer In a fugue, the entry of the theme at a different pitch, usually the interval of a fourth or fifth away, than that of the original subject.

antiphon In the Roman Catholic liturgy, a chant with a prose text connected with the psalm, sung by two choirs in alternation. The *antiphon* is usually a refrain for the psalm or canticle verses. Its melodies are often simple, with only one note per syllable.

arpeggio (*ahr-PEH-jee-oh*) [It.] A chord in which the pitches are sounded successively, usually from lowest to highest; in broken style.

arrangement A piece of music in which a composer takes an existing melody and adds extra features or changes the melody in some way.

arranger A composer who takes an original or existing melody and adds extra features or changes the melody in some way.

art songs Musical settings of poetry. Songs about life, love and human relationships that are written by a professional composer and have a serious artistic purpose, as opposed to a popular song or folk song.

articulation The amount of separation or connection between notes.

articulators The lips, teeth, tongue and other parts of the mouth and throat that are used to produce vocal sound.

avant-garde A term used in the arts to denote those who make a radical departure from tradition.

avocational Not related to a job or career.

B

ballad A strophic folk song with a distinctly narrative element. Ballads tell stories.

barbershop A style of *a cappella* singing in which three parts harmonize with the melody. The lead sings the melody while the tenor harmonizes above and the baritone and bass harmonize below.

barcarole A Venetian boat song.

baritone The male voice between tenor and bass.

barline A vertical line placed on the musical staff that groups notes and rests together.

Baroque period (*bah-ROHK*) [Fr.] The historical period in Western civilization from 1600 to 1750.

bass The lowest-sounding male voice.

bass clef A clef that generally indicates notes that sound lower than middle C.

basso continuo (*BAH-soh cun-TIN-you-oh*) [It.] A continually moving bass line, common in music from the Baroque period.

beat The steady pulse of music.

bebop style   Popular in jazz, music that features notes that are light, lively and played quickly. Often the melodic lines are complex and follow unpredictable patterns.

blues scale   An altered major scale that uses flatted or lowered third, fifth and seventh notes: *ma* (lowered from *mi*), *se* (lowered from *sol*) and *te* (lowered from *ti*).

blues style   An original African American art form that developed in the early twentieth century in the Mississippi Delta region of the South. The lyrics often express feelings of frustration, hardship or longing. It often contains elements such as call and response, the blues scale and swing.

breath mark   A symbol in vocal music used to indicate where a singer should take a breath. (⸴)

breath support   A constant airflow necessary to produce sound for singing.

C

cadence   A melodic or harmonic structure that marks the end of a phrase or the completion of a song.

call and response   A derivative of the field hollers used by slaves as they worked. A leader or group sings a phrase (call) followed by a response of the same phrase by another group.

calypso   A style of music that originated in the West Indies and which features syncopated rhythms and comical lyrics.

canon   A musical form in which one part sings a melody, and the other parts sing the same melody, but enter at different times. Canons are sometimes called *rounds*.

cantabile *(con-TAH-bee-leh)*   [It.] In a lyrical, singing style.

cantata *(con-TAH-tah)*   [It.] A large-scale musical piece made up of several movements for singers and instrumentalists. Johann Sebastian Bach was a prominent composer of cantatas.

cantor *(CAN-tor)*   A person who sings and/or teaches music in a temple or synagogue.

canzona   [It.] A rhythmic instrumental composition that is light and fast-moving.

carol   A strophic song of the Middle Ages, sung in English or Latin, beginning with a refrain which is then repeated after each verse. In recent times, the word *carol* refers to a strophic song about Christmas or the Virgin Mary.

chamber music   Music performed by a small instrumental ensemble, generally with one instrument per part. The string quartet is a popular form of chamber music, consisting of two violins, a viola and a cello. Chamber music was popular during the Classical period.

chanson *(shaw[n]-SOH[N])*   [Fr.] Literally "song" in French, a *chanson* is a vocal composition to French words. The rich history of the *chanson* dates back to the late Middle Ages and continues to the present day, incorporating many styles and composers.

chantey   *See* sea chantey.

chanteyman   A soloist who improvised and led the singing of sea chanteys.

chest voice   The lower part of the singer's vocal range.

chorale *(kuh-RAL)*   [Gr.] Congregational song or hymn of the German Protestant Church.

chord   The combination of three or more notes played or sung together at the same time.

chromatic   Moving by half-steps. Also, notes foreign to a scale.

chromatic scale *(kroh-MAT-tick)*   [Gk.] A scale that consists of all half steps and uses all twelve pitches in an octave.

Classical period   The historical period in Western civilization from 1750 to 1820.

clef The symbol at the beginning of a staff that indicates which lines and spaces represent which notes.

close harmony Harmony in which notes of the chord are kept as close together as possible, often within an octave.

coda A special ending to a song. A concluding section of a composition. (⊕)

Collegium musicum *(col-LAY-gee-oom MOO-zee-koom)* [Lat.] A musical group, usually at a university, that presents period-style performances of Renaissance and Baroque music.

commission A musical work created by the composer for a specific event or purpose. The composer is approached by the commissioning organization (orchestra, chorus, academic institution, church) or individual, and an acceptable fee is agreed upon.

common time Another name for 4/4 meter. Also known as common meter. (𝄴)

composer A person who takes a musical thought and writes it out in musical notation to share it with others.

compound meter Any meter in which the dotted quarter note receives the beat, and the division of the beat is based on three eighth notes. 6/8, 9/8 and 12/8 are examples of compound meter.

con moto *(kohn MOH-toh)* [It.] With motion.

concert etiquette A term used to describe what is appropriate behavior in formal or informal musical performances.

concerto *(cun-CHAIR-toh)* [Fr., It.] A composition for a solo instrument and orchestra.

concerto grosso *(cun-CHAIR-toh GROH-soh)* [Fr., It.] A multi-movement Baroque piece for a group of soloists and an orchestra.

conductor A person who uses hand and arm gestures to interpret the expressive elements of music for singers and instrumentalists.

conductus A thirteenth-century song for two, three or four voices.

consonance Harmonies in chords or music that are pleasing to the ear.

Contemporary period The historical period from 1900 to the present.

countermelody A separate melodic line that supports and/or contrasts the melody of a piece of music.

counterpoint The combination of two or more melodic lines. The parts move independently while harmony is created. Johann Sebastian Bach is considered by many to be one of the greatest composers of contrapuntal music.

contrary motion A technique in which two melodic lines move in opposite directions.

crescendo *(creh-SHEN-doh)* [It.] A dynamic marking that indicates to gradually sing or play louder. ⊂

cumulative song A song form in which more words are added each time a verse is sung.

cut time Another name for *2/2 meter.* (𝄵)

D

---

da capo *(D.C.) (dah KAH-poh)* [It.] Go back to the beginning and repeat; *see also* dal segno *and* al fine.

dal segno *(D.S.) (dahl SAYN-yah)* [It.] Go back to the sign and repeat.

D. C. al Fine *(FEE-nay)* [It.] A term that indicates to go back to the beginning and repeat. The term *al fine* indicates to sing to the end, or *fine.*

decrescendo *(DAY-creh-shen-doh)* [It.] A dynamic marking that indicates to gradually sing or play softer. ⊃

descant A special part in a piece of music that is usually sung higher than the melody or other parts of the song.

diatonic interval The distance between two notes which are indigenous to a major or minor scale.

diatonic scale *(die-uh-TAH-nick)* A scale that uses no altered pitches or accidentals. Both the major scale and the natural minor scale are examples of a diatonic scale.

diction The pronunciation of words while singing.

diminished chord A minor chord in which the top note is lowered one half step from *mi* to *me*.

diminuendo (*dim.*) (*duh-min-yoo-WEN-doh*) [It.] Gradually getting softer; *see also* decrescendo.

diphthong A combination of two vowel sounds.

dissonance A combination of pitches or tones that clash.

dolce (*DOHL-chay*) [It.] Sweetly.

dominant chord A chord built on the fifth note of a scale. In a major scale, this chord uses the notes *sol, ti* and *re*, and it may be called the **V** ("five") chord. In a minor scale, this chord uses the notes *mi, sol* and *ti* (or *mi, si* and *ti*), and it may be called the **v** or **V** ("five") chord.

Dorian scale (*DOOR-ee-an*) [Gk.] A modal scale that starts and ends on *re*.

dot A symbol that increases the length of a given note by half its value. It is placed to the right of the note.

dotted half note A note that represents three beats of sound when the quarter note receives the beat. 𝅗𝅥.

dotted rhythms A dot after a note lengthens the note by one-half its original value. When notes are paired, the first note is often three times longer than the note that follows (e.g., dotted half note followed by quarter note, dotted quarter note followed by eighth note, dotted eighth note followed by sixteenth note).

𝅗𝅥.   𝅘𝅥 ‖ 𝅗𝅥. 𝅘𝅥𝅮 ‖ 𝅘𝅥𝅯𝅘𝅥𝅘

double barline A set of two barlines that indicate the end of a piece or section of music.

D. S. al coda (*dahl SAYN-yoh ahl KOH-dah*) [It.] Repeat from the symbol (𝄋) and skip to the coda when you see the sign. (⊕)

duet A group of two singers or instrumentalists.

duple Notes in equal groups of two.

dynamics Symbols in music that indicate how loud or soft to sing or play.

E

eighth note A note that represents one-half beat of sound when the quarter note receives the beat. Two eighth notes equal one beat of sound when the quarter note receives the beat. 𝅘𝅥𝅮 𝅘𝅥𝅮𝅘𝅥𝅮

eighth rest A rest that represents one-half beat of silence when the quarter note receives the beat. Two eighth rests equal one beat of silence when the quarter note receives the beat. 𝄾

expressionism Music of the early twentieth century usually associated with Germany that was written in a deeply subjective and introspective style.

expressive singing To sing with feeling.

F

fanfare A brief celebratory piece, usually performed by brass instruments and percussion, at the beginning of an event.

falsetto [It.] The register in the male voice that extends far above the natural voice. The light upper range.

fermata (*fur-MAH-tah*) [It.] A symbol that indicates to hold a note or rest for longer than its given value. (⌢)

fine (*fee-NAY*) [It.] A term used to indicate the end of a piece of music.

fixed do (*doh*) A system of syllables in which the note C is always *do*. *See also* movable do.

flat A symbol that lowers the pitch of a given note by one half step. (♭)

folk music Music that passed down from generation to generation through oral tradition. Traditional music that reflects a place, event or a national feeling.

folk song A song passed down from generation to generation through oral tradition. A song that reflects a place, event or a national feeling.

form The structure or design of a musical composition.

forte *(FOR-tay)* [It.] A dynamic that indicates to sing or play loud. (*f*)

fortissimo *(for-TEE-see-moh)* [It.] A dynamic that indicates to sing or play very loud. (*ff*)

fugue *(FYOOG)* A musical form in which the same melody is performed by different instruments or voices entering at different times, thus adding layers of sound.

fusion Music that is developed by the act of combining various types and cultural influences of music into a new style.

G

glee A homophonic, unaccompanied English song, usually in three or four vocal parts. The texts of early glees, from the seventeenth century, were usually about eating and drinking, but also about patriotism, hunting and love.

glissando *(glees-SAHN-doh)* An effect produced by sliding from one note to another. The word, pseudo-Italian, comes from the French word *glisser*, "to slide."

gospel music Religious music that originated in the African American churches of the South. This music can be characterized by improvisation, syncopation and repetition.

gradual In the Roman Catholic liturgy, a chant that follows the reading of the Epistle. The texts are usually from the Psalms. The melodies often contain several notes per syllable. The term *gradual* (from the Latin *gradus*, "a step") is so called because it was sung while the deacon was ascending the steps to sing the Gospel.

grand opera A large-scale opera that is sung throughout, with no spoken dialogue. *See* Singspiel.

grand staff A staff that is created when two staves are joined together.

grandioso [It.] Stately, majestic.

grave *(GRAH-veh)* [It.] Slow, solemn.

grazioso *(grah-tsee-OH-soh)* [It.] Graceful.

Gregorian chant A single, unaccompanied melodic line sung by male voices. Featuring a sacred text and used in the church, this style of music was developed in the medieval period.

guiro *(GWEE-roh)* A Latin American percussion instrument made from an elongated gourd, with notches cut into it, over which a stick is scraped to produce a rasping sound.

H

half note A note that represents two beats of sound when the quarter note receives the beat.

half rest A rest that represents two beats of silence when the quarter note receives the beat.

half step The smallest distance (interval) between two notes on a keyboard; the chromatic scale is composed entirely of half steps.

harmonic intervals Two or more notes which are sung or played simultaneously.

harmonic minor scale A minor scale that uses a raised seventh note, *si* (raised from *sol*).

harmonics Small whistle-like tones, or overtones, that are sometimes produced over a sustained pitch.

harmony A musical sound that is formed when two or more different pitches are played or sung at the same time.

head voice The higher part of the singer's vocal range.

hemiola In early music theory, *hemiola* denotes the ratio 3:2. In the modern metrical system, it refers to the articulation of two bars in triple meter as if they were three bars in duple meter.

High Renaissance The latter part of the Renaissance period, c. 1430-1600.

homophonic *(hah-muh-FAH-nik)* [Gk.] A texture where all parts sing similar rhythm in unison or harmony.

homophony *(haw-MAW-faw-nee)* [Gk.] A type of music in which there are two or more parts with similar or identical rhythms being sung or played at the same time. Also, music in which melodic interest is concentrated in one voice part and may have subordinate accompaniment.

hymn A song or poem that offers praise to God.

I

imitation The act of one part copying what another part has already played or sung.

improvisation The art of singing or playing music, making it up as you go, or composing and performing a melody at the same time.

interlocking Short melodic or rhythmic patterns performed simultaneously that fit together to create a continuous musical texture.

interlude A short piece of music that is used to bridge the acts of a play or the verses of a song or hymn.

International Phonetic Alphabet (IPA) A phonetic alphabet that provides a notational standard for all languages. Developed in Paris, France, in 1886.

interval The distance between two notes.

intonation The accuracy of pitch, in-tune singing.

Ionian scale *(eye-OWN-ee-an)* [Gk.] A modal scale that starts and ends on *do*. It is made up of the same arrangement of whole and half steps as a major scale.

J

jazz An original American style of music that features swing rhythms, syncopation and improvisation.

K

key Determined by a song's or scale's home tone, or keynote.

key signature A symbol or set of symbols that determines the key of a piece of music.

E♭ major
C minor

L

Ländler *(LEND-ler)* [Ger.] A slow Austrian dance, performed in 3/4 meter, similar to a waltz.

largo [It.] A tempo marking that indicates broad, slow, dignified in style.

ledger lines Short lines that appear above, between treble and bass clefs, or below the bass clef, used to expand the notation.

legato *(leh-GAH-toh)* [It.] A connected and sustained style of singing and playing.

lento *(LEN-toh)* [It.] Slow; a little faster than *largo*, a little slower than *adagio*.

lied *(leet)* [Ger.] A song in the German language, generally with a secular text.

lieder *(LEE-der)* [Ger.] Plural of *lied*. Songs in the German language, especially art songs of the Romantic period. These songs usually have a secular text.

liturgical text A text that has been written for the purpose of worship in a church setting.

lute An early form of the guitar.

Lydian scale *(LIH-dee-an)* [Gk.] A modal scale that starts and ends on *fa*.

lyricist The writer of the words (lyrics) to a song.

lyrics The words of a song.

M

madrigal A poem that has been set to music in the language of the composer. Featuring several imitative parts, it usually has a secular text and is generally sung *a cappella*.

maestoso (*mah-eh-STOH-soh*) [It.] Perform majestically.

major chord A chord that can be based on the *do, mi,* and *sol* of a major scale.

major scale A scale that has *do* as its home tone, or keynote. It is made up of a specific arrangement of whole steps and half steps in the following order: W + W + H + W + W + W + H.

major second Two notes a whole step apart.

major tonality A song that is based on a major scale with *do* as its keynote, or home tone.

manniboula A rustic pizzicato bass instrument consisting of a wooden resonance box with a rose window on its front panel where there are three metallic blades that sound when manipulated by the fingers of the player sitting on it. Also called a *manniba.*

marcato (*mar-CAH-toh*) [It.] A stressed and accented style of singing and playing.

Mass A religious service of prayers and ceremonies originating in the Roman Catholic Church consisting of spoken and sung sections. It consists of several sections divided into two groups: proper (text changes for every day) and ordinary (text stays the same in every Mass). Between the years 1400 and 1600, the mass assumed its present form consisting of the Kyrie, Gloria, Credo, Sanctus and Agnus Dei. It may include chants, hymns and Psalms as well. The Mass also developed into large musical works for chorus, soloists and even orchestra.

measure The space between two barlines.

medieval period The historical period in Western civilization also known as the Middle Ages (400–1430).

medley A collection of songs musically linked together.

melisma (*muh-LIZ-mah*) [Gk.] A group of notes sung to a single syllable or word.

melismatic singing (*muh-liz-MAT-ik*) [Gk.] A style of text setting in which one syllable is sung over many notes.

melodic contour The overall shape of the melody.

melodic minor scale A minor scale that uses raised sixth and seventh notes: *fi* (raised from *fa*) and *si* (raised from *sol*). Often, these notes are raised in ascending patterns, but not in descending patterns.

melody A logical succession of musical tones.

meno mosso (*MEH-noh MOHS-soh*) [It.] A tempo marking that indicates "less motion," or slower.

merengue (*meh-REN-geh*) [Sp.] A Latin American ballroom dance in moderate duple meter with the basic rhythm pattern:

It is the national dance of the Dominican Republic.

messa di voce (*MES-sah dee VOH-cheh*) [It.] A technique of singing a crescendo and decrescendo on a held note. The term literally means "placing of the voice."

meter A way of organizing rhythm.

meter signature *See* time signature.

metronome marking A sign that appears over the top line of the staff at the beginning of a piece or section of music that indicates the tempo. It shows the kind of note that will receive the beat and the number of beats per minute as measured by a metronome.

mezzo forte (*MEH-tsoh FOR tay*) [It.] A dynamic that indicates to sing or play medium loud. (*mf*)

mezzo piano (*MEH-tsoh pee-AH-noh*) [It.] A dynamic that indicates to sing or play medium soft. (*mp*)

mezzo voce (*MEH-tsoh VOH-cheh*) [It.] With half voice; reduced volume and tone.

minor chord A chord that can be based on the *la, do,* and *mi* of a minor scale.

minor scale   A scale that has *la* as its home tone, or keynote. It is made up of a specific arrangement of whole steps and half steps in the following order: W + H +W + W + H + W + W.

minor tonality   A song that is based on a minor scale with *la* as its keynote, or home tone.

minstrel   The term *minstrel* originally referred to a wandering musician from the Middle Ages. In the late nineteenth century, the word was applied to black-face entertainers who presented a variety show consisting of comic songs, sentimental ballads, soft-shoe dancing, clogging, instrumental playing, comedy skits, sight gags and jokes.

missa brevis (*MEES-sah BREH-vees*)   [Lat.] Literally, a "brief mass." The term refers to a short setting of the Mass Ordinary.

mixed meter   A technique in which the time signature or meter changes frequently within a piece of music.

Mixolydian scale (*mix-oh-LIH-dee-an*)   [Gr.] A modal scale that starts and ends on *sol*.

modal scale   A scale based on a mode. Like major and minor scales, each modal scale is made up of a specific arrangement of whole steps and half steps, with the half steps occurring between *mi* and *fa*, and *ti* and *do*.

mode   An early system of pitch organization that was used before major and minor scales and keys were developed.

modulation   A change in the key or tonal center of a piece of music within the same song.

molto   [It.] Very or much; for example, *molto rit.* means "much slower."

monophony (*mon-AH-foh-nee*)   Music with only a single melody line (e.g., Gregorian chant).

motet (*moh-teht*)   Originating as a medieval and Renaissance polyphonic song, this choral form of composition became an unaccompanied work, often in contrapuntal style. Also, a short, sacred choral piece with a Latin text that is used in religious services but is not a part of the regular Mass.

motive   A shortened expression, sometimes contained within a phrase.

moveable do (*doh*)   A system of syllables in which the first note of each diatonic scale is *do*. *See also* fixed do.

music critic   A writer who gives an evaluation of a musical performance.

music notation   Any means of writing down music, including the use of notes, rests and symbols.

musical   A play or film whose action and dialogue are combined with singing and dancing.

musical theater   An art form that combines acting, singing, and dancing to tell a story. It often includes staging, costumes, lighting and scenery.

mysterioso   [It.] Perform in a mysterious or haunting way; to create a haunting mood.

N

narrative song   A song that tells a story.

national anthem   A patriotic song adopted by nations through tradition or decree.

nationalism   Patriotism; pride of country. This feeling influenced many Romantic composers such as Wagner, Tchaikovsky, Dvorák, Chopin and Brahms.

natural   A symbol that cancels a previous sharp or flat, or a sharp or flat in a key signature. (♮)

natural minor scale   A minor scale that uses no altered pitches or accidentals.

neo-classicism   Music of the early twentieth century characterized by the inclusion of contemporary styles of features derived from the music of the seventeenth and eighteenth centuries.

New Romanticism A genuine tonal melody composed with exotic textures and timbres.

no breath mark A direction not to take a breath at a specific place in the composition. (N.B.)

non troppo (*nahn TROH-poh*) [It.] Not too much; for example, *allegro non troppo*, "not too fast."

notation Written notes, symbols and directions used to represent music within a composition.

nuance Subtle variations in tempo, phrasing, articulation, dynamics and intonation that are used to enhance a musical performance.

O

octave An interval of two pitches that are eight notes apart on a staff.

ode A poem written in honor of a special person or occasion. These poems were generally dedicated to a member of a royal family. In music, an ode usually includes several sections for choir, soloists and orchestra.

opera A combination of singing, instrumental music, dancing and drama that tells a story.

operetta (*oh-peh-RET-tah*) [It.] A light opera, often with spoken dialogue and dancing.

optional divisi (*opt.div.*) Indicating a split in the music into optional harmony, shown by a smaller cued note.

oral tradition Music that is learned through rote or by ear and is interpreted by its performer(s).

oratorio (*or-uh-TOR-ee-oh*) [It.] A dramatic work for solo voices, chorus and orchestra presented without theatrical action. Usually, oratorios are based on a literary or religious theme.

ostinato (*ahs-tuh-NAH-toh*) [It.] A rhythmic or melodic passage that is repeated continuously.

overture A piece for orchestra that serves as an introduction to an opera or other dramatic work.

P

palate The roof of the mouth; the hard palate is at the front, the soft palate is at the back.

pambiche (*pahm-BEE-cheh*) [Sp.] A dance that is a slower version of the merengue.

parallel keys Major and minor keys having the same keynote, or home tone (tonic).

parallel minor scale A minor scale that shares the same starting pitch as its corresponding major scale.

parallel motion A technique in which two or more melodic lines move in the same direction.

parallel sixths A group of intervals that are a sixth apart and which move at the same time and in the same direction.

parallel thirds A group of intervals that are a third apart and which move at the same time and in the same direction.

part-singing Two or more parts singing an independent melodic line at the same time.

pentatonic scale A five-tone scale using the pitches *do, re, mi, sol* and *la*.

perfect fifth An interval of two pitches that are five notes apart on a staff.

perfect fourth An interval of two pitches that are four notes apart on a staff.

phrase A musical idea with a beginning and an end.

phrasing A method of punctuating a musical idea, comparable to a line or sentence in poetry.

Phrygian scale (*FRIH-gee-an*) [Gk.] A modal scale that starts and ends on *mi*.

pianissimo (*pee-ah-NEE-see-moh*) [It.] A dynamic that indicates to sing or play very soft. (*pp*)

piano (*pee-AH-noh*) [It.] A dynamic that indicates to sing or play soft. (*p*)

Picardy third An interval of a major third used in the final, tonic chord of a piece written in a minor key.

pitch   Sound, the result of vibration; the highness or lowness of a tone, determined by the number of vibrations per second.

pitch matching   In a choral ensemble, the ability to sing the same notes as those around you.

più *(pyoo)*   [It.] More; for example, *più forte* means "more loudly."

più mosso *(pyoo MOHS-soh)*   [It.] A tempo marking that indicates "more motion," or faster.

poco *(POH-koh)*   [It.] Little; for example *poco dim.* means "a little softer."

poco a poco *(POH-koh ah POH-koh)*   [It.] Little by little; for example, *poco a poco cresc.* means "little by little increase in volume."

polyphony *(pah-LIH-fun-nee)*   [Gk.] Literally, "many sounding." A type of music in which there are two or more different melodic lines being sung or played at the same time. Polyphony was refined during the Renaissance, and this period is sometimes called "golden age of polyphony."

polyrhythms   A technique in which several different rhythms are performed at the same time.

portamento   A smooth and rapid glide from one note to another, executed continuously.

psalm   A sacred song or hymn. Specifically, one of the 150 Psalms in the Bible.

presto *(PREH-stoh)*   [It.] Very fast.

program music   A descriptive style of music composed to relate or illustrate a specific incident, situation or drama; the form of the piece is often dictated or influenced by the nonmusical program. This style commonly occurs in music composed during the Romantic period.

quarter note   A note that represents one beat of sound when the quarter note receives the beat.

quarter note triplet   Three equal divisions of a half note.

quarter rest   A rest that represents one beat of silence when the quarter note receives the beat.

quartet   A group of four singers or instrumentalists.

rallentando *(rall.)* *(rahl-en-TAHN-doh)*   [It.] Meaning to "perform more and more slowly." *See also* ritard.

refrain   A repeated section at the end of each phrase or verse in a song. Also known as a *chorus*.

register, vocal   A term used for different parts of the singer's range, such as head register, or head voice (high notes); and chest register, or chest voice (low notes).

relative minor scale   A minor scale that shares the same key signature as its corresponding major scale. Both scales share the same half steps, between *mi* and *fa*, and *ti* and *do*.

Renaissance period   The historical period in Western civilization from 1430 to 1600.

repeat sign   A symbol that indicates that a section of music should be repeated.

repetition   The restatement of a musical idea; repeated pitches; repeated "A" section in ABA form.

requiem *(REK-wee-ehm)*   [Lt.] Literally, "rest." A mass written and performed to honor the dead and comfort the living.

resolution   The progression of chords or notes from the dissonant to the consonant, or point of rest.

resonance   Reinforcement and intensification of sound by vibration.

rest A symbol used in music notation to indicate silence.

rhythm The combination of long and short notes and rests in music. These may move with the beat, faster than the beat or slower than the beat.

ritard *(rit.) (ree-TAHRD)* [It.] A tempo marking that indicates to gradually get slower.

Romantic period The historical period in Western civilization from c. 1820 to 1900.

Romantic style In music history, the Romantic period dates from ca. 1820–1900, following the Classical period. The word *romantic* (in music, as in art and literature) has to do with romance, imagination, strangeness and fantasy. Music composed in the *Romantic style*, when compared with the balance and restraint of the *Classical style*, is freer and more subjective, with increasing use of chromaticism.

rondo form A form in which a repeated section is separated by several contrasting sections.

rote The act of learning a song by hearing it over and over again.

round *See* canon.

rubato *(roo-BAH-toh)* [It.] The freedom to slow down and/or speed up the tempo without changing the overall pulse of a piece of music.

S

sacred music Music associated with religious services or themes.

scale A group of pitches that are sung or played in succession and are based on a particular home tone, or keynote.

scat singing An improvisational style of singing that uses nonsense syllables instead of words. It was made popular by jazz trumpeter Louis Armstrong.

Schubertiad Gatherings held in the homes of Viennese middle-class families, they featured amateur performances of songs and instrumental works by Franz Schubert (1797–1828).

score A notation showing all parts of a musical ensemble, with the parts stacked vertically and rhythmically aligned.

sea chantey A song sung by sailors, usually in rhythm with their work.

second The interval between two consecutive degrees of the diatonic scale.

secular music Music not associated with religious services or themes.

sempre *(SEHM-preh)* [It.] Always, continually.

sempre accelerando *(sempre accel.)* *(SEHM-preh ahk-chel)* [It.] A term that indicates to gradually increase the tempo of a piece or section of music.

sequence A successive musical pattern that begins on a higher or lower pitch each time it is repeated.

serenata [It.] A large-scale musical work written in honor of a special occasion. Generally performed in the evening or outside, it is often based on a mythological theme.

seventh The interval between the first and seventh degrees of the diatonic scale.

sforzando *(sfohr-TSAHN-doh)* [It.] A sudden strong accent on a note or chord. (*sfz*)

sharp A symbol that raises the pitch of a given note one half step. (♯)

sight-sing Reading and singing music at first sight.

simile *(sim.) (SIM-ee-leh)* [It.] To continue the same way.

simple meter Any meter in which the quarter note receives the beat, and the division of the beat is based on two eighth notes. 2/4, 3/4 and 4/4 are examples of simple meter.

singing posture The way one sits or stands while singing.

Singspiel *(ZEENG-shpeel)* [Ger.] A light German opera with spoken dialogue, e.g., Mozart's *The Magic Flute*.

sixteenth note   A note that represents one quarter beat of sound when the quarter note receives the beat. Four sixteenth notes equal one beat of sound when the quarter note receives the beat.

sixteenth rest   A rest that represents one quarter beat of silence when the quarter note receives the beat. Four sixteenth rests equal one beat of silence when the quarter note receives the beat.

skipwise motion   The movement from a given note to another note that is two or more notes above or below it on the staff.

slur   A curved line placed over or under a group of notes to indicate that they are to be performed without a break.

solfège syllables   Pitch names using *do, re, mi, fa, sol, la, ti, do*, etc.

solo   One person singing or playing an instrument alone.

sonata-allegro form   A large ABA form consisting of three sections: exposition, development and recapitulation. This form was made popular during the Classical period.

soprano   The highest-sounding female voice.

sostenuto *(SAHS-tuh-noot-oh)* [It.] The sustaining of a tone or the slackening of tempo.

sotto voce   In a quiet, subdued manner; "under" the voice.

spirito *(SPEE-ree-toh)* [It.] Spirited; for example, *con spirito* ("with spirit").

spiritual   Songs that were first sung by African American slaves, usually based on biblical themes or stories.

staccato *(stah-KAH-toh)* [It.] A short and detached style of singing or playing.

staff   A series of five horizontal lines and four spaces on which notes are written. A staff is like a ladder. Notes placed higher on the staff sound higher than notes placed lower on the staff.

stage presence   A performer's overall appearance on stage, including enthusiasm, facial expression and posture.

staggered breathing   In ensemble singing, the practice of planning breaths so that no two singers take a breath at the same time, thus creating the overall effect of continuous singing.

staggered entrances   A technique in which different parts and voices enter at different times.

stanza   A section in a song in which the words change on each repeat. Also known as a *verse*.

stepwise motion   The movement from a given note to another note that is directly above or below it on the staff.

straight tone   A singing technique that uses minimal vocal vibrato.

strophe   A verse or stanza in a song.

strophic   A form in which the melody repeats while the words change from verse to verse.

style   The particular character of a musical work, often indicated by words at the beginning of a composition, telling the performer the general manner in which the piece is to be performed.

subdominant chord   A chord built on the fourth note of a scale. In a major scale, this chord uses the notes *fa, la* and *do*, and it may be called the **IV** ("four") chord, since it is based on the fourth note of the major scale, or *fa*. In a minor scale, this chord uses the notes *re, fa* and *la*, and it may be called the **iv** ("four") chord, since it is based on the fourth note of the minor scale, or *re*.

subito (sub.) *(SOO-bee-toh)* [It.] Suddenly.

subject   The main musical idea in a fugue.

suspension The holding over of one or more musical tones in a chord into the following chord, producing a momentary discord.

swell A somewhat breathy, sudden crescendo. It is often used in gospel music.

swing rhythms Rhythms in which the second eighth note of each beat is played or sung like the last third of triplet, creating an uneven, "swing" feel. A style often found in jazz and blues. Swing rhythms are usually indicated at the beginning of a song or section.

syllabic *See* syllabic singing.

syllabic singing A style of text setting in which one syllable is sung on each note.

syllabic stress The stressing of one syllable over another.

symphonic poem A single-movement work for orchestra, inspired by a painting, play or other literary or visual work. Franz Liszt was a prominent composer of symphonic poems. Also known as a *tone poem*.

symphony A large-scale work for orchestra.

syncopation The placement of accents on a weak beat or a weak portion of the beat, or on a note or notes that normally do not receive extra emphasis.

synthesizer A musical instrument that produces sounds electronically, rather than by the physical vibrations of an acoustic instrument.

T

tag The ending of a barbershop song, usually the last four to eight bars, often considered the best chords in the song.

tamburo *(tahm-BOO-roh)* [It.] A two-headed drum played horizontally on the player's lap.

tempo Terms in music that indicate how fast or slow to sing or play.

tempo I or tempo primo *See* a tempo.

tenor The highest-sounding male voice.

tenuto *(teh-NOO-toh)* [It.] A symbol placed above or below a given note indicating that the note should receive stress and/or that its value should be slightly extended.

terraced dynamics Sudden and abrupt dynamic changes between loud and soft.

tessitura *(tehs-see-TOO-rah)* [It.] The average highness or lowness in pitch of a vocal piece.

text Words, usually set in a poetic style, that express a central thought, idea or narrative.

texture The thickness of the different layers of horizontal and vertical sounds.

theme A musical idea, usually a melody.

theme and variation form A musical form in which variations of the basic theme make up the composition.

third An interval of two pitches that are three notes apart on a staff.

tie A curved line used to connect two or more notes of the same pitch together in order to make one longer note.

tied notes Two or more notes of the same pitch connected together with a tie in order to make one longer note.

timbre The tone quality of a person's voice or musical instrument.

time signature The set of numbers at the beginning of a piece of music. The top number indicates the number of beats per measure. The bottom number indicates the kind of note that receives the beat. Time signature is sometimes called *meter signature*.

to coda Skip to or CODA.

tonality The relationship of a piece of music to its *keynote* (tonic).

tone color That which distinguishes the voice or tone of one singer or instrument from another; for example, a soprano from an alto, or a flute from a clarinet. *See also* timbre.

tonic chord   A chord built on the home tone, or keynote of a scale. In a major scale, this chord uses the notes *do, mi* and *sol*, and it may be called the **I** ("one") chord, since it is based on the first note of the major scale, or *do*. In a minor scale, this chord uses the notes *la, do* and *mi*, and it may be called the **i** ("one") chord, since it is based on the first note of the minor scale, or *la*.

treble clef   A clef that generally indicates notes that sound higher than middle C.

trio   A group of three singers or instrumentalists with usually one on a part.

triple   A grouping of notes in equal sets of three.

triplet   A group of notes in which three notes of equal duration are sung in the time normally given to two notes of equal duration.

troppo *(TROHP-oh)*   [It.] Too much; for example, *allegro non troppo* ("not too fast").

tutti *(TOO-tee)*   [It.] Meaning "all" or "together."

twelve-tone music   A type of music that uses all twelve tones of the scale equally. Developed in the early twentieth century, Arnold Schoenberg is considered to be the pioneer of this style of music.

two-part music   A type of music in which two different parts are sung or played.

unison   All parts singing or playing the same notes at the same time.

upbeat   One or more notes of a melody that occur before the first barline or which fall on a weak beat that leans toward the strong beat.

vaccin   An instrument consisting of one or two sections of bamboo, blown with the lips like one would play the mouthpiece of a brass instrument. Also called a *bambou*.

vibrato *(vee-BRAH-toh)*   [It.] A fluctuation of pitch on a single note, especially by singer and string players.

variation   A modification of a musical idea, usually after its initial appearance in a piece.

villancico *(bee-ahn-SEE-koh)*   [Sp.] A Spanish musical and poetic form consisting of several verses linked by a refrain. In modern day Spain and Latin America, the term *villancico* usually means simply "Christmas carol."

vivace *(vee-VAH-chay)*   [It.] Very fast; lively.

vocal jazz   A popular style of music characterized by strong prominent meter, improvisation and dotted or syncopated patterns. Sometimes sung *a cappella*.

whole note   A note that represents four beats of sound when the quarter note receives the beat.   o

whole rest   A rest that represents four beats of silence when the quarter note receives the beat.   ▬

whole step   The combination of two successive half steps.

word painting   A technique in which the music reflects the meaning of the words.

word stress   The act of singing important parts of the text in a more accented style than the other parts.

Classified Index

Instruments

Music & History

Poetry

Popular

Sea Chantey

Seasonal, Patriotic

Vocal Jazz

Listening Selections

Index of Songs and Spotlights

Spotlights

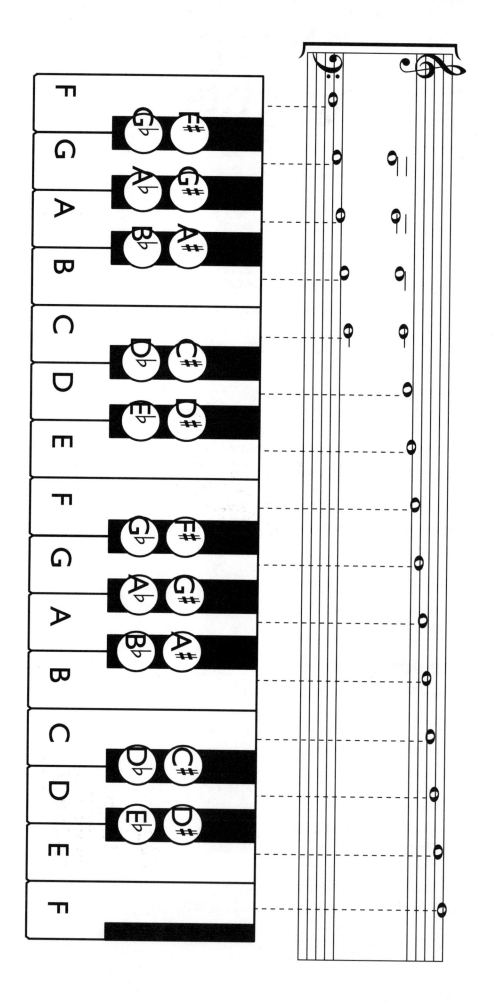